When Compassion Turns to Enabling
and
When Enabling and Alzheimer's Collide

When Compassion Turns to Enabling

Dr. Mary Willock

ABUNDANT LIFE PRESS
Port Saint Lucie, Florida

When Compassion Turns to Enabling
Dr. Mary L. Willock

All quoted Scriptures indicate the Bible translation. Scripture quotations marked:

KJV are from the King James Version, The Scofield Reference Bible, Oxford University Press, 1945, 1937, 1917, 1909. Used by permission.

NKJ are from The Holy Bible, New King James Version, Thomas Nelson, Inc., 1992, 1982, 1980, 1979. Used by permission.

AMP are from The Amplified Bible, Zondervan Bible Publishers and the Lockman Foundation, 1987, 1965, 1964, 1962, 1958, 1954. Used by permission.

NIV are from The Life Application Bible, New International Version by Tyndale House Publishers, Inc./Zondervan Publishing House, 1991, 1990, 1989, 1988. Used by permission.

ISBN: Softcover - 978-0692302484
        0692302484
ASIN: eBook - B00N1BXL4C

To order additional paperback or Kindle copies of this book, visit Amazon.com.

To learn more about Mary Willock Ministries or to invite Dr. Mary Willock to be a guest speaker on enabling or many other life-changing topics, you can reach her through www.marywillock.net.

Acknowledgements:

I thank God for His amazing faithfulness, loving kindness, and constant provision in my life. Time and time again, He has taken what the enemy meant for harm and has worked it for my good. Above all, I thank God for Jesus, my Savior and Lord.

I thank God for my husband and daughter who have lovingly supported me all the years I taught school and as we experienced my family's journey through enabling and Alzheimer's.

I thank God for Vicki Baird, Linda Brabble, and Barbara Forgus who are precious sisters in Christ. We have prayed together, wept together, rejoiced together, and seen God work in miraculous ways to help our families as they are growing up to become caring, responsible adults. They have shared their time and talents in many ways to see the enabling books finished. They have also ministered through music with me for many wonderful years.

I thank God for my Church and Pastors who have prayed for me a multitude of times and shared the joys of seeing God amazingly provide hope and answers in every situation.

When Compassion Turns to Enabling

Contents

Preface

Two book set:

When Compassion Turns to Enabling

Compassionate people enjoy helping others, but when compassion turns to enabling, that help becomes destructive. Enabling prevents others from acting in a caring, responsible manner. Compulsive rescuing and enabling can so overtake an enabler's life that there seems no way out. Families become dysfunctional. Relationships are destroyed in the process.

Information in this book will help you identify enabling and recognize the effects and root causes of enabling. Whether you are an enabler, the one who is being enabled, or the one dealing with family members who are out of control, you will learn how and why unacceptable thinking, attitudes, and behaviors must be changed. This book provides easy to understand, practical Bible-based answers and strategies to heal and restore your family. Your lives are about to change!

When Enabling and Alzheimer's Collide

Both Alzheimer's disease and enabling are destructive forces, but when they collide, the results are overwhelming. Both problems are experienced by thousands of people every day. After reading this true story, you will understand: Enabling must be stopped while the enabler still has clarity of mind. Once dementia or Alzheimer's disease is present, there will be no way to protect the enabler from the one who has been enabled.

This narrative is not a composite of many families; it is the true story of one family. The names have been changed to protect the identity of the individuals. As you read this amazing story, you will clearly understand God's desire and willingness to free your family from the bondage of enabling. Your family's situation may seem hopeless, but with God, all things are possible (Luke 1:37).

This book provides help for desperate families who are caught between Alzheimer's and the dysfunction of enabling.

Introduction

ANYTHING YOU VALUE, YOU WILL FIGHT FOR!

There is a battle that rages on for the lives and souls of our families. We can try to ignore or deny that such a battle exists, but the reality is: America's families are in crisis. Once we acknowledge that truth, then it is time for us to ask God, "How do we fight against the deceptions and seductions of the enemy?"

This book will not build your self-esteem or tell you to relax – everything will be all right. In this book you can expect straight talk: The Truth. It is written from experience and the study of God's Word. It is filled with examples you can relate to in your own life. You will be strengthened and equipped by Scriptures that confirm God's purpose, expectations, and answers for your family. Although this book may be used by counselors and in Christian colleges, it is not written in a textbook style; it is easy to understand.

Have you given up looking for truth? This is a major part of our spiritual downfall in the United States. The Bible is true. It is not make-believe stories, myths, or legends. I challenge you: For once in your life, read the Scriptures, not just as symbolic or philosophical, but as literal. <u>God is speaking to you.</u>

Although it may appear that some sections of this book do not apply to your family or your situation, you need to read all portions of this book. There will be some repetition as we revisit topics and concerns from different perspectives. Whether your situation is simple or extreme, even simple cases have the potential to reach the extreme. Enabling must be recognized and stopped! The information you gain from looking at the whole picture of enabling will help you understand why change is critical for your family members, your community, and our nation.

Allow yourself the flexibility to read beyond the gender in each example of enabling. (Forgive me for not saying he/she; I found it too cumbersome.) Enablers can be male or female. They can be any race, color, nationality, or religion. Be open to what God is saying to you about your situation.

WARNING: You may be offended by the content of this book. You may be offended to think that you have had a role in causing the dysfunction of your family. I suggest that when you feel that offense, don't throw the book away. Ask God if this relates to you, your family, or someone you know. If it does not relate to you, great! Maybe you will have the opportunity to share what you learn with someone else who needs to hear it. But if it does relate to you, ask God what He desires you to do with this information – and then do it.

God has called His people not to be easily offended. "Great peace have they who love Your law; nothing shall offend them or make them stumble" (Psalm 119:165, AMP).

This book is not intended to be a self-help book, but a God-help book. If you really want and need God's peace in your family and in your own life, then you are desperately seeking what God wants you to know and do. You will not give in to feelings or emotions, but will learn God's battle plan to save your family from dysfunction and destruction. In every challenge you face, pray and ask God for His direction. Do not react in fear, but step out in faith to see God's provision for your family. As you trust God to lead your family to victory over enabling, it won't be easy, but He will help you. And remember as you read this book, anything you value, you will fight for. I know you value your family. Get ready to trust and serve God with everything that is within you. May your relationship with God increase as you learn to trust Him in every area of your life.

Who am I? I am not a psychiatrist or psychologist. I am a retired schoolteacher with a Master's Degree in Education and a Doctorate in Ministry. During my 32 years of teaching experience, I have been a guest speaker in many churches where I shared practical strategies to restore Christian families through Bible-based parenting. Over the years, I taught students in grades K-8 and worked with their families. These experiences provided insights into many enabling situations. I also gained much knowledge about enabling through experiences in my personal family, in the families of friends and colleagues, and in churches where I have had the privilege to minister. My observations include individuals who have been enabled from early childhood into late adulthood. Seeing the desperation of these families, I have prayed for discernment to understand root causes and Bible-based solutions to stop the destruction caused by enabling. I pray that the insights God has given me will help you and your family break free from a life controlled by dysfunction. May you see God's purpose fulfilled in each family member throughout the generations that follow.

Chapter 1:
Is It Compassion or Enabling?

If you look at all of the tiny pieces of your life's puzzle, many things we do, don't seem to be so bad. But when enabling becomes a major theme, and you look at the end results, the picture may not be the beautiful family portrait you always imagined. I believe if you are reading this book, you may have already recognized yourself as an enabler, you have been accused of enabling, you are the one who has been enabled, or you are the dependable one who must helplessly stand by and watch the enabling process while you try to live your life in a responsible manner. Whatever the case, you know enabling is destroying your family, and you are very concerned about your family's future.

What will your future look like?

To help you understand some of the far-reaching results of enabling, let's start with some questions that look at the worst case scenario. These questions refer to your child, but another family member can be substituted if this person is more relevant to your situation.

If you are an enabler:

- Do you want your child to live with you for the rest of your life? Even if your child is verbally and/or physically abusing you?

- Do you want your child to live with you, keeping you in such debt that you don't know how you are going to buy food and pay your bills each month?

- Do you want to live the rest of your life in extreme loneliness because the child you enabled is so badly behaved that no one wants to be around him or you?

- Does your enabling include protecting your child from the law? Are you a supporter or an accomplice in illegal activity? Do you know that you could lose your home if the law finds illegal drug activity occurring in your house?

- Is the torment you are causing your caring, dependable child a minor distraction compared to your need to fix everything for the child who is out of control?

- Do you want your adult children to learn from you and follow your example, enabling one or more of their own children – thus impacting your family for generations to come?

- When you die, do you want to leave your loved ones in a family warzone, a warzone created by your addiction to enabling?

- When you die, do you want your family to walk away from the one you have enabled, knowing the child you have always made everything easy for has developed no sense of responsibility and no life skills?

- Would you sacrifice your need for purpose, company, and control to see your child grow up and live in a responsible manner?

2

These are real concerns. Thankfully, people do not become accomplished enablers overnight. There is still time and hope for you and your family. With a sigh of relief, you may argue that your life isn't like that – it isn't that bad. In the hustle and bustle of everyday life, you probably see yourself as just trying to manage today.

So let me ask you some different questions:

Are you a superman or superwoman who has awakened to the fact you cannot possibly meet everyone's needs, and yet you feel guilty when you say, "No"? Do you wish people around you would just grow up and fulfill their responsibilities? And yet they don't. Compassion rises up in you, and the next thing you know you are taking charge, fixing things, and making things right. How can you recognize when compassion turns to enabling? When is it time to draw the line? How can you give without becoming a victim? Is it ever time to say, "No"?

Being an active Christian in today's world is exciting, and yet very challenging; it is more than an adventure. We respond to God's call that compels us to be His hand extended to the poor, the brokenhearted, the hurting – helping to set the captives free from the bondages in their lives. It is our joy to help others. Rewarding? Yes! Exhausting? It can be. Let's see why you're so tired. What have you been up to?

In the last few months, have you?

Fixed things for
Sacrificed for
Rescued them from their mistakes
Provided for over and over again
Nagged
Tolerated bad behavior
Begged them to change
Bribed them to change
Threatened when they refused to change

3

Made excuses for
Protected from consequences
Lied to protect from consequences
Lied to keep the peace
Cleaned up after again and again
Tried to control
Given an ultimatum
Screamed and yelled, but nobody listened
Felt responsible for
Denied or ignored the truth for
Bragged about doing things for
Acted like a martyr
Suffered in silence
Pretended things weren't happening
Threatened to quit, but did it anyway
Searched through pockets, drawers, or the computer history
Walked on eggshells to keep the peace
Hovered over
Bailed out
Bargained with
Felt pity for
Felt guilty about
Feared rejection from
Or otherwise been obsessed with someone else's needs and wants

You appear to be a tower of strength, but everything is out of control. I could go on and on – but enough! Being such a caring person who loves God, why in the world would you act like this – or even think like this?

Why do we enable them?

We enable them because:
We love them.
We are nurturers.
We take pride in being a devoted parent.
We just want to help.
Your problem is my problem.
We can't think about anything else.
We can't rest until it is fixed.

4

We just want things done right
No one else will do it.
We do it to stop the complaining.
We can do it better and quicker.
We need to feel needed.
Helping gives our lives purpose.
We feel sorry for them.
They have had a rough life.
Perhaps they were sickly.
Perhaps they have been through a divorce.
Perhaps they lost a job or a home.
They have failed before.
We can't bear to see them fail again.
They really need our help.
We know how to take charge and get the job done.
It's the way we have always done it.

Some are good reasons – at some time – but not all the time. You may have noticed, while you are helping, fixing, making things right, others are avoiding their responsibilities. You, my dear friend, have become an enabler. Can you believe it?

It is time to pray.

Lord, we are turning this all over to You!

Heavenly Father,

I thank You for loving me so much that not only did You send Your Son, Jesus, to die for me, You are the answer to everything that is wrong in my life. You know me as I am, and yet You love me. Jesus, I ask you to forgive me for my sins. I accept the sacrifice You made on the cross as payment for all my sins. Jesus, I want You to be my Savior and Lord.

Lord, please give me discernment to know what is truly going on in my life. I need courage to face the truth. I need determination and endurance to see my life radically and permanently changed. I need Your direction, so that I may fulfill Your purpose in my life.

Lord, I thank You, praise You, and trust You. I love You, Lord. In the name of Jesus, I pray. Amen.

Let me clarify: Enabling is a destructive form of helping, usually allowing others to avoid responsible behavior and to avoid growing up and becoming a caring, mature person.

The Dilemma:

If you are like me, it is easy to look at your current emergency and think: Well, I am in trouble if I do, and I am in trouble if I don't. Come on, if I fix the situation, at least it is fixed. Maybe this time he will learn from it and grow up. Oh God, please make it soon! But he is 50 years old! Yeah, but that doesn't mean he has grown up. Face it — we have all enabled other people, children and adults, to avoid responsibility at some time.

It could be something as simple as a spouse continually dropping dirty clothes all over the house, leaving them for the maid. Oh, you don't have a maid, do you? Neither do I. So who is picking up the dirty clothes at your house? Are your children driving you crazy with disruptive behavior? Is a family member abusing alcohol, addicted to drugs, smoking, and always in debt?

At this point, many might say, "Hey, some of this could be more than enabling; this could be codependency." Yes, in psychological terms, where alcohol or drug addiction is involved, and the enabler becomes obsessed with the one she is attempting to help, codependency is present. Where appropriate, I will make reference to codependency, but my focus will be predominantly based on enabling from a Biblical perspective. You will better understand codependency as you learn about enabling.

6

It is time for Christians to recognize:

Anything that is a habit – a recurring problem, is a stronghold. Whatever the strongholds in your life, through Jesus Christ, they can and will come down.

If you have already recognized yourself or your family situation, you know you need help. Where can you go for help? You can get worldly answers that may involve drug therapy and months of counseling. Psychologists or psychiatrists will probably tell you enabling is your problem; it is a control issue. Secular therapists are limited to worldly solutions that attempt to resolve emotional or physical issues. God's answers are very different from that of the world. Too often the symptoms may be emotional and physical, but the real problems are spiritual problems that need Bible-based answers.

> The Bible warns, "See that no one takes you captive through hollow and deceptive philosophy, which depends on human tradition and the basic principles of this world rather than on Christ" (Colossians 2:8, NIV).

As you read this book, you will discover that control is only a small piece of the puzzle, a puzzle that must be put together, if our families are going to grow up into spiritual maturity.

I know I've got a few problems. Can I get a little sympathy here?

In my experience, there is one thing that really irritates me about enabling – you don't get much sympathy. I say, if you can't get that person you are "helping" to straighten up and live right – at least you could get some sympathy from others. But others see through the excuses. Sympathy is not going to help you. You don't need another pity party.

If I can't get sympathy, can I at least get some compassion? Compassion is a good quality, a Godly quality. Compassion does not have a destructive outcome. As Christians, we need the compassion of Christ, more than we need sympathy or empathy. God sees the root of your problem. He recognizes the seriousness of your situation, for He loves each one of us where we are. Thank God, He loves us too much to leave us there in our sin. And if we allow Him, He changes us from "glory to glory" (2 Corinthians 3:18).

What does the Bible say about the compassion of God?

The Lord is gracious and full of compassion, Slow to anger and great in mercy. The Lord is good to all, And His tender mercies are over all His works (Psalm 145:8-9, NKJ).

This I recall to my mind, Therefore I have hope. Through the Lord's mercies we are not consumed, Because His compassions fail not. They are new every morning; Great is Your faithfulness. "The Lord is my portion," says my soul, "Therefore I hope in Him" (Lamentations 3:21-24, NKJ).

Chapter 2:
Get Ready to be Changed!

How do you know when it is time to stop taking charge, fixing things, and making things right?

Some say, "I stop when I can't take it anymore, right before I explode – or more likely, a little after I explode." God does not want us to come to the point of exploding or going crazy. This breaks down relationships that may be very difficult to mend.

Others say, "OK, I'll just quit. They can take care of themselves." That might work, but you are still putting up walls. When you stop abruptly, you may have been providing so much help that your loved one does not have the life skills to continue on his own. Let's learn from the eagles: Even eagles provide their little eaglets with wonderful comfort, at first. The nest is lined with soft feathers, making it very cozy. When the time is near for the maturing birds to make their way in the world, Momma and Daddy eagle begin to pull the feathers out of the nest, leaving them with spikey branches – ouch! Not comfortable anymore! It is time for them to spread their wings and make a home of their own. As the eaglets grow stronger, the support is purposely and incrementally withdrawn.

9

Does your 6 foot tall, immature eaglet need to grow up? Maybe it is your spouse. Oh, why didn't his mother train him better? Maybe it is your children or grandchildren. Whether they live at home or on their own, do they behave recklessly or irresponsibly? Have your adult children abdicated their parental responsibilities? In too many homes, parents have chosen lifestyles controlled by sin. They have either decided not to parent or are unable to parent their children. As the grandparent who loves your grandchildren, have you taken on many of the responsibilities that should belong to your adult children? Now, you are literally raising your grandchildren. You tremble as you look at how your own children have turned out and know you have got to get it right this time. You cannot bear to see another generation lost. Or maybe it is not a family member at all. Maybe it is someone at church or in your community who is becoming increasingly dependent on you. Whether they are adults or children, there will most likely be tough love involved if they will ever be able to live on their own. God will help you.

Where do we start?

We start with you. At this point you may be asking, "Why Me? They are the ones with the problem. I want you to show me how to make them change." Ah, through Christ they will change – but first, you.

I have three questions for you:

1. How many years have you been saved?
2. Do you have a testimony beyond your salvation?
3. Can you give specific examples of God's faithfulness in your life?

Or does this sound like you?

"It is so hard to trust God! He makes me wait! I don't like waiting! I can't wait, and I don't wait. I don't like to bother God. I just jump in there and fix my own problems. Oh, and I fix other people's problems, too – my kids' problems, my husband's problems. Do you have a problem? Let me fix it for you. Your problem is my problem. Trus: me, I can help you."

You wouldn't behave like this, would you? Too many people want to approach life as a do-it-yourself project. God never meant life to be that way.

Know this: You will never be able to stop enabling others until you learn to trust God and wait upon Him in your own life.

When you race in, fix it, make it right, and don't wait on God for His provision or plan, you are actually enabling yourself. You may think this is impossible. After all, you take responsibility – you fix it. Ah, but you are not becoming the mature Christian God wants you to become. You spend too much time living on the edge of desperation by somehow trying to hurry up and fix the problems in your life or the lives of others in your family. God has a better way – His way.

Christ-like maturity and character are developed under pressure.

(James 1:2-6, AMP)

1. James, A servant of God and of the Lord Jesus Christ, to the twelve tribes, Greetings (rejoice)!
2. Consider it wholly joyful, my brethren, whenever you are enveloped in or encounter trials of any sort or fall into various temptations, [even like trying to fix everything – my comment]
3. Be assured and understand that the trial and proving of your faith bring out endurance and steadfastness and patience.
4. But let endurance and steadfastness and patience have full play and do a thorough work, so that you

11

may be [people] perfectly and fully developed (with no defects), lacking in nothing

5. If any of you is deficient in wisdom, let him ask of the giving God [who gives] to every one liberally and ungrudgingly, without reproaching or faultfinding, and it will be given him.

6. Only it must be in faith that he asks with no wavering (no hesitating or doubting).

Did you notice if the Scripture said, "If any of you is deficient in wisdom, you should run to all of your friends and neighbors for advice"? No, it did not. Or how about, "You should stay up all night worrying?" No, again.

Asking God pleases Him. Trusting God pleases Him. Waiting on God pleases Him. When you pray in faith and ask God to provide, according to His will, He pours out blessings and provides answers that are above anything your finite mind can conceive.

> For it is Christ who "is able to do exceedingly
> abundantly above all that we ask or think, according
> to the power that works in us" (Ephesians 3:20, NKJ).

God's answer is better than anything you can imagine, figure out, or frantically fix up. God's answer is worth the wait. Right now, read Proverbs, Chapter 3. It is an excellent chapter that will help you learn to trust God.

Do you want or need peace?

> And we know that all things work together for good
> to those who love God, to those who are called
> according to His purpose (Romans 8:28, NKJ).

You may say, "I know these Scriptures." God wants you to live these Scriptures.

Before we move on to other people, let's try another scenario. The last one may have sounded too much like other people, not you. How about this one?

You get news that organizational changes are taking place at your worksite. There will be downsizing, and some workers will lose their jobs. First, you panic, and then you are angry. How can they do this to you after all these years of faithful service? Your anger increases as you lash out at everyone around you – your spouse, your kids, and the family pet. You snort and stomp while using inappropriate language. When things are calm, you say you trust God, but now you have problems. You react in frustration and anger. Someone gets a hold of you long enough to convince you to pray. You pray together, and God provides. At that point, you just wish you had kept your big mouth shut and trusted God.

Good News! You will have another opportunity to learn this lesson. God is an excellent teacher. He is patient and thorough. He doesn't mind repeating the lesson time and time again until you finally learn to trust Him. This can take a lifetime, or can be learned quickly. Some will never learn to trust God at all. It is up to you. How do I know all of this? Experience. I have also learned to ask God to teach me gently. "Lord, help me listen and obey the first time." I don't enjoy repeating painful lessons. God uses whatever is necessary to help us learn. When we maintain a good attitude and learn quickly, He is a gentle teacher.

Trusting God takes faith. What does the Bible say about faith?

"But without faith it is impossible to please Him, for he who comes to God must believe that He is, and that He is a rewarder of those who diligently seek Him" (Hebrews 11:6, NKJ).

13

You may be concerned, because you just don't feel like you have any faith. Paul tells us, "God has allotted to each a measure of faith" (Romans 12:3, NAS).

Although you may not feel like it, you were given at least a measure of faith. And if you need more faith – which you will – God has provided a simple, but effective way for increasing faith:

"Faith comes by hearing, and hearing by the Word of God" (Romans 10:17, NKJ). If you want to increase your faith in God, you will read and listen to His Word.

God expects you to use your faith. "The just shall live by his faith" (Habakkuk 2:4, NKJ).

"For we walk by faith, not by sight" (2 Corinthians 5:7, NKJ).

Your actions demonstrate your faith. "Faith was working together with his works, and by faith was made perfect. You see that a man is justified by works, and not by faith only. For the body without the spirit is dead, so faith without works is dead" (James 2:22, 24, 26, NKJ).

"I am a worrier. I believe worrying shows that I care. Is that OK?"

Some people view worrying as a vital life skill, but in reality, it does not please God. Worrying is not faith; it is fear. Therefore, it is sin. Sin separates us from God and what He wants to do in our lives (Isaiah 59:2). Sin withholds blessings from us (Jeremiah 5:25). Worrying about the past or the future steals our peace and joy today.

Worrying robs us of sleep. To please God, our faith must be in Him. Worrying has to go!

"It is easy to say, 'Trust God,' but how can I really learn to trust Him?"

We'll start with the basics. As we continue through the book, there will be greater depth and detail which will also help you learn to trust God. All of this will work together to help you become a mature Christian.

1. If you have not done so already, receive Jesus as your Savior and Lord.

Ask Him to be your Savior, to cleanse you from your sins, and to be the Lord of your life.

> Jesus said, "For God so loved the world that He gave His only begotten Son, that whoever believes in Him should not perish but have everlasting life. For God did not send His Son into the world to condemn the world, but that the world through Him might be saved" (John 3:16-17, NKJ).

2. In order to trust God, you have to know Him.

Are you reading the Bible every day?

> Romans 12:2 encourages us, "And do not be conformed to this world, but be transformed by the renewing of your mind, that you may prove what is that good and acceptable and perfect will of God."

God's ways are so different than our ways. Pray before you read, and He will reveal awesome truth found only in His Word.

> Jesus said, "And you shall know the truth, and the truth shall make you free" (John 8:32, NKJ).

15

Reading the Bible will demonstrate His amazing power throughout generations. You will learn how people who lived in Bible times learned to trust God. He is the same today. God has not changed. What He did for others, He will do for you (Acts 10:34).

3. Does your family need a miracle? Pray in faith.

> Paul instructs us, "Be anxious for nothing, but in everything by prayer and supplication, with thanksgiving, let your requests be made known to God; and the peace of God, which surpasses all understanding, will guard your hearts and minds through Christ Jesus" (Philippians 4:6-7, NKJ).

When you pray, be specific. A lot of people don't want to bother God with the details and prefer to just pray that the Lord bless them. This type of prayer produces very few testimonies. When you are specific, you will know it is God answering your prayer – it is what you asked for.

How will I know it is really God's answer for me? The answer will be RIGHT. It will be amazing, beyond that which you could ask or think. Yes, God still performs miracles today, for those who believe Him.

The Bible declares that God answers all prayers.

> Jesus said, "So I say to you, ask, and it will be given to you; seek, and you will find; knock, and it will be opened to you. For everyone who asks receives, and he who seeks finds, and to him who knocks it will be opened" (Luke 11:9-10, NKJ).

Do not let Satan, the father of lies, tell you any differently. When you pray and feel distracted, ask God to help you focus. He is not looking for long prayers, just prayers from your heart. He is not hard of hearing, and He is faithful to answer.

In my times of desperation, times when my situation seems so impossible, I ask God for His answer, His will in my life. I specifically declare my need and don't try to tell Him how to supply it. That would only limit God. His ways are above my ways. He sees the whole picture. I usually tell Him I don't know how He can solve my problems, but I know He can and He will. Then I wait expectantly – looking for God's provision. As soon as I see it, I am quick to declare His faithfulness to others. It becomes part of my testimony.

4. Wait on God for His answer.

Sometimes God instantly answers my prayers. Other times, the answer to my prayer requires that I wait on Him. What do I say to people who ask me what I'm going to do? I am ready with my answer. I declare, "I am trusting God. I am waiting on God." Waiting on God requires faith.

> "Wait on the Lord; Be of Good courage, And He shall strengthen your heart; Wait, I say, on the Lord!" (Psalm 27:14, NKJ)

Exactly, what does "Waiting on God" mean? It means I wait until I hear from God before I do anything else. Do Christians actually hear from God? Yes. Jesus said that His "sheep follow Him for they know His voice" (Jchn 10:4, NKJ). God may speak to you in an audible voice or in a still small voice only your heart hears. If you have not been listening for His voice, perhaps you have been too busy fixing things. Perhaps you didn't even know it is possible to hear God's voice in current times. God still speaks. The question is: Are we listening?

> The Lord is good to those who wait hopefully and expectantly for Him, to those who seek Him [inquire

of and for Him and require Him by right of necessity and on the authority of God's Word]. It is good that one should hope in and wait quietly for the salvation (the safety and ease) of the Lord (Lamentations 3:25-26, AMP).

What can I do while I am "Waiting on God?" Pray, maintain a thankful attitude, treat others kindly, and focus on being faithful in your current responsibilities as you serve God. Expect God's best, and trust Him to work the situation out for your good.

What happens when you don't wait on God? When you run ahead of God and fix your children's problems, God has not had time to work in their hearts and lives. Your children have not had time to take responsibility for their actions. You may avoid the consequences this time, but there will be another opportunity for your child to learn the same lesson again.

When Moses led the Israelites into the wilderness, God performed many miracles. The people loved and celebrated the miracles, but it wasn't long until they started complaining, not waiting on God's plan. Read on as you learn and think about the surprising results of impatience.

(Psalm 106:11-15, AMP)

11. And the waters covered their adversaries; not one of them was left.
12. Then [Israel] believed His words [trusting in, relying on them]; they sang His praise.
13. But, they hastily forgot His words; they did not [earnestly] wait for His plans [to develop] regarding them,
14. But lusted exceedingly in the wilderness and tempted and tried to restrain God [with their insistent desires] in the desert.

15. And He gave them their request, but sent leanness into their souls and [thinned their numbers by] disease and death.

When they didn't wait on His plan, God sent "leanness into their souls." Today, too many people refuse to wait on God. When things do not work out like they expected, they are engulfed in depression. Waiting on God pleases God and demonstrates our faith in Him.

5. Focus on God and not on your problems.

"You will keep him in perfect peace, Whose mind is stayed on You, because he trusts You" (Isaiah 26:3, NKJ).

So many people get caught up in how and why the situation occurred. Chasing these answers does not produce peace in our lives.

In Proverbs 3:5-7, God teaches us how to apply faith:

Trust in the Lord with all your heart and lean not on your own understanding. In all your ways acknowledge Him, and He shall direct your paths. Do not be wise in your own eyes. Fear the Lord and depart from evil.

You don't need to know how or why. All you need to know is that God will provide the answer you need. I challenge you: Dare to trust the Lord.

Have you noticed many people feel like they have to comment on everything? Once you quit demanding that God tell you how and why, what will you talk about? Declare your trust in Him. Fill your mouth and your mind with these words: Lord, I trust You. It is not a mindset, but a statement of faith and submission declaring, "I am trusting Your plan for my life. God I know You will meet my needs according to Your riches in glory by Christ Jesus, because You promised" (Philippians 4:19).

Focus on God in the heat of the battle.

You may feel like your life is in the middle of a family warzone right now. If you focus on the battle, it will depress and defeat you. God has other plans for you. Read this true story teaching us how to respond in the middle of an overwhelming battle.

In the Old Testament, 2 Chronicles, Chapter 20, a multitude of warriors were coming to do battle against Judah.

> King "Jehoshaphat feared, and set himself to seek the Lord, and proclaimed a fast throughout Judah. So Judah gathered together to ask help from the Lord." At the end of the prayer they declared, "We have no power against this great multitude that is coming against us; nor do we know what to do, but our eyes are upon You."
>
> The Lord told them, "Do not be afraid nor dismayed because of this great multitude, for the battle is not yours, but God's." "Do not be afraid or dismayed – for the Lord is with you." They bowed before the Lord, and they raised their voices in praise as the singers went out before the army. When they began to sing, the Lord set ambushes; not one of the enemy escaped. God gave Judah rest, and God received the honor and glory for the mighty protection and victory they received that day.

Singing praises to God is an excellent way to build your relationship with God and to keep your focus on Him. It is part of a Christian's spiritual warfare. Singing praises to God moves your focus from your circumstances to God and gives you peace in the midst of your trial. You don't have to be an excellent singer. Sing songs of deliverance from your heart declaring your trust in God. Play recorded music and sing along. Find that old dusty instrument you used to play and praise God with it. Or just sing without music.

God loves to hear you sing. In faith, praise Him with your whole heart and He will deliver you from the hand of the enemy. Singing may sound too simple, but singing is God's way.

> Psalm 32:7 declares, "You are my hiding place; You shall preserve me from trouble; You shall surround me with songs of deliverance. Selah."

6. Guard your mouth.

You can keep fear from creating a stronghold in your life by guarding what you say. Too many times we pray about a need, only to immediately declare words of fear and doubt about that same situation. When we do this, we are working against the answer that God has already put into motion. God is not moved by our complaining. He is responds to our faith.

> Jesus said, "Whatever things you ask when you pray, believe that you receive them, and you will have them" (Mark11:24, NKJ).

7. Step out in faith.

You may not like what God is asking you to do, but it will be the right thing for your situation. Know this: Feelings follow actions; actions do not follow feelings. If you wait until you feel like it, you may never obey God. Step out in faith, and the feelings will follow. You will be overjoyed as God provides the answer you desperately need. You will have a testimony.

You can trust God's Word as you step out in confidence.

In our world today, the lack of honesty and integrity are causing nations to crumble and fear to abound. Only by returning to the Bible, can we know truth and place our confidence in God.

> "The grass withers, the flower fades, But the word of our God stands forever" (Isaiah 40:8, NKJ).

His (God's) faithfulness and truth endure to all generations (Psalm 100:5, AMP).

God is not a man, that He should lie, Nor a son of man that He should repent (Numbers 23:19, NKJ).

Paul confirms God's inability to lie:
Paul, a bondservant of God and an apostle of Jesus Christ, according to the faith of God's elect and the acknowledgement of the truth which accords with godliness, in hope of eternal life which God, who cannot lie, promised before time began (Titus 1:1-2, NKJ).

God's promises are true.
What He says He will do, He will do.

You can step out in confidence because there is power in His Word. God spoke the world into existence. So many times in Genesis, Chapter 1, God said, *"Let there be...."* and He created the earth. There is amazing power in His Word. As we trust in His Word and speak His Word in faith, we will see God miraculously move in our lives.

You may wonder, "If I speak His Word, does this mean I'll never have to wait on God?" No, many times waiting on Him will still be necessary – but His timing is perfect.

You can step out in faith in confidence because God will never ask you to do anything in opposition to His Word. His Word is truth and filled with wise counsel that confirms who God is and what He will do. Yes, when God tells us to do something, it may seem impossible, but our God is the God of the impossible.

Jesus said, "The things which are impossible with men are possible with God" (Luke 18:27, NKJ).

I can do all things through Christ who strengthens me (Philippians 4:13, NKJ).

"Be strong and of good courage, do not fear nor be afraid of them; for the Lord your God, He is the One who goes with you. He will not leave you nor forsake you" (Deuteronomy 31:6, NKJ).

8. When the victory comes, give God the praise, honor, and glory.

God does not share His glory with anyone (Isaiah 42:8). When you talk about luck or try to take the credit for your success, you rob God. It is God who makes you able to come through your problems as a victor instead of a victim.

How can you give Him the glory? Psalm 100:4 tells us to, "Enter into His gates with thanksgiving, and into His courts with praise." You give Him glory when you celebrate His greatness during praise and worship. You also give Him the glory by sharing your testimony. The victory is multiplied in the lives of others. Many will hear and dare to put their trust in the Lord. Seeing and sharing God's victory in your life will encourage you to trust Him again and again. Finally, you give Him the glory just like Jesus did – you complete the work He has called you to do (John 17:4).

Today, there are many who attempt to silence Christians. Christians cannot afford to remain silent. In these last days, sharing your testimony will be an integral part of your ability to defeat Satan and to experience the power of God in your life.

"And they overcame him (Satan) by the blood of the Lamb and by the word of their testimony, and they did not love their lives to the death" (Revelation 12:11, NKJ).

9. Learn from your life experiences with God.

If you don't learn from your experiences, you will forever need to go back to square one to learn how to trust God. If you are to be a lifelong learner, you cannot afford to forget the great things He has done in your life. Keeping a journal is a great idea. It doesn't have to be a daily journal, but it can be. Being able to revisit times of God's faithfulness and miracles in your life will be a great encouragement to help you trust Him in your current situation. Journals can also be a part of your legacy to your children.

Trusting God is paramount
in learning how to stop enabling others.

For your family's sake and for your sake, become that mature Christian God has called you to be and learn to trust Him. He will help you.

Chapter 3:
I Just Want to Help!

A reminder from the introduction - Please allow yourself the flexibility to read beyond the gender in each example of enabling. (Forgive me for not saying he/she; I found it too cumbersome.) Enablers can be male or female. Be open to what God is saying to you about your situation.

Now, we are ready to talk about those other people in your life – those people for whom you do everything. Have you noticed that they won't do anything for you, at least not without a major confrontation? Something is wrong. The following questions will help you determine if your help is beneficial or destructive. As in all things, pray first and ask God for His direction. If God says to do something, do what He tells you to do. Seek God, for He knows what they really need.

Do they really want or need your help?

Some of you just need to be needed. At lunch one day, I was speaking with a woman who enthusiastically stated that her adult children could not make any decisions without her. Her eyes beamed with pride as she told me that her children frantically called her to get her advice or assistance – almost every night! She smiled and said, "I have never said, 'No,' to any of my children. See how they need me." Out of her need to continue to mother her adult children, she keeps them frantically dependent upon her. Is this you? Some of you may have never recovered from the empty nest syndrome. It is time to declare that this is your Day of Deliverance. May God fill your life with other ministries, according to His will.

Are you listening to your children at all?

If they don't want your help, let them make their own mistakes. You did! "But they won't do it right." Well, you didn't either. This definitely is a control issue. Let them make their own mistakes. Don't do for them what they can and/or should do for themselves. "But, but, but…" Do you trust God?

When your children don't take your advice, are you offended?

Alienating your children will destroy your relationship with them. They want to make their own decisions. Yes, consequences will follow: some good, some bad. This is part of their learning and growing up. God can teach them, if you will quit fixing things and get out of God's way. Then, when they turn to God – because they desperately need His help, God will supply all their needs, and they will have a testimony. As a Christian parent, you will find that one of your greatest joys is hearing your children talk about what God is doing in their lives.

My mother, who loves me dearly, was a great enabler in my life. Every time I began a new project, she was ready with sympathy and advice. "That's just too much for you," she always would say. As soon as I heard those words, it wouldn't be long until I quit. One night, God gave me a dream. I dreamed there was a graph of my life displayed on a large chart. Jesus was seated in a wheelchair. He said to me, *"You cripple My work because you will not work for Me."* Through that dream, God changed my life. I told Him I was sorry and asked Him to help me change. I was no longer unstable, quitting as soon as things became difficult. I learned to pray, seek God, trust Him, and renew my mind by the reading of His Word. I learned that the things He would call me to do would definitely be too much for me. However, learning to rely on Him, He always helped me.

Don't tell your children or your spouse something is too much for them. Of course, whatever God calls us to do is too much for us. God expects each believer to trust Him and to walk boldly in faith to see His purpose accomplished in their lives. Be a partner in the journey God has prepared for your family members. Encourage them. Pray with them and for them. And the testimonies will come.

Does every conversation include a guilt trip?

Do you try to shame your family into compliance? Do you always add a generous helping of guilt with all of the advice you give? "You never call me, and you never come to visit me." Enjoy the call or the visit you are receiving. You cannot force adults to spend time with you. Instead, make the most of every call or visit with a cheerful attitude. Forget the complaints. Nobody wants to hear them. Be thankful that your children have taken time from their busy schedules to contact you.

Do they listen to you?

Or do they want you to do everything for them, but they really don't listen to anything you say. Maybe they have never listened to anything you have ever said, and yet you are constantly there for them. Listening is a sign of caring and respect. To really care about someone, you must listen to them. If they don't listen, it is time to step back. Yes, you have permission. Start withdrawing what you are providing, just like the eagle pulling the feathers out of the nest. Don't do it in anger. Do it in a matter-of-fact manner. Do exactly what you have already told them you would do.

Right now, take a moment and think about all the things you have declared you will do if your family does not listen to you. Are you threatening things that even you know you will never do? This becomes a matter of integrity. "Who, me? I'm not lying on purpose! I mean it when I say it. They know I won't really kick them out of the house." If this is the case, it is no wonder they don't listen to you. The extreme threats have probably been going on since your children were very young. If you want your children to listen to you, you will quit threatening things you know you will never do. Tell them the truth.

Does the person you are helping treat you with kind words and attitudes, or does he frequently respond in anger?

If you ask your son to do something, even a small thing, does he willingly do it, or do you end up in an argument? This places you in an abusive situation. You may excuse your son's behavior by saying, "Well, that's just the way he is. His daddy had a bad temper, too." This excuse becomes a generational curse – like father, like son. Or perhaps your grandson has had a difficult life. Do you excuse his behavior? "Well, he can't help it. His parents divorced, and things have been really hard." Things are hard for everyone – that is life. Your sympathy is not helping him. What you excuse, you will get more of.

How do you respond to your child's anger? Do you snap back in anger? You know anger doesn't solve the problem. Your anger confirms that fits of rage are OK. Do not argue with your children. Take control of the situation by declaring the conversation is over – for now. Stop, pray, and walk away until things have cooled down. You are not forgetting, but rather postponing the conversation for a time when both of you can listen and calmly discuss the situation.

When you revisit the problem, start with prayer. If he tells you he is sorry for not doing his part or for being unkind, ask for specific reasons why he is sorry. Don't say, "That's OK," because it is not OK. Honestly say, "I forgive you." Discuss what he could have done instead, a behavior that would have pleased God and you. Forgive and do not bring it up again. If he is really sorry, you will see change. If another occurrence starts, pray, calmly discuss, and forgive. Consistency is the key.

What if the person you are helping is constantly treating you with unkind words and anger?

Do not be deceived, your submissive example is not sufficient to make that person change. He perceives you as weak, to be controlled. Weakness invites aggression. He controls you with his anger. Even small children learn to do this, usually with tantrums. I've heard parents warn, "Don't make the baby mad!" You will not make the outbursts go away by trying to keep the baby happy. Instead, you are setting yourself up for a lifetime of manipulation that will never be satisfied.

One family I know figured out a plan to keep their eight year old child from acting out in church. They decided that they would not attend church together. One parent stayed home to take care of their volatile daughter. She was a child well known in the community for angry tantrums. "It is only a phase," the parents would say. The next thing you know, she became a rebellious teenager. Her parents continued to declare, "This is a phase. She will grow out of it." She didn't grow out of it.

A phase is not a Biblical concept. For the moment, it may seem easier to ignore or deny the problem rather than face it. Children outgrow clothing, but wrong behavior is not outgrown. Instead, it seeks a higher level of involvement to fulfill its constant need for satisfaction. It is much better to face the problem and train the child. Training is something that takes time. Again, consistency is the key.

Train up a child in the way he should go, And when he is old he will not depart from it (Proverbs 22:6, NKJ).

What kind of situation catapults your child into a full blown tantrum?

Your child sees an expensive toy he wants. You declare that you are not going to buy the toy. Loud crying starts. How long does it take for you to give in to his demands? Once your child recognizes weakness in you and the possibility of commanding the situation, he will make demands until you give in and give him what he wants. Whining, crying, and throwing things do not embarrass your son; they embarrass you. When you give in, it demonstrates that you do not follow through with what you say you will do. It is an integrity issue. It is sin.

It is a school night, and your daughter has homework. You insist that your daughter complete her homework before spending time with friends. She reads for a few minutes and then throws the book on the floor. You are exhausted and you don't stop her when she yells at you and angrily walks out the door. She has done this before, even after you specifically told her that she would be grounded if she did not do her homework before she went out to see friends. You gave in by not doing anything. Your daughter has learned that when you are tired, she can pretty much do anything she wants. Yes, it is an integrity matter. If you tell your daughter what to do, and she disobeys, it is your responsibility to provide the consequences you have promised. If you do not, you will have many years to see your relationship deteriorate. She may walk away from everything else she does not like in life.

Things are worse than ever!
I need help now!

People, including you, will not change until they think it is necessary.

- Are you making it easy for your children to remain as they are?
- Do you anticipate their needs?
- Do you constantly "walk on egg shells," so that your children are not inconvenienced in the slightest?
- Do you give in easily?
- Do you ignore the problem, hoping it will go away?
- Do you try to make and keep everyone happy?
- Do you avoid all conflict and anger?
- Do you follow through with consequences, or do you just try to get past this current tantrum?

If most of what I have asked is answered in the affirmative, you are being controlled by your child's anger. No matter the age of the person having the tantrum, there will be no change until it is perceived necessary. Wise parents do not assume their child knows their expectations. They train their children to know right from wrong. They train their children to know what pleases God. Wise parents are very specific, making sure their children clearly know the reason a change in behavior or attitude must take place.

What does the Bible say about anger?

In many Christian homes, in both children and adults, anger rules supreme. This is not God's way.

> The acts of the sinful nature are obvious: sexual immorality, impurity and debauchery; idolatry and witchcraft; hatred, discord, jealousy, fits of rage, selfish ambition, dissensions, factions, and envy; drunkenness, orgies and the like. I warn you as I did

31

before, that those who live like this will not inherit the kingdom of God (Galatians 5:19-21, NIV).

A fool gives full vent to his anger, but a wise man keeps himself under control (Proverbs 29:11, NIV).

An angry man stirs up strife, And a furious man abounds in transgression (Proverbs 29:22, NKJ).

Be angry, and do not sin. Meditate within your heart on your bed,   and be still. Offer the sacrifices of righteousness, And put your trust in the Lord (Psalm 4:4-5, NKJ).

So then, my beloved brethren, let every man be swift to hear, slow to speak, slow to wrath; for the wrath of man does not produce the righteousness of God. Therefore, lay aside all filthiness and overflow of wickedness, and receive with meekness the implanted word, which is able to save your souls (James 1:19-21).

So many times, parents look at each out of control behavior as an event and fail to see the pattern developing in their children's lives. It may look like a simple battle over shopping, activities, or homework. In reality, lifelong habits are being established. Your children may think they have won when they control you with their demands and anger. Wise parents know there is much more at stake than the current skirmish. Giving into their children's demands prevents them from learning to obey those in authority. If your children do not develop self-control and learn to cooperate with your authority, they will most likely never be able to maintain a good job. Their future employers will expect obedience, cooperation, and self-control. You may dismiss those outbursts as small battles, but those conflicts are actually shaping the character of your children and the relationships within your family.

If children don't learn these lessons early, when they are older, it will be easy for them to look at family members or friends and covet their successes. Many relationships and jobs may be lost, confirming that success is probably not in their future. Their increasing jealousy only makes their anger more intense. They want to be rich, but poverty chases and overtakes them. The only wealth they can grasp comes from Mom or Dad, which deals another blow to their long line of embarrassments. The habit of anger becomes a stronghold. Bitterness takes root, and the mistreatment of family members is not uncommon.

What does the Bible say about jealousy (which is also called covetousness) and bitterness?

> And Jesus said to them, "Take heed and beware of covetousness, for one's life does not consist in the abundance of the things he possesses" (Luke 12:15, NKJ).

> For wherever there is jealousy (envy) and contention (rivalry and selfish ambition), there will also be confusion (unrest, disharmony, rebellion) and all sorts of evil and vile practices (James 3:16, AMP).

> Let all bitterness, wrath, anger, clamor, and evil speaking be put away from you, with all malice (Ephesians 4:31, NKJ).

> See to it that no one misses the grace of God and that no bitter root grows up to cause trouble and defile many (Hebrews 12:15, NIV).

Whether you are the enabler or the one enabled, anger, bitterness, and jealousy will destroy you and your relationship with your family. These battles rage every day throughout America. They keep many in bondage that can only be broken by forgiving and

33

trusting in God. Unless all involved recognize their sin and ask for forgiveness, the intensity of the ongoing struggle may be unbearable.

Is your family currently engaged in a torrential storm of anger and bitterness? God sees your situation. Your responsibility is to forgive, pray for your family, read the Word, and do what is right. As you learn to step back and trust God, He is not only working in your life, but the lives of your family members. He will give you peace in the midst of the storm.

You may or may not be able to physically remove yourself from the problem. However, when your trust is in God, He will do what you cannot do for yourself – He will remove you emotionally from the situation. He will give you clarity of mind to know right from wrong, truth from lies, and the courage to do what is right in the heat of the battle. God will protect you and give you peace.

Manipulation

Instead of anger, maybe your daughter learned to manipulate you through sweet talk. Sweet talk allows her to avoid responsibility – that means work. First it's the dirty laundry; next it's the kids. Your daughter just never seems to have any time to spend with them. She is so busy. You may say, "Well, I'm just sitting around here with nothing to do." You old martyr, you! Let her do her own laundry and raise her own children. (Occasionally, however, you will still need to take care of your grandchildren, or else they won't bond with you. Balance, my dear, balance.)

By raising her own children, your daughter can, and hopefully will, learn about the parent/child relationship at many levels:

- Her relationship with God the Father
- Her relationship with you, her earthly parent
- Her relationship with her children

God will use this time of parenting as a time for growing up, if you will step back and permit it to happen. Pray for self-control. If you have been taking charge of all the details in your grandchildren's lives, you will need self-control to allow your daughter to grow up and be the parent.

"My child just doesn't have the personality type that likes to work."

Many children and adults who don't want to work are plain old lazy. They just want to play. Work is part of growing up and becoming responsible. Let me ask you a question: Are you so focused on spending quality time with your children or grandchildren, you forget about work time? If quality time is only amusement parks and fun activities, it is no wonder children cannot settle down to work. You may even excuse their out of control behavior, defending, "Aw, they're just having fun!" Has everything become fun and games – as if the world revolves around them?

Then comes fall, and it's time to go back to school. You may have allowed or even encouraged your children to have fun and be hyperactive all summer. A month or two of absolute freedom will work against their self-control and ability to focus on learning when they return to the classroom. You could argue that school is supposed to be fun. In reality, school prepares our children for the world of work. Yes, we want our children to enjoy their childhoods, but play must be balanced with a healthy portion of lessons and activities that help them learn to become good workers.

Perhaps you have tried including chores in family time. When you reflect on your last household chore adventure, did you determine it just wasn't worth the hassle? Every time you wanted them to work, there was conflict. Know this: Work is a reality of life. Too many children have been enabled to think that true value and happiness in life is based on play. They are not taught to serve and be productive family members, Christians, and citizens. What can parents and grandparents do? Instead of always assigning your

35

children work, find frequent opportunities where you can work together. Talk about work in positive terms, not as a four-letter word. Chat about your life, the experiences that have made you a better person, and how God has blessed you. Ask lots of questions to engage your children in the conversation. And in the end, celebrate the joy of a job well done.

"My child was sick and almost died. I just can't require anything from her."

Consider the following situation. God healed your daughter, and now you don't expect anything from her? This is not a testimony to God's greatness. Everyone needs to have a productive life. For many, healthy or sick, it is a learned helplessness. If you will do it for her, why should she even try? Am I saying you should never help your child? No. Everyone needs a little help now and then. Don't do for her what she can and should do for herself. God has high expectations for parents and their children. He expects us to rise above our circumstances and trust Him to help us live productive lives.

"I adopted my child. Now, he is going to have a perfect life."

Perhaps God gave you a child through adoption. Did you rescue your child from intolerable living conditions? Now that his struggle is over, you want to give him a perfect life in your home. If you continuously make his life easy, requiring no struggle or determination to succeed, he may always expect someone to make things easy and perfect for him. This is enabling. Enabling will be very destructive to him and your family. Parenting is never easy, but God can use the challenges in his life to teach your son to trust Him. All children, including adopted children, need to experience and overcome challenges in order to grow up to be caring, responsible adults. Your love for your adopted son will be demonstrated as you teach, encourage, support, and have high expectations for him.

What else, besides the desire to help, compels us to enable our children?

For many, it is guilt. Maybe you were a mother who worked instead of staying home to raise your children. Dads, of course, were expected to go to work. Many working mothers did not want their families to have to do chores just because they went to work. The more women did, the more husbands and families expected it – the house, the job, and the church. Mothers learned to multi-task all day, every day. Do you wonder if your family would have been less dysfunctional and more successful if you had not worked? How much guilt do you carry due to working and trying to be a superwoman?

Guilt cannot change the past, nor is guilt a Godly quality. When we turn our lives over to God and repent, He takes us where we are, forgives, and changes us. Whether it is guilt over sin or guilt over choices we have made, He does not want us to live our lives burdened down with guilt. As we trust Him, He gives us peace over our past and hope for the future.

Satan's goal is to have you so depressed about your past, you have no hope for your future. He is the "accuser of the brethren" (Revelation 12:10). He vividly flaunts your past in front of you. This way he can either seduce you to return to that sin or flood your mind with unbearable regrets and sorrow. Do you frequently dwell on the pain and failures of your past? Satan wants to keep you so entangled in your past that you have no strength and energy to serve God today. The good news is Jesus came to set the captives free from all bondage caused by sin. It is time to leave your past behind you – no turning back. Allowing God to free you from guilt is one more step in setting your family free from the damage enabling has caused.

Do you have a fear of repeating the past?

Many a parent has declared, "I am determined that my children will never grow up like I did!" Did you have a difficult and unhappy childhood? Did you grow up in poverty and declare, "My child will never have to do without." Did you grow up with parents who demanded that you clean your room, mow the grass, and babysit siblings? Now you insist, "My child will never have to work as hard as I did!" Did you grow up where one child was favored over another and proclaim, "My child will be an only child who never has to share anything. My child will be the center of my life."

So how did things work out for you? Have you made everything easy for your children? Have you dedicated your time, energy, and finances to ensure your children are happy? After all you have done for your children and given to your children, are they happy? Have you made things so easy for your children that when they have challenging tasks at school or home, they develop angry attitudes? Does their loud complaining and out of control behavior drive you to lock yourself in the bathroom – just to get a little peace and quiet?

When you started out, you probably just wanted to give your children a better childhood than you experienced. Keeping your children happy is humanly impossible. God never gave you that assignment. He desires that we find our happiness in Him. Only He can satisfy our need for joy and peace. This is true for adults and children. By trying to make everything easy for your children, which is supposed to make them happy, are your children now miserable?

Our children will have to face many difficult times in their lives. If they don't develop the skills necessary to face and work through their problems, they will find it easier to quit everything they start. Do you really want your children to quit by dropping out of school, getting a divorce, giving up on a good career, or abandoning their children? No. Of course not. Parents please God when they teach their children to work hard and complete difficult assignments. Your children are capable of doing so much more than you have allowed them to do. If you want happy children, teach them to trust God as they give their best effort to see completion of a job well done.

Myth: You can't love someone too much.

If you love your family, look beyond their immediate needs. If what you are doing is destructive, or will be destructive – STOP! If what you are doing is destructive, and you purposefully continue on the path you are on, you don't love them, or you don't love them enough to do what is really going to help them in the future. Love is more than satisfying an immediate need. Love is also purposely working toward a good future. Sometimes you may be involved, while other times you may need to step back and let your loved ones work through their own issues.

Chapter 4:
Discipline and Consequences Are God's Idea.

Unconditional Love or Unfailing Love?

Many people are chasing unconditional love: It does not matter what you do, I still love you. This is true for both the enabler and the one enabled.

- The one enabled may expect or even demand that others love and accept him as he is. This eliminates his need for a change in thinking, attitude, behavior, or appearance.

- The enabler may feel guilty if she does not demonstrate unconditional love to the one she enables. She may feel guilty for her role in causing the one enabled to become dependent and demanding. The enabler may also expect her family to provide unconditional love. She thinks, "After all, we are family."

Are people capable of unconditional love?

Even as we attempt to demonstrate love, if we are not careful, our love for others will turn to enabling. God's love does not enable us to sin. His love is the only love that can free us from our sins.

In this the love of God was manifested toward us, that God has sent His only begotten Son into the world, that we might live through Him. In this love, not that we loved God, but that He loved us and sent His Son to be the propitiation for our sins. Beloved, if God so loved us, we also ought to love one another (1 John 4:9-11, NKJ).

Jesus said, "A new commandment I give to you, that you love one another; as I have loved you, that you also love one another. By this all will know that you are My disciples, if you have love one for another" (John 14:34-35, NKJ).

In His unfailing love for us, God looks beyond our sin and circumstances. The Lord corrects, disciplines, and even punishes us to call us back to His place of refuge and holiness. Oh, that we would be faithful to listen and obey.

(Hebrews 12:5-14, NKJ)

5. "My son, do not despise the chastening of the, Lord Nor be discouraged when you are rebuked by Him;
6. For whom the Lord loves He chastens, And scourges every son whom He receives."
7. If you endure chastening, God deals with you as with sons; for what son is there whom a father does not chasten?
8. But if you are without chastening, of which all have become partakers, then you are illegitimate and not sons.

9. Furthermore, we have had human fathers who corrected us, and we paid them respect. Shall we not much more readily be in subjection to the Father of spirits and live?

10. For they indeed for a few days chastened us as seemed best to them, but He for our profit, that we may be partakers of His holiness.

11. Now no chastening seems to be joyful for the present, but grievous; nevertheless, afterward it yields the peaceable fruit of righteousness to those who have been trained by it.

12. Therefore strengthen the hands which hang down, and the feeble knees,

13. And make straight paths for your feet, so that what is lame may not be dislocated, but rather be healed.

14. Pursue peace with all people, and holiness, without which no one will see the Lord.

God desires a relationship with us. Part of that relationship, as with any parent and child, is correction and discipline. Parents who love their children do not enjoy punishing them. However, they know that many times, punishment is the only way their children will avoid the heartbreak of growing up to be irresponsible, uncaring, and out of control. When necessary, parents who love their children correct, discipline, and punish them.

God takes sin seriously.

Some Bible teachers have defined sin as "missing the mark." This comes from the Greek, where archers in an attempt to qualify for the army, were tested. It was said that unsuccessful archers "missed the mark." Today, one might look at this and decide that nobody hits the bull's eye every time – nobody is perfect, thus making sin a normal error in life. In the original explanation, "missing the mark" disqualified the archers from receiving the prize.

For Christians, the prize is spending eternity in heaven with God. It wasn't long until "missing the mark" was used without further explanation. Without the explanation, "missing the mark" is inadequate. It does not create an urgency to repent and obey God. To put this into perspective, compare "missing the mark" with the Scriptures that describe sin as an abomination to the Lord.

What does the Bible say about sin?

These six things the Lord hates, Yes, seven are an abomination to Him: A proud look, A lying tongue, Hands that shed innocent blood, A heart that devises wicked plans, Feet that are swift in running to evil, A false witness who speaks lies, And one who sows discord among brethren (Proverbs 6:16-19, NKJ).

For the perverse person is an abomination to the Lord (Proverbs 3:32, NKJ).

"There shall not be found among you anyone who makes his son or his daughter pass through the fire, or one who practices witchcraft, or a soothsayer, or one who interprets omens, or a sorcerer, or one who conjures spells, or a medium, or a spiritist, or one who calls up the dead. For all who do these things are an abomination to the Lord" (Deuteronomy 18:10-12, NKJ).

"But the cowardly, the unbelieving, the vile, the murderers, the sexually immoral, those who practice magic arts, the idolaters, and all liars—their place will be in the fiery lake of burning sulfur. This is the second death" (Revelation 21:8, NIV).

Can I hide my sin from God? No.

"For My eyes are on all their ways; they are not hidden from My face, nor is their iniquity hidden from My eyes" (Jeremiah 16:17, NKJ).

God knows my heart.

You may think, "I know I've sinned. After all, nobody is perfect. Surely God knows my intentions." It may give you a momentary peace to say that God knows your heart, but the question is: Do you know your heart?

What does the Bible say about your heart?

(God) He knows the secrets of the heart (Psalm 44:21, NKJ).

Every way of a man is right in his own eyes, But the Lord weighs the hearts (Proverbs 21:2, NKJ).

And He said unto them, "You are those who justify yourselves before men, but God knows your hearts. For what is highly esteemed among men is an abomination in the sight of God (Luke 16:15).

For the word of God is living and powerful, and sharper than any two-edged sword, piercing even to the division of soul and spirit, and of joints and marrow, and is a discerner of the thoughts and intents of the heart (Hebrews 4:12, NKJ).

The heart is a deceiver!

God knows the thoughts, intents, and secrets of your heart. When you think your motive is pure, He knows the real reason behind every choice you make. Some are pure, but some are not.

Sometimes we don't even know why we do what we do. You see, the heart is a deceiver. It will tell us what we are doing is right, and when we get through, it will act shocked when the real results are destructive. Practiced over time, sin desensitizes our understanding and is easily excused. It isn't long until it is difficult to discern that our actions and attitudes are really sin.

For instance, you send your adult daughter to purchase milk at the grocery store. You give her twenty dollars, knowing she is an alcoholic and that she will probably buy the alcohol you have refused to purchase for her. When you choose not to go to the store yourself, you place her in a position of temptation. For you, it is easy to justify that you are busy and can't be with her every time she goes to the store. You send her to the store alone. It is her responsibility to purchase the milk and return home. However, in the end you are enabling your daughter to, once again, get drunk.

> The heart is deceitful above all things, And desperately wicked; Who can know it? (Jeremiah 17:9, NKJ).

> He who trusts in his own heart is a fool, But whoever walks wisely will be delivered (Proverbs 28:26, NKJ).

> The pride of your heart has deceived you (Obadiah 1:3, NKJ).

Our hearts are not as pure as we would like to think. We hide secret motives and things we do, knowing the results may cause problems for others. When greed, impatience, laziness, or anger rise-up in us, we can justify almost anything. Oh, the heart is a deceiver, all right. Only God can provide the truth that will set us free from our sins. As we learn to trust and submit our lives to Him, He reveals and cleanses our hearts. He restores our relationship with Him and others.

What does the Bible say about discernment and understanding?

> The fear of the Lord is the beginning of wisdom; all who follow his precepts have good understanding. To him belongs eternal praise (Psalm 111:10, NIV).

> Teach me, O Lord, to follow Your decrees, then I will keep them to the end. Give me understanding, and I will keep Your law and obey it with all my heart. Direct me in the path of Your commands, for there I find delight (Psalm 119:33-35, NIV).

> I obey Your precepts and Your statutes, for all my ways are known to You. May my cry come before You, Lord; give me understanding according to Your Word. May my supplication come before You; deliver me according to Your promise (Psalm 119:168-170, NIV).

> And this I pray, that your love may abound still more and more in knowledge and all discernment, that you may approve the things that are excellent, that you may be sincere and without offense till the day of Christ, being filled with the fruits of righteousness which are by Jesus Christ, to the glory and praise of God (Philippians 1:9-11, NKJ).

God knows your heart, but your children see your actions.

Whether our children are young or have grown to be adults, our children are aware of the sin in our lives. We may think that we hide our sins from them. We may think that those sins really don't matter. But our children are learning from us. Even when they declare, "I'll never be like you!" they will.

God uses consequences to correct His children.

God knew we would disobey Him. He knew that even after we were saved, there would be times when we would disobey Him. God will not send Jesus to the Cross again to pay for our disobedience. It is finished. Now, asking for forgiveness and changing our behavior is necessary. God forgives us when we repent, but that does not eliminate consequences.

> And whatever you do, do it heartily, as to the Lord and not to men, knowing that from the Lord you will receive the reward of the inheritance; for you serve the Lord Christ. But he who does wrong will be repaid for what he has done, and there is no partiality (Colossians 3:23-25, NKJ).

God, in His wisdom, and since the beginning of time, placed road signs and roadblocks called consequences to deter us from wrong attitudes and wrong actions. But if we are determined to do things our own way, even if it destroys us, He will let us experience the full destructive power of our sin. Yes, He loves us, but He will allow our lust for pleasure, violence, and doing things our own way to overtake us – if that is our heart's desire.

> It is a joy for the just to do justice, But destruction will come to the workers of iniquity (Proverbs 21:15, NKJ).

> The curse of the Lord is on the house of the wicked, But He blesses the home of the just (Proverbs 3:33, NKJ).

> And even as they did not like to retain God in their knowledge, God gave them over to a debased mind, to do those things which are not fitting; being filled with unrighteousness, sexual immorality, wickedness, covetousness, maliciousness; full of envy, murder,

strife, deceit, evil-mindedness; they are whisperers, backbiters, haters of God, violent, proud, boasters, inventors of evil things, disobedient to parents, undiscerning, untrustworthy, unloving, unforgiving, unmerciful; who knowing the righteous judgment of God, that those who practice such things are deserving of death, not only do the same but also approve of those who practice them (Romans 1:28-32, NKJ).

God desires that we fear Him.

The Bible tells us, "The fear of the Lord, is the beginning of wisdom" (Proverbs 9:10, NKJ). Does fearing God mean we worship Him with awesome reverence? Yes, but it means more than that. God wants us to listen to Him. We are to take God and His Word so seriously that we know our lives totally depend on Him. With God, there is hope. Without God, there is no hope. When we choose to trust God, our faith pleases Him and builds our relationship with Him.

Why don't people change?

A life consumed by sin, indicates a person who does not fear God. Maybe some people just don't know what they are doing is sin. However, even when confronted with their sin, many refuse to stop their sinful behavior. They prefer self-will over God's will. The Bible declares, "Because they do not change, Therefore they do not fear God" (Psalm 55:19, NKJ). For us to say we love God, and participate in ongoing sin, we are not being honest with ourselves or God. God sees our sin. He expects us to repent – be sorry, and change. To prove we have changed, Christians are to "Bring forth fruit that is consistent with repentance [let your lives prove your change of heart]" (Matthew 3:8, AMP).

How does God want us to demonstrate our love for Him?

> Jesus said, "If you love Me, keep My commandments" (John 14:15, NKJ).

We are deceived if we say that we love God and do not listen to Him or obey Him.

Disciplining your children is an act of love.

God has called parents to nurture and guide their children. If that was all it took to raise children to be caring, responsible adults, it would be wonderful. But as demonstrated throughout the generations and in the lives of families all over the world, correction, discipline, and punishment are also part of raising children. God, our heavenly Father, loves us enough to correct, discipline, and punish us. He has set the example for earthly parents, as well. Disciplining your children is an act of love.

What does the Bible say about parents disciplining their children?

> He who spares his rod [of discipline] hates his son, but he who loves him, disciplines diligently and punishes him early (Proverbs 13:24, AMP).

> The rod and reproof give wisdom, but a child left undisciplined brings his mother to shame (Proverbs 29:15, AMP).

> Discipline your son, for in that there is hope; do not be a willing party to his death (Proverbs 19:18, NIV).

> There is severe discipline for him who forsakes God's way; and he who hates reproof will die [physically, morally, and spiritually] (Proverbs 15:10, AMP).

11. Then the Lord said to Samuel: "Behold, I will do something in Israel at which both ears of everyone who hears it will tingle.

12. In that day I will perform against Eli all that I have spoken concerning his house, from beginning to end.

13. For I have told him that I will judge his house forever for the iniquity which he knows, because his sons made themselves vile, and he did not restrain them" (1 Samuel 11-13, NKJ).

Will you be the one to lead your family out of sin?

Many of our Christian children, even though they were brought up in the church, have become caught up in sin. Now, they are adults. Their lives and their children's lives are dysfunctional to the point of destruction. This will continue down the generations until someone is courageous enough to repent, ask for God's forgiveness, and choose to live according to God's Word. Will that be you? Will you be the one to lead your family out of sin?

Chapter 5:
Why Don't Parents Discipline their Children?

Do you have cute children or cute grandchildren?

Of course, you do.

Too cute to correct or discipline?

Real Quotes from Real Parents = Real Excuses

"My child is so cute, I just can't discipline her."

When our children are sweet and innocent, too young to really understand what they are doing or saying, it may seem funny when they copy the actions or conversations of adults. It may include inappropriate language, hitting parents, being sneaky, or something else. When parents giggle about behaviors they deem to be cute, they encourage more of those same behaviors. Now picture that cute little toddler as a teenager. That same bad behavior won't seem so cute. If not stopped, those behaviors will only get worse.

> Even a child is known by his deeds, Whether what he does is pure and right (Proverbs 20:11, NKJ).

53

Some would like to blame it on the "terrible-twos," "theatrical threes," or whatever you want to call the age. It is an easy excuse that has been used for generations. It is also a wrong placement of blame. All children do not experience the "terrible-twos" and "theatrical threes." Active parenting is needed. The parent is responsible for correcting wrong behaviors as soon as they occur and for setting a positive example. Parent with-it-ness is extremely important. Children need to know that their parents are present and aware of what is going on at all times. If children think their parents are not paying attention to them, they learn to take advantage of the moment. They learn to be sneaky and do whatever it is their parents do not allow. Even if you are not watching them, they are watching you to see your reaction to their behavior.

- Children of all ages benefit from swift and reasonable consequences.

- Young children will not connect the deed with the discipline if you wait too long to correct their behavior.

- When discipline is delayed for older children, it gives them too much time to come up with excuses to justify their actions.

- All hopeful children know that if the discipline is delayed long enough, Mom or Dad may forget it happened. Or their parents may dismiss the wrong behavior as past history. If you want to effectively correct behavior, it is better to address problems in a timely manner.

Finally, if your motto is, "Do as I say, not as I do," you are confirming that unacceptable behavior is allowed in your family. You are giving your children an open door to sin. Sin is never cute and always destructive. It may be time for your family to redefine – cute.

"My children would never lie."

Please come back to reality! Everyone is capable of lying. When you insist that your children are not capable of lying, it gives them freedom to lie. Now, your children can lie all they want, and they know you will never believe it.

Let's define lying: To lie is to make a statement or give an impression that is not true. Usually, deceit is involved.

Many times people are adamant that there is a difference between lies and white lies – you know those little white lies for convenience sake. White lies are lies, and all lies are sin. When our children have been led to think that white lies are not really lying, they are deceived. This confusion blurs the difference between right and wrong. If we want our children to do what is right, what is honest and true, we will not tolerate lying in our homes.

How can parents discourage lying? Once you discover your child has lied to you, require her to prove what she says is true. For instance, your daughter lies and tells you she has finished her homework. Her teacher notifies you that your daughter's homework has not been turned in for a week. Now, your daughter must prove her homework is finished. She must give you her completed homework every night. You take a few minutes to review the work to make sure it is legible and generally right. After she corrects the wrong answers, you sign at the bottom of the page indicating you have seen and reviewed the assignment. The papers are immediately placed in her backpack by the front door and ready to return to school the next morning. Will this work with other problems where lying is suspected? Yes. Requiring your child prove she has behaved responsibly will work with a variety of situations.

What does the Bible say about lying?

> Lying lips are an abomination to the Lord, But those who deal truthfully are His delight (Proverbs 12:22, NKJ).

> A false witness shall not go unpunished, And he who speaks lies will not escape (Proverbs 19:5, NKJ).

"Always trust your children."

Really? Did you always make decisions that pleased your parents? Did you ever do anything sneaky because you knew your parents would not approve? And you think your children are different? We have to be honest with ourselves – our children are human. They sin.

Wise parents become detectives and investigate any questionable situations. They consider past history. When you are honest with yourself and keep the right perspective, you will not deny the possibility of your child getting into trouble. This is especially reasonable if he tried the same sneaky things last week. Your child may be testing you to see if you meant what you said.

If you truly want to know what is going on in your children's lives, pray for discernment and the wisdom to deal with the challenges of parenting. God has a purpose and plan for our children. We cannot afford to subvert God's plan by ignoring reality. Active parenting is challenging, but worth the investment of our time. Active parenting pleases God. And we get great kids!

God wants us to trust Him without reservation. But our children? Trust your children, but take the time to confirm. They need to know that we love God, and we love them so much that we are fulfilling God's purpose for them. We investigate to make sure that they are not caught up in the ever present temptation to sin.

56

Bottom line: Always trust God. Trust Him to reveal hidden temptation in both your life and the lives of your children.

"Rules are made to be broken."

Just as a ruler is designed to keep lines straight, rules are designed to keep your life straight. As soon as a parent declares the old adage, "Rules are made to be broken," you give your children license to keep the rules they like and ignore the rules they do not like.

What does the Bible say about self-will?

> There is a way that seems right to a man, But its end is the way of death (Proverbs 16:25, NKJ).

> He who turns away his ear from hearing the law [of God and man], even his prayer is an abomination, hateful and revolting to God (Proverbs 28:9, AMP).

Parents who proclaim to their children that rules are made to be broken will find that their children easily transfer self-willed thinking to all situations. This is an excuse to live a reckless, perhaps even lawless, lifestyle.

Parents, who laugh at rules and mock the thought of sinful behavior, fall into this same category. Allowing or even encouraging perverse language, interest in pornography, sexual activity, and experimenting with drugs and alcohol make many a "cool parent" a contributor to the destruction of their own child. When parents wink and laugh at sin, they communicate to their children that experimenting with worldly temptations is just a normal part of growing up. The addictions and abortions that follow will become huge strongholds that may be impossible to break. Depression will be ever present. All this, in the name of fun, destroys the plan God has for both the parent and the child. God does not wink or laugh at sin. Many times the parent initially attempts to ignore or deny that there are any real consequences for these behaviors. The consequences of a sinful lifestyle will always catch up with the person involved in sin.

Since the day God spoke to Adam and Eve in the Garden of Eden and told them not to eat of the tree of the knowledge of good and evil, we have had rules. Rules are designed to protect us. Rules are created to help us live and work together as caring, responsible members of the community.

Rules that are well written usually stand the test of time and apply to many generations. When rules need updating, people who have authority and responsibility adapt, add, or delete rules to make them applicable to current needs. In America, voting is one way we participate when rules need to be changed. The Bible, however, continues to stand the test of time. God's rules do not change according to generations, but will continue until the end of time. Blessed is the family who honors God by obeying Him.

What does the Bible say about rules and obedience?

> Children, obey your parents in all things, for this is well pleasing to the Lord (Colossians 3:20, NKJ).

> Jesus said, "If you love Me, keep My commandments" (John 14:15, NKJ).

> My son, forget not my law or teaching, but let your heart keep my commandments; For length of days and years of a life [worth living] and tranquility [inward and outward and continuing through old age till death], these shall they add to you. Let not mercy and kindness [shutting out all hatred and selfishness] and truth [shutting out all deliberate hypocrisy or falsehood] forsake you; bind them about your neck,

write them upon the tablet of your heart (Proverbs 3:1-3, AMP).

Jesus said, "Blessed (happy and to be envied) rather are those who hear the Word of God and obey and practice it! (Luke 11:28, AMP)

"I don't care!"

Both parents and children have learned to escape reality by announcing, "I don't care!" It is a disrespectful statement that asserts, "I don't care what you think or what is right. I'm going to do what I want!" This attitude of rebellion takes us right back to the sin of self-will. It does not seek to please God. "I don't care," only seeks to please self. Parents, who set a good example, refrain from such a reckless statement. Parents who want their children to face real issues with caring attitudes will not allow their children to make this declaration. The entire family benefits when both parents and children care. What must we care about? Our relationship with God is vital. Our relationships with other people are important. We must care about and seek Truth. Our attitudes, actions, and choices are important, because we are important to God.

When we choose God's will over self-will, it is called dying to self. He is to be first and foremost in our lives. Though we may find some worldly success in pursuing self-interest and self-will, God does not reward success that is achieved outside of His will. It is all about God. "He must increase, but I must decrease" (John 3:30, NKJ). To please God, we are to trust and obey. Are there rewards? Yes! He rewards our obedience here on earth and in heaven, as well.

"He didn't know."

He didn't know someone could get hurt – he was just playing. He didn't know copying another student's test answer was cheating – he was just checking to see if the other student had the same answer. He didn't know he was stealing – no one told him that he couldn't take the jacket.

A great way to get out of trouble in any situation is for the offender to say he didn't know. Everyone will feel sorry for him because he obviously was never properly taught. So he gets the lesson again. That should solve the problem, but next time, when the same thing happens, and someone else catches him in the same wrongdoing, he will use the old fallback: "I just didn't know." It is an excuse that works almost every time. A lack of knowledge is not the problem. Parents and teachers need to recognize this as manipulation. We need to hold children responsible for lessons they have already been taught.

One year, when I was teaching third grade, a new student arrived in my class. Every day, he found ways to hurt other students. As the students entered the class, he would position himself to attack. When reprimanded for hitting, he said that he did not know that hitting was wrong. The next day, he was surprised to find out that kicking was wrong. The third day, who would have known that tripping a student with a backpack, was wrong? A child does not get to third grade without being taught that physical violence is wrong. This was quite a performance that ended in multiple consequences. Somewhere he learned that by professing ignorance, he could do what he wanted and probably get by with it. This behavior did not continue in my classroom.

We need to expect cumulative learning from our children. In too many schools, students are given weeks to get their behavior under control before consequences are ever implemented. This is wrong. It creates a poor start for the new school year. It wastes learning time. When year after year students have been taught the rules, parents and teachers should expect and require acceptable behavior. Consequences should follow when behavior is unacceptable. If the rules and consequences are taught and posted, beginning in the primary grades and continuing throughout the school years, giving students one more chance only ensures that behavior problems will continue. Young children may not be able to read the posted rules, but they can learn to obey by reviewing the expectations and associating pictures with the rules. Whether they are younger or older students, consequences should be age appropriate. Good behavior should be expected, encouraged, and occasionally rewarded.

What does the Bible say about professing ignorance?

> Therefore, to him who knows to do good and does not do it, to him it is sin (James 4:17, NKJ).

> If you say, "Surely we did not know this," Does not He who weighs the hearts consider it? He who keeps your soul, does He not know it? And will He not render to each man according to his deeds (Proverbs 24:12, NKJ)?

"He really doesn't mean all those bad things he says."

Excuses! Excuses! Excuses! What is in the heart of a person whose mouth constantly spews perverse language? The Bible answers it clearly:

> A good man out of the good treasure of his heart brings forth good; and an evil man out of the evil treasure of his heart brings forth evil. For out of the abundance of the heart his mouth speaks (Luke 6:45, NKJ).

Unless you are honest with yourself and your child, you will never end the ungodly dysfunction that exists in your family. Abusive words, threatening words, and cursing words all provide evidence of a perverse and wicked stronghold. You may try to defend your child by saying, "He only says these words when he is irritated. He's not thinking straight when he is angry." These are definitely excuses.

What does the Bible say about excuses?

> "He who justifies the wicked, and he who condemns the just, Both of them alike are an abomination to the Lord" (Proverbs 17:15, NKJ).

> Because with lies you have made the righteous sad and disheartened, whom I have not made sad or disheartened, and because you have encouraged and strengthened the hands of the wicked, that he should not return from his wicked way and be saved-in that you falsely promise him life (Ezekiel 13:22, AMP).

Quit denying the problem and making excuses. When you excuse bad behavior, that excuse is sin. If you are making excuses, God desires that you repent of your sin and actively trust Him to help you honestly deal with problems.

What about your child's perverse language? Of course, consequences must follow, but only God can cleanse your child and change his heart. What your child says matters – it matters to God. Can children repent? Absolutely, they can. Repentance is God's plan for people of all ages.

What does the Bible say about your mouth and what you say?

> Death and life are in the power of the tongue, and they who indulge in it shall eat the fruit of it [for death or life] (Proverbs 18:21, AMP).

> The fear of the Lord is to hate evil; Pride and arrogance and the evil way And the perverse mouth I hate (Proverbs 8:13, NKJ).

Whoever curses his father or his mother, his lamp shall be put out in complete darkness (Proverbs 20:20, AMP).

The lips of the righteous know what is acceptable, But the mouth of the wicked what is perverse (Proverbs 10:32, NKJ).

"You can't expect children to have self-control!"

Really? Learning self-control early in life helps children to be teachable and cooperative throughout their lives. As we discipline our children, they learn what is good and bad – what is acceptable to God and what is not acceptable to God.

Self-control is a gift from God (2 Timothy 1:7, AMP). Like faith, the more you use self-control, the more self-control you have. This is true for both adults and children. Not only do parents need to model and teach self-control, they must expect and require self-control to ensure proper character development in their children.

Excuses, pride, and denial of problems are three of the greatest enemies of self-control. Children who are enabled by these tactics find demanding tirades and explosive tantrums a frequent companion.

When children have self-control, it is much easier for them to cope with unexpected irritations and life-changing disappointments. They learn to turn these distractions into faith building opportunities where miracles happen, problems are solved, and God is glorified.

A wise person uses self-control to restrain emotions, while looking for a better way to resolve an issue. To a more aggressive individual, this person may appear weak. This is not the case at all. In self-control, there is great strength. Self-control is purposed, Godly, and part of a successful, stable life.

In today's society, where numerous homes are one-parent homes, many children lack self-control. God created the family and placed a Mom and Dad together to lead, protect, and nurture their family. As parents provide a united front and support one another in foundational beliefs, children grow up in an environment that is less likely to cater to their whims and demands. Is it impossible for single-parents to adequately raise children to have self-control? No. It is not impossible. We must recognize, however, that without support from the other parent, the single parent has to be very careful and determined not to become a permissive parent. Parents who overindulge their children by giving in to unreasonable requests or allowing their children to avoid responsibilities will experience heartache that could have been avoided. Being a single parent is not easy, but God will help you as you stand firmly on His Word.

Attending church on a regular basis provides all parents with additional, faith-based support. In church, we have someone to pray with us. In church, we can hear from others who have learned much about the challenges of parenting. We can learn from parents who have stayed the course to see the good fruit of their labor – adult children who love and serve God with their whole hearts. It becomes a generational blessing as these adults teach their own children to do the same.

What does the Bible say about self-control?

> Be self-controlled and alert. Your enemy the devil prowls around like a roaring lion looking for someone to devour (1 Peter 5:8, NIV).

> For God did not give us a spirit of timidity (of cowardice, of craven and cringing and fawning fear), but [He has given us a spirit] of power and of love and of a calm and well-balanced mind and discipline and self-control (2 Timothy 1:7, AMP).

> But the fruit of the Spirit is love, joy, peace, longsuffering, kindness, goodness, faithfulness, gentleness, self-control. Against such there is no law (Galatians 5:22-23, NKJ).

"My child is bored. You can't expect her to behave when she is bored."

Just because your child is not happy is no excuse for poor behavior. Most students who say they are bored are looking for entertainment – not something difficult to do. Boredom is an attitude problem.

Children, who have been taught to check their feelings, find it easy to quit when things do not please them. Do you quit your job when difficulties or interruptions occur? Of course, not. Our children also need to be able to persevere in the face of hardships. What causes your child to quit? Beyond boredom, does your child give up and quit when there are changes in plans, obstacles, distractions, disappointments, and other challenging times that require determination and endurance? Learning to persevere during difficult times is part of growing up and developing character qualities that will help your children become successful in life.

"My child does not know how to use self-control."

Could your child behave for one day if he knew he was going to get a great reward? Does your child behave during parent-teacher conferences or when the pastor comes to visit? If children or adults can behave at any time, they know how to behave. When they do not use self-control, they are making a choice. It is usually a choice driven by their feelings or logic – sometimes twisted logic.

Does your child react without thinking? People who develop a pattern of physical and/or verbal outbursts usually have a habit of out of control behavior. They do not check their feelings, but move

65

straight to explosion. Is there any hope for changing behavior when it has become a habit? Yes. Even individuals who react without thinking can experience a dramatic change in behavior when consequences are consistent. It is hard for most parents to be consistent, but it is the key for improving self-control. How long should you be consistent? Until the behavior changes.

Many parents give their children doctor prescribed medicines to ensure that their children use self-control. I am not against using the medicine, but it will not solve all behavior problems. The medicine must be accompanied by consistent parenting, if the behavior is to permanently change. None of this is easy, but it is worth your investment of time and effort. Trust God to help you develop the consistency you need to really help your child mature and become a responsible adult.

"I always say I'm going to punish him, but I never seem to be able to follow through."

What happens when parents do not follow through with consequences? It destroys trust. When you say that you are too busy or you changed your mind, it sounds like good excuses. Your children are learning that they don't have to keep their word when they are busy or when they change their minds. When your children misbehave again, you will be angry and frustrated. Sadly, you will probably not follow through this time either. Your children will probably speak rudely to you, and their behavior will get worse because they know you will not do what you said you would do.

To make it worse, your children no longer listen to you. Your children have learned that they do not need to listen to you, because you do not tell the truth. You threaten to punish them, but it is only words. Not following through with the consequences is a matter of integrity. If you want your children to listen and respect you, you will be true to your word. With discipline comes respect.

When discipline is not consistent, children learn to manipulate their parents. The dividing line between right and wrong blurs. If it was really all that bad, you would make sure it did not happen again. Now, the reality of your love is in question. If you really loved them, you would discipline them.

Your children are learning parenting skills from you. Unless you learn to discipline your children, this will become a generational curse that is passed on through your children and down to future generations.

"I don't believe in consequences. Consequences are cruel punishment."

Know this: Consequences are God's plan to teach us right from wrong. They are part of the life lessons that people need to experience in order to grow up and appreciate God, parents, and life. You may think you are helping your loved one by removing consequences. When you do this, you are working in direct opposition to God – a position that will destroy your life and your testimony.

"I just talk to my children. I never punish them."

Does your child always listen to you? Take a moment to think before you answer this question. Talking to your child and expecting a change in behavior probably won't be enough to ensure change.

In general, talking to your children and explaining what they did wrong, with a discussion about what they should have done right, is good. However, I have taught many students who when asked, could tell you in detail what they did wrong and what they should have done. They knew it was wrong. They just didn't want to behave. When the only punishment children face is a good "talking to," children are more likely to feel like they are getting away with no punishment at all.

What else encourages bad behavior? Choose pet names carefully.

Pet names can become a self-fulfilling prophecy. A student was misbehaving in class. I sent him to the office where his disruptive behavior continued. The administration called his father to come to school and take him home. When he walked into the office, the father laughed and yelled across the large waiting room, "Hey, Monster! What's up?" Dad promptly took him to McDonald's, where the student was rewarded with lunch. Later that day, the office staff informed me that this happens all the time. What a deal! Just misbehave and you get lunch with Dad at McDonalds. And no more school for the day! Not good.

Name calling and rewards for bad behavior enable more bad behavior. Whatever you allow or encourage, you will get more of. This works whether the behavior is good or bad. You are responsible when you encourage your child to continue sinful behavior. And those names: Monster, Bad Boy, Bad Girl, Rotten, and Hyper. You are prophesying over your children. And you can have what you say!

While on the subject of names, I have heard so many parents tell me, "At my house, we are on the buddy system." Greetings include, "Hey Buddy!" or "What's up Girlfriend?" When you do this, you are destroying your authority – your God given authority. If you are only a friend to your children, your children will not learn to obey you. If they don't learn to obey early in life, they will have great difficulty at school, on the job, and with the law. They may never learn to obey God. You are sacrificing a lot for a few moments of silly name calling.

You may think that honoring your parents is soooo old fashioned. The Bible tells us, "Honor your father and your mother that your days be long upon the land which the Lord your God is giving you" (Exodus 20:12, NKJ). God wants your children to honor you. Do you want your children to have long lives that please God?

Teaching your children to honor God requires respectful behavior toward God, parents, and others.

"What's the point? Nobody uses good manners anymore."

Good manners are still appreciated by caring, responsible adults. If you want your children to be able to cordially get along with others, they need to know and use good manners. Please, thank-you, you're welcome, and excuse me are some of the ways to keep a conversation pleasant and express appreciation to the other person. When good manners are used by parents on a regular basis, children naturally learn those manners. They also learn that kindness promotes positive relationships.

"Sometimes, I'm just too tired to decide."

Have you tried to make your young child a decision maker too soon? There are many decisions that young children can make. They are decisions that do not place anyone or anything in danger. These decisions are obvious: Do you want vanilla or chocolate? Do you want to play at the park or at home? Often parents escalate the opportunity for decision making to determine where the family will eat dinner or what the family will have for dinner. Maybe you are too tired to make the selection and find it easy to let your child decide. This in and of itself, is not a problem, but when your child starts making all of the decisions determining dinner, you are placing your child into a position of authority. When this happens, it isn't long until the parent is too tired to make other important decisions. In the meantime, the child learns to enjoy the position of authority and power. The family is not meant to have equal say in all decisions. Parents have the responsibility for paying the bills, keeping the family safe, and making sure that everyone works together in a cooperative, productive manner. This also includes attending church on a regular basis.

What happens when you treat children as small adults? Children do not have the experience to make wise decisions or the responsibility for the results of these decisions. Parents should include children in age appropriate problem solving and decision making so that they learn how to make wise decisions. However, the authority to have the final say remains with the parents. Children who learn this early in life find it a lot easier to come under the authority of the parents as they grow older. Learning to obey our parents is essential in learning to obey teachers, bosses, and most important, to obey God.

"Preteen dating? They're just having fun."

Does your preteen want to date? What if everybody else is doing it? Yes, and look at the condition of our nation! Even if everybody else is doing it, that doesn't make it right. Parents who want their children to do well in school, attend college or career training, and have a successful job, keep these goals in front of their children. They do not allow or encourage (enable) early dating. They know that once dating starts, children lose interest in school, and sexual activity may lead them on a path to abortions or STD's. This is not what you planned for your children. The responsibility of the parent is to see that their children get a good education. Later, there will be time for dating. Right now, the focus needs to be on education – if you want your children to grow-up and be able to provide for their families.

What about allowing children to entertain others in their bedrooms? I have known children as young as kindergarten age who were sexually active. Although you may have protected your own children, you cannot be sure what influences have been present in the other child's home. Use wisdom. Unsupervised time easily leads to unacceptable behavior, no matter what the age.

"I guess he just likes to learn things the hard way."

Some children are strong-willed and only learn important life lessons the hard way. When you try to compensate for your child's poor choices, you are rewarding poor behavior. Yes, it is painful to watch our children go through problems, when you know that their challenges could have been resolved with a little patience, endurance, wisdom, common sense, and/or self-control. Experience makes an excellent teacher when the experience includes consequences. Then in the future, when similar issues arise, your child will hopefully consider the consequences before acting. When children learn to stop and think before they act, things will be better. Better yet – stop, pray, and think.

How about a family project? Parents can teach and reinforce good decision making by thinking aloud as they talk through the problem solving process. This way, your children experience working through a problem with guided help. Usually this help comes in incremental steps, stopping along the way to think and talk about it. Teaching your children to analyze and make good decisions promotes independence and improved problem solving. The consequences still come, but this time, they will be the product of a job well planned and well done.

Some people think that school is the only place where problem solving should be taught. You limit your child when you don't share the skills and knowledge you have learned in your life.

What are some of the benefits of solving problems together at home?

- You and your child work together in a one-to-one setting. At school, the teacher works with many students. Even if you and your child have trouble talking together, patience, positive talk, and problem solving can help to improve conversations and relationships.

- Solving problems together allows your child to observe you as you practice modifying plans, procedures, or materials. To be a good problem solver, you must be able to adapt when the problem presents new challenges or unplanned surprises.

- The problems or projects you select at home will be different from those at school. Don't just announce the problem/project and give instructions on how it will be accomplished. Ask questions. Talk about possibilities. Take measurements. Draw diagrams. Plan for clean-up. Now, this is quality time well spent while working together.

What kind of problems would be good for home problem solving?

- How can chores be divided to make them fair for the whole family?

- How can we save money at the grocery store?

- Are there families in our neighborhood or at our church that our family could help? How?

- How can we make sure that everyone gets to school on time?

- What supplies do we need to paint a room?

- How can we make our back yard look better?

- There are plenty of arts and crafts kits available at a reasonable price, but even better, think of a project you can do to benefit your family, house, yard, or others.

Additional suggestions:

- Like everything in life, be sure to start with prayer. Ask God for direction, skills, and the ability to successfully complete this project. Ask God to protect you both when you use tools or need to travel.

- Problem solving is not something to be feared and worried over, but something to be worked through. If today is not a good day for you, select a date when you will not be rushed.

- Electronics, cell phones, and texting will only compete with the quality time you have planned. Agree to turn electronics off and put them away until your session is completed for the day.

- If you are working outside, consider the weather. Too much rain or excessive temperatures may not be conducive to the project. Plan ahead, but be flexible.

- Make sure ample adult supervision is available for all projects. This includes use of tools, use of money, transportation, etc.

- Be very careful to make plans that can be completed in a reasonable amount of time. Unfinished projects only cause frustration. Money is wasted and the valuable lessons which teach your children to finish what they start are missed.

- Be very aware that you are teaching more than problem solving skills. By your words and by your actions, God can use you to teach your child listening, kindness, calmness, sharing, cooperating, patience, determination, researching, flexibility, and endurance. You are also teaching your child to recognize God's presence in the everyday things in life and to give Him the glory for helping you successfully complete your task.

"Every issue becomes a WAR." Pick your battles:

If everything is a battle, your family has a habit of arguing. This is a stronghold that needs to come down. Ask God for wisdom and strategies. Everything should not be a battle. Do your family members have to be asked over and over and over again, placing you in the position of nag? You may think that you wouldn't be a nag if the other person would just do the responsible thing.

Do you have any late sleepers? I learned years ago to start with, "Last call!" It works. Try it. If your children normally go back to sleep every time you call to wake them up, they really don't know how many times you have tried to get them out of bed. No point in fighting on this one. Whatever you do last, start there. No screaming needed. I usually start with, "Last Call!"

Evening routines can eliminate arguing at bedtime.

- Establish consistent bedtimes.

- A warm bath right before bed, instead of a shower, encourages sleep.

- Limit physical activity before bed.

- Read books that are calming.

- Finish snacks at least one hour before bedtime.

- No caffeine after 4 p.m.

- Limit evening phone calls. All phones off by 8 p.m.

- Discuss family problems earlier in the afternoon or evening. Time for thought and resolution promote peaceful sleep.

- Pray and read the Bible together. Jesus is the Prince of peace.

Do you feel like your family is keeping the electric company in business? Do you have family members who won't turn off the lights? Obviously, they aren't the ones who pay the electric bills. Yes, teach and remind young children. For adult children, paying part of the electric bill is appropriate. For your spouse, continued nagging will not change the number of times he/she forgets and leaves the lights on. Don't tell your spouse that you will no longer nag on this topic – just quit nagging. Nagging only demeans your spouse. Nagging sets the stage for hostility in other disagreements. Instead, compliment him when he turns the lights off. If you want your family to listen to you on other issues, important issues, pick your battles. When they hear that you need their help on something, or that you are concerned that the family has a serious situation, they will be more likely to listen and to work with you.

"Instead of arguing, I just take the path of least resistance."

The path of least resistance is a well-known path to most of us. Just about everyone has walked down it at one time or another. When life gets difficult, challenging, or unbearable, do you divert to a position that avoids conflict? Let's face it: Parenting is not easy. Life is not easy. What is easy? For the moment, when you just cannot take any more, ignoring bad behavior seems easy. Many parents happily declare, "I'll just take the path of least resistance. I want to be a peacemaker."

Know this: Taking the path of least resistance requires no faith.

"Without faith, it is impossible to please Him (God)" (Hebrews 11:6, NKJ).

As parents, we discipline our children because we love them. The path of least resistance does not demonstrate our love and will not raise our children to become caring, responsible adults.

God's way for raising children requires faith in Him. God's way requires courage, determination, perseverance, and so much more. Years ago, experts told us to ignore our children's bad behavior and they would lose interest and eventually stop. It was an easy fix that fixed nothing. Ignoring the facts does not change the facts. Bad behavior is bad behavior. Ignoring bad behavior only enables our children to become more deeply involved in sin. It is peace at any cost. The consequences of ignoring or tolerating sin are a poor trade for a moment of peace and quiet.

Our children are learning who is in control. When you take the path of least resistance, you are not in control. Whether we are talking about behavior or attitudes toward learning and school, you either get these problems under control early, or they will only get worse, much worse, as your children get older. The path of least resistance merely diverts our attention long enough to get past the current demand or conflict. Bad behaviors remain unchanged. In order for our children to learn to recognize sin in their own lives, we must identify the wrong doing. We use active parenting to make sure these attitudes and behaviors are stopped. Our children need to know that their bad behavior does not please God, and we will not tolerate it.

At this point, you may say, "I knew it! It's my wife's fault! She always takes the path of least resistance. She lets the kids get away with everything." And why did she choose the path of least resistance? The husband may have spent years undermining the authority of his wife by making fun of her household rules. He may have even allowed or encouraged misbehavior when his wife was not present. Or worse, he may have encouraged his children to misbehave right in front of Mom. God wants husbands and wives (including grandparents) to present and maintain a united front. If you don't hold the line and require what is right, nobody else will. Then comes the day when your undisciplined child goes to school and comes up against the authority of the teacher. It will be a disaster! And when that same child rebels against the authority of the law – there will be serious consequences.

When you've "heard every excuse in the book!"

In many homes, children find it easy to excuse their attitudes, behavior, and failure to complete assignments. Where did they learn to make all of those excuses? Was it from you or your spouse? It is very possible that is was. Children, even at a very young age, learn to make excuses when they discover that excuses will set them free from consequences.

Does your child say, "I don't feel well," and you move into Super Mom or Super Dad status? Not feeling well is not the same as being really sick. Not feeling well is not a good reason to stay home from school. How many times have you gone to work not feeling well? You go to work because it is the right thing to do. You have work assignments to finish, and your paycheck is dependent upon you completing your work.

What other excuses get your attention? "I'll do it later." "I'm on the phone." "I just can't deal with it now." "I'm busy. I'm watching TV." "I'm tired." "This is boring!" None of these mean that your child cannot get up and finish the task that needs to be completed. This is no time for you to give up and do it for your child – that is enabling. If it is your child's responsibility to do something, they need to quit checking their feelings, set aside the TV, video game, cell phone, computer, or book, and just do it! Making excuses is a learned skill. If you want your children to follow your directions, you will give consequences for noncompliance.

"Not in my home!"

When unacceptable behavior and attitudes continue for a very long time, with no end in sight, many parents become overwhelmed with frustration. In exasperation many have declared, "You can do whatever you want when you leave home, but while you are under my roof, you will do as I say." Parents have been saying this for generations.

Making that declaration multiplies your problem in two ways. First, can your child/teenager really do whatever they want when they leave home and still be in right relationship with God? Will they be in right standing with the law? The answer to both is, "No."

Subsequently, it isn't long until leaving home means freedom. Living at home means bondage. Leaving home becomes their focus, and attending school becomes the obstacle they must escape. Instead of a positive attitude toward school, anger and resentment fill every thought. Freedom screams in their ears. As soon as they can get out of school, they can leave home and be free to do whatever they want. This lie robs homes across America every day. Too many children quit school. Now, their lives take a direction that their parents never expected or planned.

Parents who love their children train them to respect rules, school, finishing what they have started, and preparing themselves to be responsible family members and citizens. Be very careful what you say. Keep the goal before them. Your children are not through with school until they have life skills and career skills. When dropouts discover that their income is very limited, it isn't long until they move back home. It is most likely that they have changed. Moving back home may include sinful lifestyles and addictions. If you thought it was bad before – now it will be worse. Instead, encourage your children to stay in school and get a college education or training to work in a skilled trade. When they finally move out on their own, they will be equipped with life and job skills.

"I have other children to raise." / "I have done all I can do."

Are you too busy? Too tired? Maybe just too tired to be consistent? Know that Satan is neither too tired nor too busy, and he is making welcome the children you do not have time to parent. Now is the time to train and discipline your children, while they are young. It will be much more difficult, and almost impossible, if you wait until they have reached their adolescent years. Parents who love their children do not give up. Instead they set the example, hold firm to God's standards, require good behavior and attitudes, pray, and trust God.

The Bible says, "Correct your son, and he will give you rest; Yes, he will give delight to your soul" (Proverbs 29:17, NKJ).

78

"I really tried."

Do you start off with good intentions? When inappropriate behaviors do not change, do you give up? Maybe you lasted two weeks – maybe not that long. Your child's behavior problems did not increase to such a severe level overnight. Turning the behavior around, may not happen overnight.

Personally, I still believe in miracles. When I pray, I know that God hears me and sets into motion the answers that I need.

> Paul the Apostle wrote, "My God shall supply all your need according to His riches in glory by Christ Jesus" (Philippians 4:19, NKJ).

If you have enabling issues in your family, you need this stronghold to be broken in your lives. God said that He would supply your need. The answer to your need may come instantly or over time. If it requires an extended amount of time, do not allow frustration to overtake you. As a parent, you cannot afford to try for just two weeks and then give up. Keep your focus on God, and praise Him for bringing you through to a successful end. In no place in the Bible is the word "try" used when walking in faith. We are to trust God until the answer comes.

> Giving all diligence, add to your faith virtue, to virtue knowledge, to knowledge self-control, to self-control perseverance, to perseverance godliness, to godliness brotherly kindness, and to brotherly kindness love (2 Peter 1:5-7, NKJ), until the answer comes.

The perfect consequence:

I know you have waited for this answer. Parents should choose non-abusive consequences that are related to the offense, reasonable, and have an impact on your child's thinking. It should be a consequence your child does not want repeated. Discipline should not be delivered in anger, but as the expected result following inappropriate behavior.

Consequences – Some ideas:

- Time out in a Calm Down Area
  (Remember, the clock does not start until the offender is calm.)

- Loss of a privilege

- Loss of an item the child likes

- Physical work assignments

- Writing assignments (apologies and/or a statement of what I did wrong and what I can do to prevent myself from behaving that way in the future)

- Absence from family outings

- Absence from school outings

- Loss of activities to include: sports, music, drama, dance, cheerleading, etc. (This may be a temporary or permanent loss of activity according to the seriousness of the offense.)

- Loss of electronics

- Loss of allowance

Many parents would like for me to give them the perfect consequence to change behavior. The key is not the perfect consequence. The key is consistently providing the consequence you have promised.

Are the consequences you promised more like threats?

Are the consequences unrealistic or inappropriate? If so, it is time for change. Inform your children that they can expect changes in discipline. Use the following or create your own discussion.

- Explain to your children that you love them and want them to grow up to be caring, responsible adults. You want your home to be a peaceful place where everyone cooperates, and everyone can have a good day.

- From now on when they misbehave, you will pray about the situation and calmly decide the consequences.

- You will deal honestly with them and do exactly what you say you will do.

- Punishment will be fair and used to help them improve their behavior and attitudes.

- Excuses will not be allowed. Honesty will be expected and required.

- Children will correct their own wrongdoings – if at all possible.

- Apologies will be accompanied by a sincere attitude and willingness to change. Apologies will include why they are sorry and describe how a change in attitude or behavior will take place. Children will write the apology to document the plan they have agreed to complete.

- Consequences will increase if discipline is not received with a good attitude.

- Consequences will increase if behavior and attitudes do not improve.

- You will not fix things for them so that they can avoid punishment.

- You will read the Bible with them so that you both can learn how to please God.

The Bottom Line:

If you love your children,

You will discipline them consistently.

Chapter 6:
Blended Families

Although the following suggestions are intended for blended families – All families can benefit from these basics.

Both men and women often feel guilt over divorce. Many single parents are trying to compensate for everything their children missed, due to the absence of one parent. Many enable their children, trying to outdo their ex-spouse. With the divorce rates so high, it is no wonder that so many homes are dysfunctional.

In blended families some parents are carrying the weight, while other parents are not fulfilling their responsibilities. You can hope by your example and expectations that your children are learning to be caring, responsible adults. You now have the added challenge of knowing that your children are being influenced by both sets of parents.

How can you improve cooperation with your blended and extended family?

- Stay involved. Just because you have to deal with two separate families and their issues and opinions, does not mean that this is the time to relax or retreat. Your child needs to know that you love him enough to stay involved in his life.

- Be diligent to train and protect your family. If you find yourself too busy or too tired to stay involved, you will enable others to control your family's future.

- Take time to get to know each other. Learn their names and learn about their preferences; share yours, too. This does not mean you have to do everything they want or like. It is a way of connecting – showing that you are interested in them and what concerns them.

- Don't rush the relationship, expecting instant love. Honest compliments are usually better received and preferred to physical displays of affection. Be observant to recognize and understand what makes your family comfortable.

- Talk to your children. Look them in the eyes and listen to their concerns and fears. Don't act like these are not important issues, because they are important to them. Set your cell phone aside; no texting either. Let your conversation be more than instruction and correction. If they had a success or a failure at school, talk about it.

- In coordinating between two or more households, things can get very hectic. When you are busy, taking time to listen seems almost impossible. Your children still need to know you care about them and you value what concerns or interests them. When your children want to talk, and you are very busy, honestly tell them that you are busy. Assure them that you want to hear everything they have to say. Tell them you need (2) minutes to come to a stopping point, and then you will be able to talk. If you need a reminder, set a timer.

- Require your children to listen to you, your spouse, their other parents, and other family members. Active listening is demonstrated when the listener's eyes focus on the person speaking. Both the listener and the speaker turn their bodies toward each other. Occasional responses should include: agreement, disagreement, I understand, or something else appropriate to let the ones sharing the conversation know that both are still engaged. This is true for parents as well. If you want your children to respect you, listening is one of the basic ways to show respect for one another. And finally, model good listening. If you don't listen to your spouse, neither will your children.

- Do not argue with your children. When the intensity of the discussion increases to the level of argument, take authority over the conversation. Speak in a firm, but calm voice and declare that this conversation is over – for now. When everyone has had time to calm down and think about what was said, you may choose to revisit the topic. When you argue with your children – you lose. You are the parent. Of course you are going to disagree at times, but you have the responsibility for holding your family to Godly standards and expectations. The Bible is your standard. When you read and apply the Word of God to your situation, the disagreement is no longer with you. God expects His people to come under the authority of His Word.

- Discipline should not be immediately commanded by the new step-parent. When the birth parent takes the lead and maintains regular expectations, transitions will be easier. Take time to work with your new spouse to adjust or set limits.

- Your new children may have developed habits that do not please you. Perhaps every time you correct your daughter, she loudly declares, "You're so mean to me!" Perhaps she does this in public when you won't buy her something. Don't make a scene or give into this habit of manipulation. When you get home, either you or you and your spouse, calmly talk to her about her actions. If you tolerate rude comments, you will enable them to continue. Establish expectations and consequences. Make the consequences something reasonable that will impact her way of thinking – a consequence she will not want repeated.

- Talk to your children's other parents. Talk about positive things you have in common. Don't try to dominate conversations. You are in this together. Include your children in some, but not all of these conversations.

- Keep focused on what is important and keep a good attitude. Are there important issues that need to be discussed? Make sure you get to those first so that you have ample time to address any concerns.

- Don't compete with your children's other parents. Don't try to buy the most expensive presents or take them on the most expensive trips. Quality time also means time doing everyday chores and house projects together. The focus is doing things together, not who spends the most money.

- Look for honest ways to compliment their other parents when you observe correct parenting strategies. Everyone needs to be encouraged now and then. If you see something that deserves a compliment, express your approval with a cheerful, appreciative attitude. The more you identify what is praiseworthy, the more likely you are to see it repeated.

- Hold firm, but maintain a positive attitude on important parenting issues. Every family has basic, foundational beliefs that should be honored. You do not have to compromise your beliefs, but acknowledging special celebrations or participating when appropriate could be a great time of bonding for both families.

86

- Plan for the future. Don't wait until it is time for your children to attend college before you discuss financial and academic issues. Important life decisions should be discussed and planned. Last minute decisions that could have been managed by planning ahead may cause tempers to rise and relationships to deteriorate. Create a college savings plan now.

- Diligently monitor your children's academic and social lives. This will help your children stay focused on academics and possibly earn scholarships. Good parenting and successful children don't just happen. Good parenting takes diligence and hard work on the part of everyone involved. Parents, who are faithful to set the goal, save money, and require good grades, are more likely to be able to eliminate the need for college loans. These loans, while convenient, usually prove to be a mountain of debt even many years after graduation.

- Be considerate by being on time for appointments and pick-up/drop-off times for the children. Always make sure the children are safe and under adult supervision before leaving the area.

- On occasion, find a time when all parents and children in the family can relax and have fun together. It doesn't have to be expensive. A potluck picnic with yard games may provide a non-confrontational atmosphere where everyone benefits. Limit or do not allow alcoholic beverages. Everyone needs to be on their best behavior.

- What if you really cannot get along with the other parents? Limit times when you are together. Invite a third party, such as a pastor, youth pastor, or counselor to be in attendance at the meetings. Sometimes people will guard what they say and do when a witness is present.

- Whether the relationship with the other parents is positive or not, speak in a positive manner about their other parents when your children are present. Both sets of parents are important to your children.

- You and your spouse should present a united front. Decisions about parenting should be made early in your relationship – preferably before the marriage. Discussions should be ongoing, attempting to anticipate basic decisions before the needs arise. Issues should be dealt with in a timely manner, not giving your children time to manipulate and gain an advantage. If enabling becomes an issue, caught early, honest talk with your spouse will help to eliminate heartache later.

- Accounting for age, all children should be treated equally in discipline, responsibilities, and privileges. Fair treatment encourages caring attitudes and family cooperation. Unfair treatment sets families up for enabling that will destroy caring attitudes and the need to fulfill responsibilities. Although many parents think they can hide the inequitable ways they deal with their children, it does not take long for children to recognize unfair treatment.

- Parents who establish family rules and expectations find it easier to discipline their children. Though children may not like the consequences, they know that all siblings who commit the same offense will be treated the same – it is fair. It is also fair when all family members are expected to fulfill their assigned responsibilities. Finally, it is fair when all family members are acknowledged for behavior or assignments well done. In most cases, fairness is a matter of integrity. It doesn't take long for children to recognize and appreciate fair treatment. Parents who work to maintain fairness among family members find it much easier to maintain an environment of cooperation in the home.

- Be consistent. Don't make rules one week and change them the next. There is enough confusion with different rules in different households. If possible, have a calm discussion to decide rules that could apply to both houses. If you wait until an issue arises, the emotional involvement requiring an immediate decision, may make alignment of rules less successful.

- Limits and boundaries are important. Children, whose parents set boundaries, know that their parents love them. Your children may not like the boundaries, but deep down, they know that limits and boundaries are created for their good. Don't make ultimatums or promises you cannot keep. Your children are learning about honesty and integrity from you.

- Agree to disagree. Just like any husband and wife, two families will not agree on everything. Make an effort to find basic areas of agreement that will benefit both families.

- Every weekend should not be a trip to a theme park. Quality time also includes doing chores, home repair, decorating, playing games or sports, helping others, or any activities that encourage talk and relationship building experiences.

- Enjoy your new family structure without trying to make it match your previous family life. Expectations based on fantasy will only slow your progress in becoming a well-functioning family.

- In your need for acceptance, don't reward your children too much or too soon. You create high expectations when you overindulge your children. They will learn to expect this level of attention as the new normal. Reward, but be reasonable.

- Don't be offended if your step-children talk about or compare you with their birth parent. Let them know by your words, actions, and attitudes that you love, support, and care for them. Your children will feel more at ease when they know that your goal is not to replace their original parent.

- As a family, discuss and set reasonable goals. Listen to each other. Work together and insist on respect, good effort, and good attitudes. Celebrate successes and appreciate talents.

- A second marriage does not usually allow too much time for a lingering honeymoon. Do not let your love and your attention for your spouse become so overwhelming that you do not have time for your children. Your enthusiastic attention and time spent with your whole family will pay off in better cooperation and behavior from your children.

- Whether it was a divorce or a death in the family that preceded your new marriage, be compassionate, but do not become an enabler. Words of comfort, encouragement, and realistic expectations will help during this challenging time of transition.

Chapter 7:
Are You Enabling Your Adult Children?

Enabling and Money:

You may be financially providing for a family member. Maybe your son or daughter needs help for a season because of a lost job or experiencing a house fire. Perhaps your loved one needs help to recover from a natural disaster or has gone through a devastating life change beyond personal control. When you reach out to help, this is compassion.

Other reasons may make it necessary for your adult children to return home. As soon as you hear about the possibility of their return, your motherly or fatherly instincts may rise up in you. You excitedly exclaim, "Our kids are coming home to live with us!" Before they arrive, it is important for you to take time to honestly look at the situation and openly discuss it with your spouse. You do not want to destroy your own marriage in the process of helping your children. As you pray and work together, both of you need to recognize the challenge and be in agreement as to how much and how long you are willing to help. Drawing the line is not the same as shutting your child out. Instead, limits are meant to help your child regroup and return to independent living in a timely manner. The boundaries are meant to help preserve relationships throughout your entire family and to preserve your family's financial stability.

Setting boundaries before your adult child moves home:

Having to return home and start again can be a very stressful time for all involved. To prevent hard feelings later on, you and your spouse need to meet with your adult child and discuss concerns and expectations before the move.

Topics may include:

- Attitudes
- Plans and strategies for seeking employment
- Plans to return to school or training to learn additional job skills
- Smoking and alcohol/drug use
- Cooking and cleaning expectations
- Landscape and lawn care assistance
- Use of the car
- When friends are allowed to visit
- Attitudes
- Manners
- Church attendance
- Bedtime and morning routines
- Music volume
- Reasonable use of household utilities
- Are pets allowed? Who will be responsible to take care of them?
- And whatever else concerns your family

A plan for finances needs to be established for spending and bill paying during the time your son is unemployed. Once employed, the plan needs to be modified by adding a savings account. Planning and preparing for a move back to independence provides all adults involved an expectation and reasonable hope that a return to independent living is really going to happen.

Your child may not be returning home alone, but bringing children and a spouse. In this case, you and your spouse need to meet with your son and his spouse before the move and come to consensus over as many concerns as possible. These topics are in addition to those in the previous list. Although the parents are in charge of the children, the grandparents own the house.

Topics related to adult children with childen may include:

- Who is allowed to discipline?
- What are appropriate consequences?
- What basic manners and chores will be expected?
- How will they be transported to and from school/special events?
- Who will take care of the children before and after school?
- Who will help the children with their homework?
- Where will everyone sleep?

Although Grandma loves her grandchildren, she should not be expected to be a full time babysitter. Like any experienced childcare service, Grandma should be paid. Of course, hers is a labor of love, but none the less, a labor. This will help eliminate Grandma's feeling of being used. It will also limit any extra funds the parents have for entertainment. If Grandma does not need the money, she can save it in a college fund for her grandchildren. This ensures saving for a very worthwhile cause. If your son or daughter-in-law is unemployed, they shouldn't need too much babysitting. But if they do, they can trade babysitting for extra work around the house, thus freeing Grandma for some free time of her own.

Now, from the above information or your own ideas, devise a plan and list of expectations for your son and his family. The list will make living together a more positive experience. Even though you may enjoy having your son at home, do not make it so comfortable that he never wants to leave.

Did they quit their jobs or their marriage?

Both are serious life changes. If abuse was involved in either situation, then compassion is appropriate. But these days, it is too easy to give up when things are difficult. Every job and marriage has its challenges. Too much sympathy in either situation may help to convince the one who quit the marriage or the job, that things will be better at home. Mom and Dad will take care of me. Parents, what is your goal? If it is to revisit the joy of having your children home, know that they may be home for a long time. What is your goal? Let's explore a few situations before you answer.

Did he quit his job?

Perhaps he spent months complaining about the demands of his job. You listened with such sympathy, it only confirmed that he should not have to work so hard or put up with people who weren't nice and respectful to him – he deserved better. You could have prayed with him and watched for God's provision. That would have encouraged him to maintain his job until God provided relief or another job. What happened? The more he complained, the more your encouragement made it seem that it was time for him to quit. Enough complaining and sympathy will convince anyone to quit, no matter the consequences. Now, with so few job opportunities available and so many unemployed people competing for work, it may take years to find another position that pays enough to provide for his family.

If your son is unemployed, pray with your son and his family. Ask God to provide a new job. If your son is a Christian, have your son pray. You can agree with him in prayer. You will help your son grow up spiritually when he sees God answer his prayers.

Encourage your son to get additional training. The job market is constantly requiring new skills. Expect him to be actively searching for a job, with daily effort to find work. He may have to take a position that pays less than he previously earned. Today, some people have to work two jobs to earn enough to pay their bills. Sadly, quitting a job with no prospects of another position has left him and his family in a vulnerable position.

This is a life lesson: Do not quit. Wait for God's provision.

What else can you expect? God has a way of teaching us to trust Him by revisiting unlearned lessons. He expects His people to trust Him and overcome in every challenging situation, even when the job is difficult, even when people treat us unkindly. If and when the next job leaves your son desperate for a change of employment, pray with your son. Trust God for His answer and the ability to overcome in the face of hardship. Pray for God to provide a mentor, someone who has more job experience and can help your son continue in his current position. Ask God for favor with everyone your son comes in contact with and all that have influence over his job and his life. Wait on God and expect miracles.

The field of education has always provided many situations where quitting the job would have seemed expedient for the moment, but destructive for future employability. I remember in my first years of teaching, an experienced teacher came to my rescue. I was very frustrated with the continuous changes in the school system. Every change seemed to make teaching more difficult, with no positive learning gains for the students. It was always more paperwork – which equaled more busywork for teachers. An experienced teacher told me to hold on; schools have always been in a constant climate of change. If you don't like this change, in a few years, it will be gone and some other change will take its place. Just do your job with excellence. Do the best you can for your students. It was true. My goal was to teach for 30 years, but I taught for 32. It was challenging, and yet rewarding. I had the opportunity to be a Christian teacher in the public schools. Daily, I prayed and submitted myself to God's will. I looked for His faithful provision. He enabled me to continue, when I thought that I could not. (God's enabling is the good kind of enabling.) God has called us to be overcomers. You and your family have that same calling.

Did she quit her marriage?

Again, too many people give up when situations become difficult. Pray with your loved ones. Ask God to provide a Christian counselor who will not only show them what God's Word says, but who will help hold them accountable for their actions. Divorce places children at risk. Don't be deceived: Many children are not resilient and do not bounce back easily. When parents don't keep their marriage vow/commitment, their children learn to quit when things get difficult. It becomes a generational curse. The children may quit school and turn to drugs, alcohol, or suicide for comfort. They may become promiscuous, feeling it is better to risk disease than to risk divorce – divorce that so devastated their lives. Divorce should be the last resort. The word divorce should not be frequently used in conversations; it only encourages divorce as a viable option. Prayer should be a weapon of warfare. By faith, we do not give up on our marriages just because relationships or circumstances are difficult.

Has unwise spending placed them in this situation?

Does unwise spending continue? Is it excessive charge card debts and money spent on alcohol, cigarettes, new cars, name brand clothes, video games, movies, or dinners out – the good life? And what is their response? Do they tell you that it is "their money"? After all, they are adults. This is a stronghold. This is a good place to pull back support. You are not helping them become more responsible. The more help you give, the less they need to get free

96

from the strongholds that keep them in financial bondage. As long as you provide for their wants and needs, they have no need to seek God or get their lives straightened out.

Is the person you are helping, financially contributing to your household?

I have heard so many times that parents don't want to charge their adult children to live in their home. Most frequently used excuse: "I don't want them to think that I want their money. Besides we are financially well off. We can afford it." If this is true then take the rent and food money and secretly put it into an account for them. When they are ready to buy a house, you can give it back to them. You now have permission to charge them.

Did you know that people who have access to their total salary as spending money are in danger of never being able to manage their money when living on their own? If you do not charge them, you are enabling a continuation of financial irresponsibility. They will spend lavishly on cars, electronics, and entertainment – saving little or nothing. You will be frustrated. Your relationship will be strained, if not seriously jeopardized. What you think is a wonderful act of love may be soon considered something you owe them. Gratitude quickly disappears and those old teenage rebellious attitudes and behaviors may reappear in your home.

What if they have no income?

Life is more than just paying bills. They can also do chores, fix things, and make a continuing effort to give back. And they can do this with a good attitude. No, things are not perfect, but when everyone works together to get through the tough times, families grow closer together.

An enabler, however, finds it easy to excuse attitudes and behavior.

What might an enabler say? "She doesn't have time to help out or do chores." "She's been depressed and needs to spend time with her friends." The truth is your daughter needs to be productive. She needs to grow up and become a responsible adult. What else might an enabler say? "It's OK. He can't clean up around the house. Men just don't do that. And if I don't prepare his food, he will starve. He has to eat." Know this: His future spouse will appreciate your efforts to see that he is more than a couch potato. At the very least, she'll want a husband who has basic living skills and a willingness to cooperate with his family. In healthy relationships, we work together. Giving should be reciprocal: I help you, and you help me. It probably won't be totally equal, but you should see good, consistent effort.

What happens when you provide their total financial support?

God will have to take them to a greater level of financial need in order for them to see that He truly is their Provider. If you provide for all their needs, there will be no testimony of God's greatness. And then, when you can no longer provide, they may be very angry with you. Maybe you have run out of funds, or maybe you are frustrated, thinking enough is enough. It is very likely they will demand that you owe it to them. How far will things have to go before they grow up and take responsibility for themselves? As long as you enable them, it will not happen.

Is it OK for me to use my tithe money to help my children?

You may look at your children and think that God won't mind if you forego giving your tithes in order to give the money to your children. After all, isn't that the same as giving it to a charity? And your children are so needy.

What does the Bible say about tithes and offerings?

> Will a man rob or defraud God? Yet you rob and defraud Me. But you say, In what way do we rob or defraud You? [You have withheld your] tithes and offerings. You are cursed with the curse, for you are robbing Me, even this whole nation. Bring all the tithes (the whole tenth of your income) into the storehouse, that there may be food in My house, and prove Me now by it, says the Lord of hosts, if I will not open the windows of heaven for you and pour you out a blessing, that there shall not be room enough to receive it (Malachi 3:8-10, AMP).

God has designed His own financial prosperity system. God is so sure of His system, that He tells us to prove Him. This is how it works: God expects us to faithfully give tithes and offerings to the church. We trust Him with our finances and our lives. When we have a need, we pray and ask God to provide for that need. Since we have already trusted God with our finances, He multiplies blessings back to us. These blessings produce physical, spiritual, and financial prosperity in our lives. We demonstrate our trust in God by being faithful to give tithes and offerings.

Parents who spend their tithes on their children's needs are robbing God. When they subvert their tithes to other things, no matter how needy the person or worthy the project, they set their entire family up for disaster. They rob God in their own lives. And by their example, declare to their children that tithing and obeying God are optional. Spending your tithes on your children's needs may appear to be a quick fix, but it has far reaching, negative results.

Should parents loan their adult children money?

These questions will help you discover the right answer:

- Does your daughter currently owe you any money?

- Has your daughter repeatedly proven herself untrustworthy?

- Is your daughter already doing everything she can to live responsibly with the resources she currently has?

- Does she attend church? Does she tithe?

- Do alcohol, drugs, cigarettes, excessive shopping or entertainment dominate her spending habits?

- Does your daughter have a good attitude toward you and the rest of your family?

- Is the loan going to be a hardship on your family?

- Will you have to borrow money to be able to provide the loan?

- Is the loan going to take money from her college fund or the college fund of another child?

- Are you and your spouse in excessive debt?

- Will you use your credit card to provide the loan?

- Will you create a realistic payback plan/contract?

- Will your daughter sign the payback/plan?

- What are the consequences if the payment is late or defaulted?

- Can the money be legally acquired any other way?

- Do you and your spouse agree that the need is real and practical? If the loan is for something that is not essential, this would be a good time for your daughter to learn to save money for something she desires.

- Do both you and your spouse want to give your daughter a loan?

- Have you and your spouse prayed about this loan? If you have not prayed, this is first on your list of things to do. You will also need to pray with your daughter before the contract is signed.

Do You See a Pattern?

By now, you should be seeing a pattern of reasons to give or not to give your daughter a loan. If you decide to give her a loan, a payment schedule with documentation of payments needs to be created. Both you and your daughter need to understand that if she does not fulfill her part of the contract, your relationship may be strained or damaged.

If you decide not to give your daughter a loan, do not let guilt enter into the relationship. By praying and then understanding the options and reasons for and against providing a loan, you and your spouse will be doing the right thing. If your daughter becomes verbally abusive because you have not given her a loan, you will know that she is not mature enough to be trusted with a loan at this time.

How can parents break the financial bondage that is destroying your family?

If your daughter has moved home, and you have not set up boundaries, you are probably in the heat of the battle right now. You may be seeing a lot of the out of control behavior that got your daughter in trouble in the first place. Is it too late? No. First, pray for God's direction. If you are married, pray with your spouse. Next,

101

write a letter to your daughter with the expectations already provided in this chapter. By writing the letter, you will have time to fully think through and establish reasonable expectations. This letter should be a joint effort, with you and your spouse in agreement. In the letter, be sure to identify specific responsibilities your daughter needs to perform. Don't think that she just knows – she doesn't. Give her a copy of the letter as you calmly inform her of your expectations and reasonable consequences when she does not act in a responsible manner.

So, where do you turn when you are desperate?

God? You say that you trust God, but waiting on God is a huge part of trusting Him. When a problem arises, do you give God time or space to move in your life? In your daughter's life? Are you bailing your daughter out of every situation, never allowing her to experience the consequences? Constant enabling is not faith driven – but fear driven. If you, with your lightning speed, just fix it, that makes you faster than God. But the fix is only temporary. You need God's power in your life to help your daughter become a caring, responsible adult. His timing is perfect, and when He provides, there will be no doubt that it is God.

Tell me this, if you continue to fix the situation every time, when will your daughter learn to trust God? When you die? Every time you fix the problem, your daughter will get another opportunity to learn this lesson again. It may be worse, a lot worse, the next time.

Let's review: Will waiting on God be easy? No. But if you are desperate for change, you will trust God to help you stop enabling the behavior that is destroying your daughter and her family. When she has her next self-inflicted emergency, pray with her. Of course, if it is a medical emergency, get help right away; but if not, choose to wait on God for the answer. When she asks you, or someone asks you, "What are you going to do?" say, "We're going to wait on God. We're going to trust God for His answer." Do not panic. Do not try to fix anything. Frustrated with the simplicity of this answer, you may think that you just can't stand-by and watch. Then don't look! Focus your eyes on God and your mind on other important things. Pray, praise, and trust God. Keep a thankful attitude, for only God can rescue you from the stronghold of enabling. How will you know that it is really God's answer for you? As I said before, the answer will be RIGHT. It will be amazing, beyond that which you could ask or think. Yes, God still performs miracles today, for those who believe Him.

> "Trust in the Lord with all your heart, and lean not on your own understanding; In all your ways acknowledge Him, And He shall direct your paths" (Proverbs 3:5-6, NKJ).

What if things get worse before they get better? Some people have to hit rock bottom before they look up to God for help. Hold fast to Romans 8:28. "And we know that all things work together for good to those who love God, to those who are the called according to His purpose." You see, when you quit enabling irresponsible behavior in others and submit yourself to God's purpose, you will see change. He will change you and the one you have been enabling. And when you follow His will for your life, you will see miracles. He will work things together for your good. He promised.

Is everything you are doing pointing your adult daughter to Christ?

Is she receptive? Many people do not want to talk about God. They just want you to meet their needs. Are your daughter and her family making an attempt to get their lives reconciled to God? Or are they just letting, or even demanding, you meet all of their needs? They may see no reason to seek or serve God. They think that they are doing OK without Him. We know that they are not doing OK without God.

Is she going to church?

Is her answer that she just doesn't have time to go to church? Is she too busy with her job, the kids, and activities? God wants to teach her to put Him first. If her job, the kids, and activities always come first, this will become a generational curse. While we are on this topic, are you going to church? I hope so. If not, it has already become a generational curse.

If going to church is part of your family life, is your daughter learning about tithing and giving? Tithing and giving are part of developing a relationship with God, trusting Him for His provision in their lives. If you don't trust God with your finances, you probably don't trust Him in other areas. At this point, you may interject, "She can't afford to tithe." The truth is she can't afford not to tithe. You have just read Malachi 3:8-10. When you rob God of tithes and offerings, you are cursed with a curse. When you bless God with tithes and offerings, He will pour out blessings upon you that will be so abundant that there will not be room enough to receive them. Do you want your daughter and her family to experience abundant blessings? Do you want your daughter to prosper? Of course, you do. Giving is not optional. If her finances are in the depths of disaster, God has provided a way out. He is calling you and your children to prove Him by giving tithes and offerings.

> Jesus said, "Give, and it shall be given unto you;
> good measure, pressed down, and shaken together,
> and running over, shall men give into your bosom.
> For with the same measure that ye mete withal it shall
> be measured to you again" (Luke 6:38, KJV).

In the church, the lack of financial giving has become epidemic. If we want our families, our churches, and our country to prosper, then we will do it God's way. We will give!

104

Last chance!

Whatever disastrous event occurred to cause your daughter to have to return home, God can use it for her good. Maybe your family did not attend church when your children were growing up. Maybe you accepted Jesus as your Lord and Savior later in life. Have you been praying for your children to be saved? God can use this time while your daughter is living in your home to give her an opportunity to receive Jesus as her Savior and Lord.

If you were saved later in life, God has probably changed you in many ways. You have been blessed. Let your children see the changes God has made in you. Don't revert to old habits of angry yelling, but by your words and actions, let her see that there is hope in Jesus Christ. Pray before meals, but also join together sometime during the day or evening to pray for problems and concerns. Guard your words so that worry does not overtake you. Speak words of faith, declaring your trust in God. When prayers are answered, share praise reports in your family time. Expect your children and grandchildren to attend church with you. Use your time wisely. This may be their last chance!

Is enabling limited to a specific gender, race, nationality, socio-economic level, or religion?

No. Parents of every type and economic level may find their love for their children overrides their common sense. Some would say – then that is not real love. I would have to agree in most circumstances. Parents love their children according to their own perception of love, most of it based on the experience they had growing up in their families. Love is about more than family influence. Television, books, and movies have dramatically affected how we perceive love – this love is based on fantasy. For reality, we go to God's Word.

What does the Bible say about love?

Love is patient, love is kind. It does not envy, it does not boast, it is not proud. It is not rude, it is not self-seeking, it is not easily angered, it keeps no record of wrongs. Love does not delight in evil but rejoices with the truth. It always protects, always trusts, always hopes, always perseveres. Love never fails (1 Corinthians 13:4-8, NIV).

What else concerns you as your adult child returns home?

"Help! My son won't take his medicine!"

Where codependence and mental health issues are involved, it is very important for your returning adult son to continue to take his medications. You and others may have prayed many prayers for him. You may be trusting God for deliverance from these problems. This is not a time for either one of you to quit taking your medicine. If, and when, God completely heals your son, it will be obvious. When God performs a miracle, it can be confirmed by doctors. It will be a testimony of God working in your lives. Until there is a confirmation of healing, the medicine should be taken in faith. Trust God to cause the medicine to help your child manage his life.

"I can't change her – she's an adult."

When our children turn 18 or 21, we say that they are adults. For children who have planned, prepared, developed work skills, and are able to take care of themselves, this is a wonderful time in their lives. However, too many children have grown in height, but not in maturity. They just want to escape from home. They think of themselves as, "The Man!" or "The Woman!"

When these children become adults, it is a scary time for parents who suspect that their overgrown kid will probably return home in some kind of trouble. A month or two of relief abruptly ends as their daughter shows up on their doorstep. Will she be cooperative? Will she listen? At this point, many parents are so afraid of stepping on their child's fragile self-esteem that they hesitate to give any advice. Their daughter quickly settles in, but still wants to retain her new "adult status." It isn't long until Mom and Dad give up in exasperation declaring, "I can't change her – she's an adult."

We know that change is a normal part of life. If your daughter is unable to live on her own and is returning home, she obviously needs some changes to take place in her life. As the wise parents, setting limits and boundaries before your daughter moves in will help her understand that you know she is an adult. You expect more from her than you did when she was younger.

After she moves back into your home, your advice to her must not be a constant stream of commands. Instead, calmly share the wisdom you have gained by experience. By your words and attitude, demonstrate your concern for her, yourself, and for your family. Everyone must cooperate for this living arrangement to be successful. This may prove to be a time of humbling for the entire family. Pray together as a family. Be specific when you pray. Pray for and with your daughter, teaching her to look for God's provision in her circumstances.

What if she doesn't want to pray? Make family prayer as one of the expectations you have for her. What if your family has never prayed together before? This is a good time to start. God can change your daughter in ways you have never even imagined, but you have to welcome Him into your family.

Do we really need counseling?

One of the things you don't want to happen is for your family to have an emotional explosion where relationships are permanently damaged or destroyed. You want to help your daughter, but you do not want to lose any other family members in the process. In relationships where enabling has been out of control for many years, if the enabler is not careful, she will end up with no children who want to be in relationship with her. You might think this is impossible, but consider the following: In the end, the enabled one, tired of depending on Mom for everything, will desperately want to be free of Mom's hovering presence in her life. Her only interest in Mom may be in the financial gain she can extract from her. The dependable one may finally decide that the constant conflict and chaos between the enabler and the enabled sibling is destroying his personal time, resources, and peace. This is no way to live! In self-preservation, he may separate himself from Mom. What about the rest of the family? They will probably agree with the dependable one.

How can you avoid this? Do not wait until your family has a total meltdown before you seek help. Family and individual counseling may be vital to helping your family. There are plenty of Christian counselors who help restore family relationships. Ask your pastor to recommend a counselor or other counseling resources. If you really want change, you will need to do more than you have previously done – or else you will get the same results. Where alcohol and drug addictions are involved, counseling for overcoming codependency will be a necessary part of the restoration process.

What if your returning son lies to you, just to be able to move back home?

So your adult son agreed to follow the house rules and promised to fulfill certain responsibilities in exchange for allowing him to return home. Within days of his return, it was obvious. Everything he promised was a lie! Now what?

Learn from this experience.

1. Pray. Ask for God's help and direction.

2. Face reality. He did not break the rules by accident – he lied.

3. If you have enabled him for most of his life, it is no wonder that he lied. Past history allowed him to believe that you really did not mean what you said. If you are serious, this will be his last chance.

4. There is no time to waste; it is time for a family meeting. Your son needs to know that things have changed. You have changed. God has changed you. (Give him a copy of this book and a Bible.) If he really wants to or needs to stay in your home, things will be different. He will follow the rules.

5. Be specific. He needs to know the rules and responsibilities he must fulfill, if he is going to live in your home. Use your original list of rules and responsibilities or create a new list. Add other rules where needed. Make sure it is a written document, a contract. If he wants to stay, he will need to sign it. You will sign it also. Have it notarized; this confirms that you mean business. You are serious. Inform him that if he breaks the rules, the locks will be changed, and he will need to find another place to live.

6. What about warnings? The contract is the warning. Since he has already proven himself untrustworthy by lying, you need to protect yourself and your family.

7. What if he blames you? You did not break the rules. He chose to break the rules. He never intended to follow the rules. He chose to lie.

8. What if he isn't happy? Remember, you are trusting God to help you stop being an enabler.

9. Too harsh? If you give in now, you may experience a lifetime of your son controlling you and your household.

10. If he becomes abusive or breaks the law, call the police and press charges.

What if your son did not lie to you, but over time, has quit cooperating with household rules and responsibilities. You may have even returned to enabling. If this is the case, you will need to reread this book. If your child has not already read this book, he will need to read it to learn how enabling has affected him. He needs to know the truth. He needs to know that there is hope for him.

Chapter 8:
Are You Enabling Your Spouse?

Everybody grows up, but not everybody matures. Does this describe your spouse? Perhaps you find yourself working full time, taking care of the yard, the car, and the house, while the one you love watches TV, plays video games, or surfs the Internet and consumes calories that will never be burned. Perhaps you even take care of the children and cook the meals with no offer of help, while your spouse is involved in sports, shopping, or talking on the phone. When you were looking for a spouse, you couldn't think about anything but romance. Now, the reality of everyday life may have caused you to question, "What went wrong?"

To this point, I have focused on parents and children. I encourage you to read this entire book, since enabling also impacts couples in many similar ways. Why the similarities? In many homes, the enabler takes on the role of the parent. The spouse is immature either in thinking or willingness to perform the normal and reasonable roles and responsibilities of an adult. The spouse takes on the role of the child and becomes the enabled one.

Roles and Responsibilities: Who Does What?

In some homes where traditional roles and responsibilities are working for both husband and wife, that is great! Do you have this

111

system at your house? Does it really work for both of you? That is a question only you and your spouse can answer. But in this day and time, I am purposely trying to avoid traditional gender specific roles. I am aware that many families have an agreement where the responsibilities are divided according to the strengths of each person. For example: Joe loves to cook, while Chloe prefers to mow the grass. Since opposites do attract, allowing each adult the opportunity to operate according to personal abilities or interests, while depending on the spouse to do the same, can work very effectively. There are, of course, roles and responsibilities that neither may enjoy, but must be done. A mature couple recognizes this and finds ways to work together to see that these needs are met. The converse is also true. When couples share a common interest, such as cooking, they can create delicious meals, enjoy regular time for bonding with each other, and provide still another bonding time where the entire family appreciates the results.

God is glorified when we work together as a family, demonstrating through our love for each other and our love for Him, that we can live lives that are pleasing to Him. Whether one spouse vacuums the floor and the other spouse washes the dishes, is not important. What is important is that we accomplish household duties with good attitudes. When our children see us cooperating with each other, they learn to do the same. This way, we are not asking anything from our children that we do not already do ourselves.

Is that how things are at your house, or do yelling and arguing dominate the scene? Perhaps it is your spouse that needs an attitude adjustment. Perhaps it is you. Let's talk about strategies that may help to reduce the enabling and stress you are experiencing at home.

Do you take over your spouse's responsibilities?

At your house, do you have jobs that need to be done? Are you the one who always ends up doing them? Are you enabling your spouse to have time to play video games or watch TV, while you are working yourself to death? If you need your spouse to mow the grass, give him a choice: Either mow the grass or hire it done. You may think that there is no money to pay someone to mow your grass. Take the money from entertainment, eating out, multiple cell phones or other luxuries. Your spouse may decide that mowing the grass is worth the effort – if he can maintain his toys. It is time we learn to prioritize and differentiate between wants and needs, preferences and essentials. One person cannot do all of the household work, alone. If you have children capable of mowing the grass, the same exchange works – they can mow the grass or they can give up their luxuries as you hire it done.

What else needs to be accomplished at your house? Talk to your spouse and work together to make one list for you and one list for your spouse. Make the list now for upcoming needs or projects. These chores may be determined by ability or interest. Duties that nobody really wants can be divided to better equalize the task assignment. Don't forget to make age appropriate lists for your children. Each may work down his own list, selecting the task he will do next. Place a star by any that is a priority and must be done now. A list works in a couple of ways. Some people do not respond well to verbal requests. A written list provides everyone the opportunity to select the task they will do next and the joy of crossing projects off when the tasks are completed. I know everyone knows about making lists, but many people are too lazy to make one. Even you may find this a great way to get organized and see long overdue projects finished.

Is your spouse obese? What about your children?

- Do you buy your family all kinds of treats and desserts and then get angry when they gain weight?

- Do you fill lunch boxes with chips, high calorie sodas, and candy?

113

- Do you load the refrigerator with good things, just daring anyone to eat them?

- Do you love to celebrate every holiday with an abundance of baked goods?

- Do you like to buy or bake goodies, but don't eat them yourself? Is that how you keep your weight under control?

When you enable your family to gain weight by providing an abundance of food that will pack on the pounds, you are to blame. Will they complain when you reduce your purchases to a minimal amount of treats? Probably, but you will know that you are doing the right thing.

What can you do? Buy healthy whole grain snacks. Buy fresh fruit, but limit high calorie juices and soft drinks. Yogurt, raisins, nuts, or granola bars will help hold your children over until dinner time. Reduce portion size at mealtime. When it is holiday time, make enough for one meal, with minimal leftovers. Most people won't gain weight from one meal. It is five nights of rich foods and desserts that cause your family to gain weight. After dinner, encourage a walk or some active play time. Don't constantly use desserts as a reward. Don't comfort someone's disappointment or sorrow with high calorie treats. Eat to live, not live to eat.

Is your spouse or child involved in illegal activity?

- Has this family member been arrested? Many times? Do you race to rescue your spouse or child and bail him out of jail? Yes, jail is a terrible place. You just can't bear to let your loved one stay in jail, so you "fix it" one more time. He returns home, unchanged. Jail is meant to deter people from committing crimes. Jail is a consequence for bad behavior. When you immediately rescue your loved one from any consequence, you have not given God any space or time to work.

- Do you charge the bail fees on your already stressed credit cards or borrow the money from someone else, placing you further in debt?

- Did you use your house as collateral to secure bail? If your spouse or your child has been arrested, but does not show up in court, you could lose your home. Wow! This is serious. For a spouse or child who has been in and out of trouble, you are risking your future by arranging for bail. You cannot afford to lose your home.

- Does your enabling include protecting your spouse or child from the law? Are you a supporter or an accomplice in illegal activity? Do you know that you could lose your home if the police find illegal drug activity occurring in your house?

Do you protect your spouse from the consequences of his own actions?

This next section contains many questions about your life. They are not meant to bring condemnation, but to help you identify enabling behaviors that God wants to help you change. If you recognize areas that need improvement, and they seem impossible, beyond your control, you are in miracle territory! Rejoice. As you submit these things to God, He stands ready to deliver you from the bondage caused by enabling and heal relationships in your family. Expect miracles. You are not alone. God will help you.

- Does your spouse stay up late playing video games, drinking, or gambling, making him unable to get up in the morning for work or church? Do you call and make excuses?

- Do you always give your spouse one more chance? Even if you told him last time, "This is your last chance!"

- Do you say, "I don't approve of his behavior," but then turn right around and give him money to support his addiction?

115

- Do you make excuses to friends and family, thinking that they are fooled? Is it hard to keep the stories straight? Do your children or spouse hear these excuses?

- Do you blame others, even though you know your spouse has done this before? Do you say these things in front of your children, knowing that they know the truth? They have already experienced the problem. Now, your integrity is in question. Your children are learning from you.

- Do you accept your spouse's excuses? "I'm taking drugs because I'm depressed." "I'm spending great amounts of money because I'm stressed at work." As long as you accept her excuses, it will get worse. Your acceptance of her excuses indicates acceptance of her sin.

- Does your spouse use stress at work as an excuse to abuse you? Have your ears become a dumping ground for problems and complaints over which you have no control? Is physical violence involved? God never meant for you to be a dumping ground or a punching bag.

- Are you caught up in a cycle of violence and forgiveness? Are you the victim? Does he abuse you and then win you back with sweet talk? You are God's child and deserve to be treated with kindness and respect. Even though you may be afraid, unless you seek help, the cycle will continue.

- Perhaps you have taken enabling a step further. Have you joined your spouse in gambling, taking drugs, or viewing pornography – allowing sin to control both of your lives?

- Have you quit going to church because he doesn't like to go? The truth is your spouse is addicted to sin. When you quit attending church, it confirms that church really isn't that important. You both need the help that only God can provide.

- Is your need for financial security more important to you than protecting your children from the sexual abuse of your spouse? That dirty little family secret will not stay secret forever. Your children need you to protect them, NOW!

- Is your need for financial security more important to you than protecting yourself from the verbal and physical abuse of your spouse? Your children see the abuse and will either follow Dad's example or yours. This is not what happens in normal, healthy family living.

- Is the verbal and physical abuse in your home showing up at school? Do your children bully other children? Your children may determine that they no longer like school because they have no friends at school. Will your children quit school and have dead end jobs because of the abuse in your home?

- Do you secretly drink or take pills to stop the emotional pain from living in an abusive situation? You are placing yourself and your children at-risk. Your children may be hurt while you are not cognizant enough to protect them. You may overdose and leave your children with just one parent – the one who abuses them.

- Whether your bank accounts are joint or separate, do you and your spouse spend, spend, spend while saving nothing for your future or your children's educations? That spending does not satisfy the needs of your family. The things you drag home will soon be worn out, broken, no longer fit, out of style, or just not what you thought they would be. Quit telling yourself that you deserve all of these luxuries. Your family deserves a stable future. Your family needs to know that planning for the future is a part of normal living and requires sacrifice. The sacrifice will be well worth it when your children have good jobs and can take care of their own families in a responsible manner.

- When you shop for groceries, do you bring home cigarettes and alcohol to keep him well stocked? You may think you are doing him a favor – at least he is not out driving or being seduced by something or someone else. He is safe at home. While he consumes your food money, your children are getting an understanding of how to be an alcoholic. They are

117

also getting an up-close view of how you respond to his angry tirades when the cigarettes or alcohol run out. If you truly love your husband or wife, you will not enable or condone your spouse's sin. Frivolous spending sprees, gambling, alcohol, drugs, and pornography will destroy your marriage and your family. Are you financing your spouse's sin, while your family suffers?

Excuses will never solve your problems. The out of control behaviors listed here, will only multiply in your family when your children begin to believe that this is normal in all families. It is not normal and not acceptable to God. To prevent these behaviors from controlling your family down the generations, get help NOW! Stop the enabling NOW!

What about rehab?

After your spouse goes through counseling or rehabilitation to separate himself from his addiction, how do you respond when he comes home?

- Do you tempt him to return to the bondage he has escaped?

- Have you enabled him in any way since he returned home?

- Do you leave alcohol in the house – even drink in front of him?

- Do you smoke or do drugs in front of him?

- Do you invite friends to the house who are caught up in their own addictions?

- Have you secured your finances so that he does not have access to funds to purchase alcohol or drugs?

- Do you remind him of the way he was instead of encouraging him for the improvement he has made?

- Have you given up?

118

Your spouse cannot be free if you tempt him to return to his old addictions. If you thought it was bad before, read what the Bible says will be the result of going back to former sins:

> Jesus said, "But when the unclean spirit has gone out of a man, it roams through dry [arid] places in search of rest, but it does not find any. Then it says, I will go back to my house from which I came out. And when it arrives, it finds the place unoccupied, swept, put in order, and decorated. Then it goes and brings with it seven other spirits more wicked than itself, and they go in and make their home there. And the last condition of that man becomes worse than the first. So also shall it be with this wicked generation" (Matthew 12:43-45, AMP).

> A man is a slave to whatever has mastered him. If they have escaped the corruption of the world by knowing our Lord and Savior Jesus Christ and are again entangled in it and overcome, they are worse off at the end than they were at the beginning (2 Peter 2:19-20, NIV).

What do you do while your spouse is at rehab/counseling?

- Do you pray for your spouse every day?

- Do you ask God to change you, to free you from the addiction of enabling?

- Do you consistently attend church?

- Do you read the Word every day to renew and strengthen your own mind?

- Have you contacted any counseling or support groups for help for your children or yourself?

119

If you could stop your spouse's sins on your own, you would have done so already. Church counseling, AA, Al-Anon, Nar-Anon, and many local support groups are free or at low cost. If you truly want help and change, you will make the contact.

What else should you do while your spouse is at rehab/counseling?

Your spouse needs you to do the things that strengthen your trust in God. At the same time he is improving through counseling or at rehab, he needs you to improve. When he returns home, both of you need to demonstrate that you are truly changed. Your family will not benefit if he returns to the same old reactions and arguments. If your spouse is to stay true to his commitment and remain separated from the things that have held him in bondage, he needs for you to learn how to live without enabling him.

What else concerns you?

"My husband will not take a leadership role in our family. If I don't lead, it doesn't happen. How do I get him to lead?"

First, we need to define what we mean by leadership. Leadership should mean making decisions after praying, studying, and determining the best option to provide for your family. This works well if both husband and wife take the time to learn and listen to God and each other before they decide – that takes work. Many people are not willing to invest the time and effort it takes to make a wise decision. No family benefits from quick decisions based on feelings instead of facts.

It would be nice if all parents trained their children by word and example to use wise problem solving strategies. This is not a reality in many homes because many parents did not have benefit of such training from their parents. How can they teach what they never learned?

What does the Bible say about leadership in the home?

As one consequence of Adam and Eve's sin in the Garden of Eden, God declared that Adam would rule over Eve (Genesis 3:16). This declaration changed their relationship. Fast forward about 4,000 years. In Galatians Chapter 3, we read about another radical change.

> For you are all sons of God through faith in Christ Jesus. For as many of you as were baptized into Christ have put on Christ, There is neither Jew nor Greek, there is neither slave nor free, there is neither male nor female; for you are all one in Christ Jesus (Galatians 3:26-29, KJ).

You may read this Scripture and think that, other than God, there is no other leadership established in our homes. This is not true. In the following Scripture, the beauty and love of Christ declares the quality of the leadership that should be in the home.

> Wives, submit to your own husbands, as to the Lord. For the husband is head of the wife, as also Christ is head of the church; and he is the Savior of the body. Therefore, just as the church is subject to Christ, so let the wives be to their own husbands in everything. Husbands, love your wives, just as Christ also loved the church and gave Himself for her (Ephesians 5:22-25, NKJ).

In Christian homes, God has placed the husband in a leadership role. Christian leadership is to be motivated by love of God and love of family. As husbands and wives work together to benefit their family, decision making will include prayer and study of available options. Decisions will not be made contrary to God's Word. When families submit to God's leadership and trust Him for the results, even if their decision is wrong, God will work it out for their good (Romans 8:28).

I find it very interesting that the Scripture immediately preceding Ephesians 5:22, states that all Christians are to submit to one another in the fear of God (Ephesians 5:21). Although husbands have the ultimate responsibility for the home, when we love God and each other enough to submit to one another, the decision making process easily includes discussions between husband and wife to understand the benefits and possible results of their final choice.

Not all husbands are willing to pray, study/research, and discuss options. Husbands who use Scripture to dominate will soon find themselves with nobody who wants to follow. When this happens, many husbands give up and require the wife to make all decisions to escape being wrong; thus, enabling the husband to avoid responsibility. The wife, in desperation, makes the decision. Does this produce peace in the home? Not necessarily. When angry outbursts or silent sulking follow every decision – the family suffers. After years of this cycle, many spouses, whether husband or wife, determine that they cannot continue in this heart-wrenching dysfunction. This was never God's plan for the family.

If your relationship looks more like this than the one in the preceding paragraphs, through Christ, there is still hope. It requires a humble spirit, time, and effort. Together, determine that you want to please God as you make your decisions. The next decision that needs to be made will start with prayer, study/research, and a discussion of options. Do you or your spouse fear discussion? Know this: Discussion does not suggest weakness. Discussion demonstrates strength and willingness to communicate. The discussion should be without prejudice – presenting the facts as you know them. Both husband and wife must willingly submit to the authority of God's Word, trusting Him for the answer. Because you have prayed, expect God to make it clear which option is the most beneficial for your family. If it is not clear, return to step one and learn more as you pray, study, and discuss your options. When it is time for the decision to be made, ask God to stop you if it is the wrong choice. Thank God for His answer and watch for anything that looks like or sounds like – "stop." If you hear or see "stop," Stop! If you do not receive a message to stop, proceed. Trust God and step out in faith, trusting that your decision is the right thing to do. Maintain attitudes and conversations filled with faith and thanksgiving, trusting that God will intervene and work things out for your good (Romans 8:28). Your children will witness your change in attitude and willingness to work together. This will help your children to learn God's way for solving problems and making decisions.

What kinds of decisions does this process work to resolve?

- Purchasing a house, car, or insurance
- Saving for college, retirements, or trips
- Disciplining your children
- Changing jobs or churches
- Planning for an adult child's return home
- Planning for a living facility for an elderly parent

I could go on and on, but the truth is – it works for all decisions. If you want God's blessing on your lives, seek His counsel and direction about everything. Consult God first and expect His best.

When you know you need God's help:

As you have read about the results of enabling your children and enabling your spouse, you may feel God's convicting power in your life. You recognize that you need God's help to change. Know this: When God reveals areas that need change, His mercy and grace are present to forgive, heal, and restore. True answers and change always start with prayer.

To the Enabled Spouse: PRAY WITH ME

Dear Heavenly Father,

I come to you in the name of Jesus. I recognize that my sin has overtaken my life. My sin is disobedience to You. Forgive me for my sins of (name your sins), and help me to change. Only You can help me change. Remove my addictions to (name the addictions). When temptations come, help me to stop and acknowledge You and Your help in my life. Help me to walk away from sin and turn my thoughts and words to praising You, trusting that You are doing a complete work in me. I know You can do it, and You will do it. I don't have to know how or why. I trust You. Help me to make wise decisions that please You. Help me to discern when something is not of You and reject it. Provide me with Godly support and counseling. I trust You for full deliverance from all the evil addictions in my life.

Lord, I recognize the spirit of death that has tried to overcome me with depression. In the name of Jesus, I command that spirit to go and never return. Lord, fill me up with Your precious Holy Spirit. Help me to be sensitive to You and all You desire for my life. Help me never to return to my old sins, but fill my life with Your Word and Your purpose.

Lord, forgive me for the anger and bitterness that have controlled my life. Lord, forgive me for making excuses and living in denial. Forgive me for parading my sins in front of my spouse and my children. Help my children not to have dysfunctional relationships in their own families because of what they have seen in our home. Help these sins not to become a generational curse. Help my children to grow up to love and serve You. Help me to no longer dwell on what is past, but follow Your leading all the days of my life. Help me to become the person You have created me to be. Lord, I trust you to restore peace, joy, and hope in my family and me. Make my life a testimony of Your greatness. Thank You, Lord. I love You. Thank You for loving me. Amen.

To the Enabler: PRAY WITH ME

Dear Heavenly Father,

I come to you in the name of Jesus. I recognize that I have enabled my spouse to sin. I have been addicted to enabling. My sin is disobedience to You. Lord, forgive me for I have wanted to please my spouse more than I have wanted to please You. I have enabled addictions to (name the addictions).

Lord, I recognize the spirit of death that has tried to overcome me with depression. In the name of Jesus, I command that spirit to go and never return. Lord, fill me up with Your precious Holy Spirit. Help me to be sensitive to You and all You desire for my life. Help me never to return to my old sins, but fill my life with Your Word and Your purpose.

Lord, forgive me for the anger and bitterness that have controlled my life. Forgive me for enabling my spouse, which is preventing Him from turning to You and becoming the person You created Him to be. Lord, forgive me for making excuses and living in denial, especially in front of my children. Help them not to have dysfunctional relationships in their own families because of what they have seen in our home. Help these sins not to become a generational curse. Help my children to grow up to love and serve You. Help me to no longer dwell on what is past, but follow Your leading all the days of my life. Help me to become the person You have created me to be. Restore my relationship with my spouse (and if not saved, save him/her). Lord, I trust you to restore peace, joy, and hope in my family and me. Make my life a testimony of Your greatness. Thank You, Lord. I love You. Thank You for loving me. Amen.

Let's talk:

In the past, where you didn't speak up to avoid confrontation, problems were not addressed or settled. Your silence may very well

125

have enabled the behavior to continue a good deal longer than a simple, honest confrontation. Whether your spouse and you are living together or not, and you are still married, you need to be able to talk. Now, when sharing your ideas and concerns, follow these basic conversation rules – or create your own rules for conversation.

1. Pray first. If the other person will not pray with you, pray before you meet.

2. Be on time.

3. Meet in a safe place where there are not a lot of distractions.

4. No one controls the entire conversation.

5. Take turns listening and sharing in quiet voices.

6. Be respectful. No name calling or attacks.

7. Be honest and share openly.

8. Don't rush. Think about what you are saying and hearing.

9. Turn cell phones off. Be focused on this conversation.

10. Maintain adequate eye contact.

11. Ask questions to clarify meaning.

12. Make notes. If you have questions later, you will accurately remember what was decided. Review all decisions at the end of the meeting.

13. Have realistic expectations. Let your motives be constructive, knowing it is the future of your family you are talking about.

14. Do not blame, and spend a lot of time talking about the past. Instead, learn from the past mistakes that you as a couple have made – in order to prevent making them again.

15. Try to understand the other person's point of view, as you tactfully separate facts from emotions.

16. Do not treat this meeting as a competition. With singleness of purpose, work to identify and practice ways to improve your relationship with your family.

17. Meet again to discuss progress.

18. Encourage and celebrate all successes.

Chapter 9:
Enabling Impacts Your Entire Family.

In the following section, we will look at the perspective of the enabler, the one enabled, the dependable family member who has desperately tried to stop the enabling, and other family members. Keep in mind that each perspective is a general statement, not meant to be a comprehensive study. These observations may not seem relevant to all the situations in your life, but you may be able to see similarities as God reveals exactly what you need to do to restore your family.

Some enabling relationships may be in the early stages of dysfunction, while others have been dysfunctional for years. All of the relationships need healing and forgiveness. As you submit yourself to God, ask Him how each topic applies to you and your family.

Perspectives we must recognize and consider.

The family:

The family may not like the world being made aware of their problems, but unless problems are exposed, they will never be dealt with. Solutions will never be found. Embarrassing? It can be.

Necessary? Yes! Besides, as you read Chapters 10 and 11, you may be amazed to learn how many people already know about your family's problems. They are waiting for you to rescue and make safe both the enabler and the one enabled.

Who is the Dependable One?

The Dependable One Described:

- Honest
- Keeps his promises
- Responsible
- Trustworthy
- Faithful
- Good listener
- Is kind and seeks to cooperate with others
- Knows how to be firm when necessary
- Dependable in times of blessing as well as in times of distress
- Admits it when he is wrong, and to the best of his ability, makes corrections
- Is organized.
- Is skilled in problem solving, bill paying, and basic life skills
- Seeks professional and spiritual help when needed
- Trusts and relies on God for all decision making
- Consistently makes every effort to do the right thing in all situations

So who is the dependable one in your family? If this description does not sound like the one you currently rely on, then he is not the dependable one. As parents age and become less able to take care of themselves, it is only natural for them to trust at least one of their children to help with important matters. There is no guarantee that parents will actually have a dependable person at the time they need assistance. If there is no dependable person, and an adult family member assumes a leadership role in the family, this could be a hostile takeover that may require legal intervention.

When the time comes, how can you know that a dependable son or daughter will be ready and capable to assist you? That depends on you. Did you train any or all of your children to be dependable?

Have you done your part to make sure you have organized your information so that the dependable one can step in and easily manage your household? Remember, he will probably have personal responsibilities with his own job and family to manage. Taking over as executor of your estate is challenging, but attempting to manage your household while you are alive is even more demanding.

To the Parent:

- Have you worked with an attorney to set up a Trust and/or a Durable Power of Attorney?

- Have you created written instructions to help him navigate your finances, preferences, and any other specific concerns?

- Do you have Living Will?

- Do you keep a bill book?

- Are your important papers filed in one location or are they scattered all over your house?

- Do you have the original copy of your current will?

- Do you have an attorney? An Elder Law Attorney can provide legal advice that is specific to your situation. This attorney can also create a Durable Power of Attorney, help you set up and manage your Trust, suggest documentation strategies, and recommend resources that are available in your area.

You may have done extensive planning for your death, but have you discussed your preference for assisted living or nursing home care if dementia or Alzheimer's disease makes it impossible for you to live on your own? At this point, you may bristle and declare that you are going to stay in your own home. Memory loss issues can be very deceptive. Memory loss can make you think that your current "senior moment" is a one-time event – when in reality it is becoming a pattern, threatening to overtake you. The problems become evident when you forget to take your medication, bathe, or pay your bills.

Increasing memory loss may make you vulnerable to people who do not have your best interest at heart, leaving no one in whom you can trust. If you are an enabler, it is possible that the ever increasing addictions and demands from the one you have enabled will require that you be placed in assisted living to protect you from him. You may think, "This is impossible! I know my child loves me!" Not only is it possible; it is very likely. Plan for your future by training your children to be caring, responsible adults – your future depends on it! Expect to see evidence of those qualities now, or find someone else you trust and on whom you can depend to make important decisions and arrangements for you when you are no longer able to make them yourself.

To the Dependable One:

Through the years, you may have watched in horror as your parent enabled your sibling. Your parent may have even said, "When I'm gone, he'll grow up. Let someone else deal with the problem." Your parent created the problem, and her abandonment of responsibility for the problem is like placing a death sentence upon you, her dependable son. The situation may already have destroyed the life of your enabling parent. God does not want this to happen to you. You cannot change what has happened. You can pray and ask God to deliver them from this stronghold. You can pray that God help them and restore them to right relationship with Him and each other. It won't be easy. Any help that you give will be most frequently described as tough love. Others may not recognize it as love at all, but for your sake and the sake of the rest of the family, you cannot afford to have this severe dysfunction continue to destroy your family for generations.

As the enabling increases, so do the challenges:

The following may be difficult for you to read, but it is happening in homes where enabling has reached the extreme.

The dependable son watches as his aging parent becomes isolated and not taking care of herself. Mom keeps saying that she will teach her enabled son some life skills, but a closer look may indicate that she has quit taking care of her own needs to focus on her enabled son's needs. She says she will teach him to manage his finances, but she doesn't even pay her own bills anymore. They both spend money with reckless abandon. She gets very frustrated with him because he will not take his medicine, but she quit taking her medicine a long time ago. Mom doesn't even try to teach him to take care of his house. She has given up and does all of his laundry, dishes, and housework. How much worse can it get? She may even clean up after decadent evenings where alcohol and drug use were prevalent. She just can't stand to see him live in such filth – so she cleans. The dependable son is horrified to see his parent controlled by the sin of his enabled brother. It is more than the dependable son can bear to see, much less is able to stop.

When family comes to visit Mom, the enabled one hovers over the gathering. It is a tactic of manipulation. He will not allow Mom and family members to be alone. The enabled son knows that he will be the topic of conversation. Through verbal abuse, or worse, he drives the family away. They can no longer visit with Mom. She cries out, "Please don't leave," but then soon turns her attention to pacify her needy, out of control son. Again, Mom is further isolated.

The dependable son recognizes that Mom's love and compassion for her enabled son have turned into obsession. The term Martyr comes to mind:

M-Mom

A-Always

R-Runs

T-To

Y-Your

R-Rescue

While Mom is willing to sacrifice everything for the child she has enabled, she risks losing the rest of her family. Is jealousy involved? Even young children know when one parent favors another sibling with extra time and finances. So, is jealousy involved? Yes, but not necessarily. The parent may be quick to declare she loves all of her children equally. Since Mom is sure that her caring and dependable son is fine, she is also sure that her dependable son does not need her. She determines to concentrate all of her resources and efforts on the one who is out of control.

For her dependable son, all of this is very hurtful. Too often, the enabling parent does not even listen to her dependable son. This indicates a lack of respect for the son who strives to help her. And yet as the isolation grows and the enabling worsens, her dependable son sees the inequity. Mom hardly, if at all, notices when her dependable son is displeased compared to her total focus when any hint of displeasure is evident in her enabled son. The dependable son makes his decisions based on restoring both his parent and enabled brother to responsible living. The enabled son makes his decisions based on wants, lusts, and feelings.

As the dependable son diligently labors to protect his mother from his brother's verbal, physical, and financial abuse, codependence causes a very close bond to form between the abuser and the abused. The dependable son is heartbroken when he sees his mom listen to and agree with his brother's "wisdom." She is addicted to enabling and does everything she can to protect her enabled son from any good that her dependable son can provide. When the dependable son places both of them on a reasonable budget, it is not unusual for Mom and her enabled son to form an alliance. Mom grows to trust the one she so lovingly enabled. And when she deems it necessary – lies to her dependable son. Together, they conspire to override the financial control of her dependable son. It is heart-wrenching for her dependable son.

The dependable son recognizes that he must separate the two of them in order to protect his mother from his brother. Over time, he realizes, more than protecting his mother from his brother, he needs to protect his mother from herself. She tolerates any and all abuse from her enabled son, as she hurries right back to help him. She will destroy anyone and anything that tries to stop her from protecting her son. It is an impossible situation. Mom's extreme compulsive behavior demonstrates her own desperate need for memory or mental health evaluation.

If the parent is older, it is very likely dementia or Alzheimer's disease is a factor. Knowing that does not make the situation any easier for her dependable son. It just increases Mom's need for protection. In her confused mind, she freely gives every cent she owns to try to satisfy the son she has enabled. He doesn't want to change – he wants more money. Not only is she wasting her life and her money, her compulsion for enabling is further dividing her family. With the situation so impossible, what can her dependable son do? He can pray and ask God to somehow get through the confusion in his mom's mind and to help her know that what he is doing is right. She needs to cooperate with him. Only God can reach her now.

The dependable son may no longer feel loved by his parent. He tries to stop the insanity of enabling, protect his parent, and survive in the process. All the while he is also trying to protect his own family from the ugliness he sees. What about love? It pierces his heart to hear his mom frequently declare she loves both of her children the same. It might have been true during the early years, but how can she love them equally now? Does she love them just the same when her dependable son does everything within his power to help his mother, while the son she enables continually verbally and financially abuses her? She loves them just the same! What might be a comforting statement in most families is hurtful in the family where enabling is taking place. Even so, her dependable son, for his own sanity, needs to tell Mom he does not want to hear that statement again. He must tell her how it makes him feel. Mom needs to hear honest talk, told in a loving manner. If she says it again, remind her again. Mom really needs to know how her actions are impacting you.

To the Dependable One:

Do you wonder if your labor is worth the battle? If you do, the answer is a definite – Yes! You are pleasing God by faithfully and diligently doing what is right. Press on and trust God to bring you through this situation. Do not get caught up in enabling the sins of your mother or brother. Keep your eyes on God, for only God can change your family. Do what God directs you to do and leave the rest to Him.

Should all children receive an equal inheritance?

I am not sure where we got the idea that the inheritance should be shared equally. In the Bible, inheritance was divided in a variety of ways.

To be fair, I believe the child who selflessly gives time, energy, and finances to help his parents should be the one to receive the greater portion of the inheritance. I have seen too many caregivers who singlehandedly spend years sacrificing all to help their parents only to end up heartbroken and in debt as they receive an equal share. They may pass it off and say they were doing it because they loved their parents. But in the end, it still stings. Those who do the work should receive a greater inheritance. Perhaps if children knew this was the way the inheritance would be divided, they would be a little nicer and more cooperative with their parents through the years. You could argue that the other siblings were working and could not take time off to help or even visit. That was a choice. They could have contributed financially, and they could have used some of their vacation time to give the dependable sibling a respite. Don't wait too late to update your will. Do it while you still have clarity of mind. Reward those who deserve a greater portion in their inheritance.

What about my needy child? Some parents compare the financial status of one child with another to determine who has greater needs, and therefore should receive more of the inheritance. Usually, major differences in finances indicate the result of life choices. Poor life choices should not require that the needy child receives more money. He will probably squander it, just as he has done with his own finances. Besides, it is very likely that the parent has already given additional funds on many occasions to the needy son. Early on, parents should work to maintain fair distribution. Perhaps if money is given to the needy child during his lifetime, parents could also set aside money in an account for the more responsible child. This would help to balance the inequity in the situation.

What about the sibling whose family has extreme financial issues due to medical bills? It is possible that the inheritance should be greater for this sibling. If the medical issues are due to drug use or other abusive behaviors, then additional funds would not be fair.

After the will, comes the actual distribution of property. I have seen the dependable one labor for weeks to close out the family home, only to have siblings come in and claim the best of what the parent owned. Did they consider the feelings or work of the sibling who labored so long and hard? No. It was wrong. The executor of the will needs to make sure this does not happen.

Memory Loss is Progressive.

If your parent is elderly and dementia or Alzheimer's disease is involved, your parent is not the person she used to be. In all likelihood, she has forgotten what it was like to live a normal life. Not only is her life changed by memory loss, until she is separated from the one she enables, she will still retain compulsive enabling behaviors. She has done it so long – she just can't stop. She also cannot make wise decisions and may find comfort in relying on the one she has enabled. This serves as an open door to more verbal, physical, and/or financial abuse. Isolation worsens because she is no longer able to drive, but demands that she continue to live in her own home. Cooped up in her house, she has few visitors or conversations, thus making the lack of mental stimulation a factor in her increasing memory loss. Lying has become a habit she cannot break. She lies to the son she enabled to keep the peace. She lies to her dependable son because she knows he cannot and will not approve of his brother's sin-filled life.

In the midst of the enabling years, she thought she had it all figured out. She knew what she was doing – protecting her child. She refused to seek help when help was available. She had clarity of mind, thinking she could protect herself. Now memory loss has taken over, and she cannot protect herself from her enabled son. He takes advantage of her at every opportunity, leaving her with nothing. Not only does she need protection from him, now more than ever, she needs protection from herself. He steals her food money and uses it for drugs and immoral living. He is never satisfied. She refuses to believe it.

Dependable son, have you tried to get help for your mom time and time again, but no one with any authority will protect her? Unless God provides a miraculous solution, only death or moving her to an assisted living facility will separate her from your abusive sibling. Assisted living facilities will protect the privacy and identity of the residents. If necessary, the assisted living facility will protect her from the child she enabled. Safety is a priority. They will call the police if there is a disturbance. Or you could move your mom in with you, inviting the whole enabling problem to overtake your household. If violence or threat of violence is involved, you may be placing your whole family at risk.

How will it all end?

The enabler would like nothing better than for her dependable son to be a partner in enabling. This would confirm that the obsessive compulsive enabling she has been denying for years was the right thing to do. Not only would she like for you to be an accomplice, she will be expecting you to receive your enabled sibling as part of your inheritance. Wow! The enabler finally has peace. You, on the other hand, will be destroyed. You have a choice: You can either join her in enabling or expose enabling at every opportunity and fight the good fight to see the enabling stopped.

In my family's situation, I chose the good fight. I had no answers. Situations were way beyond anything that I could manage or control. I had faith in God. I knew He would help me. I submitted to Him every circumstance, need, sorrow, and concern, making me totally dependent on Him. God performed miracle after miracle on my behalf. It was a long battle, but in the end, my mom was released from the death-grip of the enabling situation she had created. She now lives in an assisted living facility where she enjoys activities, people to chat with, and great food. She rarely mentions the son she enabled. She is happy and at peace. There is hope for you. Know this: God is not overwhelmed by the depth and severity of our problems. He sees our weakness, and He meets every need we entrust to Him. God knows how to take care of His own.

Dear Dependable One,

Know that God loves you and sees everything you are going through. Do not faint or give up hope. Today, in America, prophecies are being fulfilled as men's hearts are failing them for fear (Luke 21:26,). We know that the economy is barely surviving. We know that people are out of work and cannot find jobs. We know that many people have lost their homes, and adult children are moving back home to live with their parents. You may be caught between two generations: you have aging parents, and your adult children are returning home. Some Baby Boomers are committing suicide because they cannot continue living – caught in the middle of these two turbulent situations. DO NOT GIVE IN TO THE SEDUCTION OF SUICIDE! Be strong and of good courage! Fall upon the mercy of the Lord. Pray, seek God, read His Word, and wait for His answers. Only by the grace of God will you be able to break the enabling stronghold in your family. Thank and praise God for every victory, whether small or large. Share your testimony with others. Write it down. It will be an encouragement to you as you look back and see how the hand of Almighty God faithfully helped you. Praise Him in the midst of your fiery furnace trial, trusting that God will bring you through.

To the Spouse of the Dependable One:

When we get married, we expect our future will be filled with good times to enjoy with our spouse. We also know that there may be some challenges ahead, but we expect to trust God and to work with our spouse to get through these difficult times. Enabling in any family can place stress and strain on the marriage. Blessed is the dependable one whose spouse is well grounded in the Word and is supportive of the hard decisions that he will have to make.

In my family, I have been blessed to have a husband who was actively supportive when I needed him to step in and physically help solve problems. At appropriate times, he also stepped back, trusted me to do what was right, and gave me some space to work with my family's issues. He listened and gave advice, but he didn't make demands. Above all, he prayed for me and with me. I pray that if you are going through an enabling situation right now, you will be strong in the Lord. Pray for and with your spouse. Support your spouse, trusting that God will bring you both through to a positive end.

Are you engaged to a dependable person whose parent is an enabler?

What about those who are considering marrying into a family where enabling is already an obvious problem? Be very careful that you look at the reality of the situation – not from the perspective of romance and fantasy. You may think that you will just separate yourselves from the rest of the family, and things will be fine. That may or may not happen. Now, while there is time, you need to have some serious discussions with your intended before making a decision that you will regret for the rest of your life. You need to make sure you and your future spouse agree as to how you will deal with enabling issues. What will happen to the enabled sibling when the parent dies? Will you take up enabling this person or will you allow the enabled one to take responsibility for and suffer consequences of his own actions?

When you talk about raising children, make sure your intended is not a product of his home environment. Is he ready to protect your future children from all consequences, while making everything easy and fun for them? If enabling is not recognized and stopped, it will become a curse that will destroy the future of your family.

To the Enabled One:

When the person who now enables you started making things easy for you, it was probably because this was the way your enabler knew how to show love. As she made things easy for you and protected you from consequences, you became very dependent on your enabler. You probably do not enjoy being dependent – but see no way out of this arrangement. There is no point in living with regrets and dreads. Just by your choosing to read this book, you are learning much about the prison of enabling that holds you captive.

How can you get free? Acting out in anger toward your enabler will not solve your problem. Making further demands of people around you will not free you from the enabling trap. If you really want change and the opportunity to grow up, you need to know it will not be easy. God will help you, if your trust is in Him.

To the Enabled Adult Son or Daughter: PRAY WITH ME

Heavenly Father,

I come to you in the name of Jesus. I recognize that sin has overtaken my life. Forgive me Lord for taking the easy way my entire life, only seeking what pleased me. I have been lazy, rebellious, stubborn, wasteful, greedy, demanding, angry, and bitter. My sin is disobedience to You. Forgive me for hurting (name those you hurt). Only You can help me change. Remove my addictions to (name the addictions). When temptations come, help me to stop and acknowledge You and Your help in my life. Help me to walk away from sin and turn my thoughts and words to praising You, trusting that You are doing a complete work in me. I know You can do it, and You will do it. I don't have to know how or why. Help me to make wise decisions that please You. Help me to discern when something is not of You and reject it. Provide me with Godly support and counseling. I trust You for full deliverance from all the evil addictions in my life. Lord, help me to become a caring, responsible person. God, help me to become the person You have created me to be. Make my life a testimony of Your greatness. Thank You, Lord. I love You. Thank You for loving me. Amen.

In the name of Jesus, these Strongholds must come down!

Only by the grace of God will you be able to break the enabling stronghold in your life. Pray, seek God, read His Word, and wait for His answers. Thank and praise God for every victory, whether small or large. Share your testimony with others. Write it down. It will be an encouragement to you to see the hand of Almighty God helping you. Start going to a Bible-believing church that has teaching and support to help you face and overcome life's challenges.

Forgive the person who enabled you and those who did not try to stop the enabler from reducing you to total dependence. When someone tries to enable you in the future, refuse the easy way and politely, but firmly, do the right thing for each situation. When someone asks you if you are tired and need to rest, don't check your feelings. Just smile nicely and say, "I'm fine." Keep doing what you know is right. You can rest later. Don't allow others to do for you what you can and should do for yourself. Be strong and of good courage! You are literally fighting for your life. It will seem impossible at times, but God will help you.

Are you dating, engaged to, or married to someone who has been enabled?

If you are dating or engaged to someone who has been enabled, perhaps the enabler has been waiting for someone to come along and take over enabling her adult son. If you are not careful, you will be dragged into the role of enabler, and your life will become emotionally dysfunctional.

Perhaps his mom loves her role and is holding on to her adult son with a death grip. Perhaps her son is enjoying the lifestyle the enabler has created. If you try to come between them, they may find ways to destroy you.

Know this: If drugs and alcohol are involved, the person you so dearly love is probably not capable of loving you. When his every thought is focused on getting high or getting the money to get high, there will be much heartache in your life. Any prosperity you have will be quickly consumed. Any children you have will learn, by his example, to abuse alcohol and drugs. Substance abuse will affect the generations to follow. If you are dating or engaged to someone who has been enabled, you need to think seriously about what your future may look like if you continue in this relationship or even marry him.

If you are already married to someone who has been enabled, God has not called you to live a life full of emotional and physical abuse. No matter how much love you give, you cannot fix what is wrong and cause him to love you. When you honestly admit the seriousness of your situation, you may need to find a place of safety to allow you to physically and emotionally heal from this relationship. Pray and ask God for His will in your life. Ask Him to provide discernment, direction, and the courage to follow through in what He wants you to do.

If you are determined to stay in this relationship or decide to return to this relationship, there are family resources and support groups available in most communities. You need a support group to give you the encouragement and training that will make you better able to deal with your situation. Contact your church for availability of resources in your community. In the end, the only way to protect yourself may be to move to a new location and make a new life for yourself and your family.

Chapter 10:
Why Can't the Community Accept My Child?

While the enabler and the one enabled think it is all about them, in reality, many people are affected. You cannot hide serious problems from the world for very long. You may find some concerned people who want to help and even try to help, but give up in desperation as an attempt to secure their own safety and sanity. In this chapter, we will look at perspectives and concerns as related to the police, the health workers, the school, and the church within the community.

How are other people affected by the presence of enabling?

The following example may seem extreme, but it is a reality in many communities: Enablers cannot hide their enabling forever. A trip to the grocery store or bank will cause eyes to widen as the enabled adult son freely demands what he wants, cusses at his parent and the workers, and dares anyone to do anything to stop him. The enabler expects the community to understand and give sympathy. When bystanders see the situation, they feel helpless. If the mother and son are frequently seen causing a commotion in the store, other shoppers may even be repelled by the mother's addiction to protect and provide for her out of control son. Why hasn't something already been done? Especially if elder abuse is involved? Many times the only way stores and banks can protect their customers is to no longer allow the offender to return to their place of business. This in no way solves the problem or protects the enabler, but it is a matter of survival for the business owner.

Why don't they call the police? Business owners and workers are afraid to get involved. They just want the parent and son to leave. Yes, they may be concerned, but if the business gets involved, the store or bank will be further disrupted by the presence of the police. Getting involved will also require time to testify in court. The enabled son will probably receive minimal jail time, and there may be some type of revenge in the future when the offender returns to the community. This can be a cycle of abuse in which no one wants to be entangled.

Stores, banks, and neighbors all think that the enabler and son must want help – surely they want help! The enabled son just wants what he wants – money, alcohol, junk food, cigarettes, drugs, or whatever else he currently lusts after. The enabler is embarrassed; however, her need for peace overtakes her need for help. She tries to fix the situation by saying, "My son has problems." She finds comfort in any sympathy she can garner. And finally, yes finally, leaves the store thinking she can escape any more public attention. She does, but only until the next time when she allows her enabled son to accompany her to town.

What does the Bible say? The community knows.

He who walks in integrity walks securely, But he who perverts his ways will become known (Proverbs 10:9, NKJ).

A man will be commended according to his wisdom, But he who is of a perverse heart will be despised (Proverbs 12:8, NKJ).

The way of a fool is right in his own eyes, But he who heeds counsel is wise. A fool's wrath is known at once (Proverbs 12:15-16, NKJ).

A wise man fears, and shuns evil, but the fool is hotheaded and reckless. A quick-tempered man does foolish things, and a crafty man is hated. (Proverbs 14:16-17, NIV).

 The wicked man craves evil; his neighbor gets no mercy from him. (Proverbs 21:10, NIV).

Is there any hope when the whole community knows? Yes!

When a man's ways please the Lord, He makes even his enemies to be at peace with him (Proverbs 16:7, NKJ).

A challenge for the Enabled One:

Am I saying that we should view our community as the enemy? No! Many people in the community care about you. If pleasing God by our words and actions is enough to make our enemies live at peace with us, then how much more will our community live at peace with us when our choices and lifestyle please God? Enabled one, God declares you will see change in your community's attitude toward you, when it is visible that you are demonstrating positive changes in your life. Speak kindly and respectfully. Use good manners. Make your requests known and wait patiently. You may not see an instant change, but over time, as you change, they will become more accepting of the new you.

145

As we look at the perspectives of different community members, keep this Scripture, Proverbs 16:7, in mind. It is a promise from God. There is hope.

The Police:

With elder abuse such an important concern, it is only natural we expect the police to rescue our elderly parents when they are threatened by the one they have enabled. I believe that the police are interested in keeping everyone safe. Even though they may want to intervene, there are reasons they will not protect the parent by arresting her son. I do know that police in different areas of the country may have different ways of dealing with elder abuse, but I am reporting to you from my own experience with family members who have been involved in enabling.

Why won't the police arrest them?

Many parents who have become victims may call the police, but refuse to file a police report against their child. This happens in many domestic violence cases. If you refuse to file a police report and/or will not agree to show up in court, the police can do nothing.

It is worse when dementia is involved. Let me give you an example. Your parent with dementia or Alzheimer's may be able to call and tell you about an abusive situation that just happened, but by the time you arrive, memory loss takes over and all your parent will say is, "Everything is fine." Which of course, it isn't. Even if you contact the police, you did not witness the abuse. If your parent won't or can't confirm it, your account is only hearsay.

Let's factor in enabling. When the police have observed a parent cater to her adult son's every demand, especially giving him excessive money and valuables – a precedent has been set. Now, when the parent declares that her son has stolen from her, why

146

should the police believe it? This is especially true if the enabled son insists she gave it to him. Now, no one will believe it was theft.

Isn't this elder abuse? The elder abuse designation does not apply if the elder does not live with the abuser. The elder is not dependent upon the abuser for her place to live. The reasoning: The parent can protect herself by going home. For the compulsive enabler, it is difficult for her to go home. She is sure she is still needed at her son's house.

Verbal abuse is not a reason for someone to be arrested, unless a threat of violence is involved. Even though you feel violated when an angry person pummels you with perverse language, you will probably not be able to silence him with an arrest. The police, however, will work to de-escalate the situation. That only stops the abuse while the police are present. As long as the parent makes it known that she will "handle it," the police will let her.

If the parent calls the police department often, but does not file a police report, the police and the abuser may develop a congenial relationship. They become "buddies." This is not a good situation and does not protect the parent.

The police do not want to complete cumbersome paperwork if the victim will not show up in court to testify. Officers may ask the parent if she would rather have the abuser home or in jail. In her confused state of mind, Mom wants her son home – home and behaving himself. However, that is not what she gets. She just gets him returned home with no change in behavior.

A restraining order is difficult, but not impossible to get. You must have documentation of specific incidents that necessitate a restraining order. Getting proof can be challenging. There may be a past history of extreme violence combined with recent threats. If documentation of actual violence is not recent, no restraining order will be issued.

I respect the work our police officers do; however, there are many reasons they may not be able to protect an elderly parent who has spent a lifetime enabling her out of control adult son. So how do we protect the enabler from the one she enabled?

The best answer:

The enabling must be stopped while the enabler still has clarity of mind. Once dementia or Alzheimer's disease is present, there will be no way to protect the enabler from the one who has been enabled.

Social Workers:

Caring social workers can be a valuable resource to help dysfunctional families. Social workers assist individuals and their families as they adjust to problems in their lives. The services provided may be related to serious physical illness, substance abuse, mental illness, child abuse, physical challenges, antisocial behavior, or a variety of other needs. Social workers can offer counseling and therapy, inform individuals and family about available community resources, and make connections for people who need help.

Aging parents who can no longer drive may receive information about free or inexpensive transportation to the grocery store or a doctor's appointment. Social workers can direct clients to Meals on Wheels or other feeding programs. This usually works well for a homebound, elderly parent until she can no longer manage on her own.

What about the enabled one? If he is generally homebound and considered disabled – even if he is disabled due to alcohol and/or drug abuse – the same services can be arranged for him. The social worker, however, cannot require him to take advantage of these programs. He will need to be responsible to get to the bus on time or get out of bed to answer the door and receive food from Meals on Wheels. Another dilemma, social workers cannot make the enabled one act in a civil manner nor prevent him from verbally abusing the volunteers who deliver his daily meal. Abuse of any community volunteers will facilitate the loss of the service, a standard consequence for unacceptable behavior.

Social workers may be an immense help in developing life skills for the one who has been enabled. That individual will still be responsible to cooperate by showing up at meetings, attending therapy, developing and using appropriate social skills, and giving good effort. Some clients learn to manipulate the system for a while, but the reality of their success is determined by their behavior in the community.

Doctors:

Doctors are very concerned when possible abuse of family members is involved. They must report any suspected abuse. If patients are secretive and careful not to admit the presence of abuse, the doctor's ability to adequately assess the situation is very difficult.

Will the doctor tell me when my aging parent should no longer live alone?

Not necessarily. When the patient is elderly, dementia or Alzheimer's disease is a real possibility. Doctors are concerned, but unless your health community has a good system for identifying these conditions, doctors are very hesitant to declare a patient can no longer manage her own life. Doctors are very concerned that they will get sued if documentation is not adequate.

What are your options? The dependable one can have the parent declared incompetent by the courts. You must be very careful to differentiate between the need to protect your parent from the enabled one and the need to protect your parent from her diminishing capacity. Can she take care of herself, make good decisions, take medicine, and manage finances? If your parent is competent, then attempting to have her declared incompetent would not be the correct route to take. If your parent is not competent, then you will need ample documentation to prove diminished capacity. This must include: medical, financial, and witness statements.

What are some of the signs of memory loss?

- Confusion
- Forgetting – short and/or long term memory loss
- Difficulty concentrating
- Loss of vocabulary
- Loss of bill paying ability
- Loss of ability to consistently take prescribed medicines
- Inability to do routine tasks that used to be easy – bathing, getting dressed, brushing teeth, setting the table, washing the dishes
- Loss of good judgment – reckless spending
- Increasingly fearful or increasingly trusting – does not discern danger
- Too many close calls while driving the car
- Getting lost in areas that were formerly well-known
- Wandering
- Loss of large or fine motor skills
- Repeating the same task
- Asking the same questions over and over
- Difficulty in learning new tasks
- Difficulties reading, writing, listening, speaking
- Loss of problem-solving ability
- Isolating self from family or friends
- Change in personality or mood – depressed, anxious, aggressive

If you observe some or many of these behaviors, you may want to have your loved one evaluated for dementia or Alzheimer's disease. Keep a notebook with names, dates, phone numbers, addresses, medical reports, receipts, and any other confirming documents. By collecting documentation as soon as possible, you will be better prepared when you need to confirm your parent's inability to live alone.

When your aging loved one is an enabler, your task will be even more challenging. You will need to keep similar records about the one enabled. Often times, when the one enabled recognizes the possibility of losing control of his parent, he may resort to aggression or violent acts to maintain his lifestyle. Once the dependable sibling steps in to bring sanity to the situation, the enabled one will know access to excessive finances and protection from consequences will soon end. The enabled one may declare war.

The dependable one has enough to do to make sure his parent is safe. Dependable one, your job is to do what is right. Remember – When you please the Lord, God makes even your enemies to be at peace with you (Proverbs 16:7, NKJ). Rely on this Scripture and declare it when you find yourself in the heat of the battle. God will protect you and give you peace in the midst of your circumstances.

The School:

It would be wonderful if all children, parents, and teachers worked together to ensure the success of each child. I hope this book will help parents and teachers recognize enabling as a root cause for many of the problems they see in the classroom.

What happened in our schools? When America began to focus on entertainment instead of hard work, public schools were quick to follow. Schools thought they could reduce the number of behavior problems needing administrative attention by requiring all lessons be made fun and easy. Parents liked the reduction in homework and the good grades that appeared on their children's report cards. Thus began the "dumbing down" of education in America. Thus began a system of enabling that seemed to make everyone happy – for a while. Students avoided the responsibility of completing difficult lessons while they had a great time. Since the grades were inflated by easy lessons and easy tests, it wasn't long until students were unable to master even the basics. Multiplication tables, phonics, spelling, English grammar, and cursive writing were just a few of the lessons deemed not really important. Without these lessons, reading, math, and writing all suffered. Hey! Those are the basics! What were we thinking?

As things got easier, it wasn't long until parents and children returned to complaining about the remaining "work load." It interfered with afterschool sports and activities. By now, some students didn't like their "fun, but easy classes," and once again, began complaining to parents. These students did not desire more difficult work. They wanted lessons that kept them happy – lessons that satisfied their ever increasing need for fun. Everyone was sure that fun, easy lessons would cause students to behave and keep them out of the office. Of course that wasn't enough, so by consulting educational experts, it was determined that consequences were the problem. Teachers were specifically told, "There will be no consequences for inappropriate behavior."

Know this: Lessons that are fun and easy will never replace learning to overcome challenges. School is supposed to prepare students with skills and strategies to succeed, even when assignments are difficult, especially when assignments are difficult. When everything is made easy and fun, students are not prepared for real life. They do not become responsible adults who face difficult situations and refuse to give up until they succeed. Instead, when schoolwork gets difficult, they quit. When the marriage gets difficult, they quit. When the job gets difficult, they quit. In real life, consequences follow serious decisions like these. Families are plunged into poverty and dysfunction.

When schools removed consequences they removed any understanding of why students needed to do the right thing. Students were robbed of character building lessons that would change the way they viewed life. They did not need determination, perseverance, endurance, patience, kindness, or cooperation. Real life requires all of these and more. God uses consequences to develop positive character qualities in us. Through consequences, we learn how to be caring, responsible adults. Even if the schools do not recognize the destruction these educational changes caused, parents who love their children will choose not to make everything easy and fun. They will not remove consequences from their children.

Can we blame the schools for enabling students to avoid academic skills and character development? Yes, but as you see, parents had their part in this enabling problem. Parents wanted to reduce stress at home by suggesting, and sometimes demanding, school be made fun and easy. Schools and parents both need to recognize their role in enabling our children and seek to restore both good behavior and academics in the classroom.

So what else causes the parent/teacher breakdown? In many families, parents are overwhelmed with the cares of life. These cares include stress at work, divorce, loss of child custody, loss of job, and other family problems. It is easier for parents to declare that the teacher is the professional. She should be the one to make my out of control child behave in class and get good grades. This is not a new problem. The behavior and academic issues for this child have probably been an ongoing problem for many years. Now, the child's current teacher is expected to fix it. The child's behavior may have been uncontrollable for so long that the parents feel powerless, and they retreat to a position of monitoring. They say, "Send us daily and weekly progress reports." As the teacher diligently documents every issue and strategy she is using to try to effect positive change, it is not unusual for the parent to lose interest and not want to be bothered hearing about their child's ongoing behavior problems. Oh, they still want the progress reports, but signing off is about the limit of their participation. It isn't long until the progress reports keep arriving at home, and they are neither signed nor returned. Can't the teacher just handle it? This is unreasonable. Now picture this scenario multiplied by many students who need the same help and monitoring within the class. Teachers cannot do this alone. Parents and teachers must work together.

What can parents do?

- Actively monitor your child's lessons and progress.

- Parents of elementary school students need to review all tests and homework.

- Your child should make corrections to all missed questions or problems. Don't just provide answers. Instead, your child should bring home the appropriate books or use the Internet to find correct answers. If the questions are multiple-choice, have your child tell you which answer is right and why the other answers are wrong.

- Read every night with your child. Fantasy is nice on occasion, but it will not make your child excellent in academic subjects. Biographies of people who have made a positive difference in our country are great to reinforce character qualities. Science and history books expand your child's interests, as they strengthen their understanding of real world knowledge.

- Read and discuss vocabulary. Ask questions such as who, what, where, when, why, and how.

When parents become active in working with their children at home, both academics and behavior usually improve.

Parents of upper grade students also need to make sure their children do their homework and study for tests. Parents who faithfully review their children's tests, progress reports, and report cards will learn about their academic progress in a timely manner, before it is too late to pass the course or the grade.

You may say that the lessons have become too difficult. You are no longer able to help your child study. The following suggestions will help you.

Instruct your child to:

- Arrive at class ready to learn. Have sharpened pencils, paper, notebooks, textbooks, completed homework, and anything else you know you will need. Before the lesson begins, take your materials and supplies out of your backpack and make them readily accessible. Too much learning time is lost in the first few minutes of class when students are not prepared. Be ready to start on time.

- Sit at the front of the class to avoid distractions.

- Listen and take notes.

- Ask questions. Remind your child that other students probably have the same questions, but many are afraid to ask. Your child may be doing the whole class a favor. Perhaps everyone will do better on the test.

- Check your backpack before you leave school so that you do not arrive at home without the materials needed to do your homework. Make sure you have packed necessary books, papers, page numbers for homework assignments, and a calendar listing dates when projects are due. Don't just assume that everything is in your backpack. Check!

- If needed, use the afterschool homework hotline or afterschool tutoring. These resources are provided by most school districts. Check your school district for other available help.

- Use online resources that provide step-by-step information relevant to your child's lesson.

- If necessary, hire a tutor. The longer you wait to get your child back on track, the greater the deficit in learning will become.

Can't we just trust our children to study? No. Even if your child knows how to do the homework, there are too many distractions that can consume study time. Study requires focus. Remove any distracting electronics, to include cell phones. If your child really needs to phone a classmate for homework assistance, the call should be brief, allowing both to return to completing their homework. What about doing homework with a friend? The "buddy system" can be beneficial, but it needs adult supervision to ensure everyone stays on task.

What happens when parents do not monitor their children's homework time?

What might start as time doing homework together, may end with too much idle chatter and very little homework being accomplished. Even parents of earlier generations knew children could easily get off-task. But things are different today. How bad can it get? Too much time spent in "hanging out" may cause your preteen or teenager to lose their desire to do well in school. Conversations may start out as simple complaining that lead to plans or even acts of violence. Idle talk may tempt children to experiment with sexual activity, alcohol, and drugs. All are easily attained, while parents hardly notice until it is too late. With-it-ness is not a parenting skill that is only for parents of young children. It is just as important to actively supervise older children to ensure they do not give into seductions of sin that will destroy them. In the old days they used to say, "Idle hands are the devil's workshop." It is even truer, today. The results are seen in the news almost every night.

What does the Bible say about idle conversations?

> Jesus said, "But I say to you that for every idle word men may speak, they will give account of it in the day of judgment. For by your words you will be justified, and by your words you will be condemned" (Matthew 12:36-37, NKJ).

> In all labor there is profit, But idle chatter leads only to poverty (Proverbs 14:23, NKJ).

What does the Bible say about "hanging out" with friends?

> The righteous should choose his friends carefully, For the way of the wicked leads them astray (Proverbs 12:26, NKJ).

> He who walks with wise men will be wise, But the companion of fools will be destroyed (Proverbs 13:20, NKJ).

> Fear the Lord and the king, my son, and do not join with the rebellious (Proverbs 24:21, NIV).

> Do not be deceived: "Evil company corrupts good habits." Awake to righteousness, and do not sin; (1 Corinthians 15:33-34, NKJ).

I can't afford a private school. What if my child must attend public school?

Whatever the school, speak in a positive manner about your child's school, teachers, and schoolwork. You can actually destroy your child's motivation and ability to learn by complaining about the teacher or school. If you are a Christian, do not think that there are no Christian teachers in public schools. Many Christians teach in public schools. If you frequently complain about your child's teachers, you may be working against the very person God has placed there to help your child.

How do parents enable their children to avoid responsibility at school?

1. Parents demand that the teacher allow work to be taken home for completion. The child never learns to work with the clock or the joy of finishing a day's work in a day's time. Procrastination becomes a constant companion that steals productivity.

2. Parents do homework for students. Sometimes, parents do complete projects for their children. Homework is practice. It is meant to reinforce and review what was learned in class. Children need additional practice if they are going to do more than experience the lesson. We want our children to master the skills and progress from there.

Although projects can provide a nice bonding time for families, the child needs to create most of the project. Parent instruction, guidance, and supervision of tools are good, but when an eight year old shows up at school with a project that rivals any professionally built endeavor, the parents have done too much.

What if the parents just complete the project for their child? In order for children to become good workers, they must experience the joy of getting the job completed. If not, they will never finish what they start, making it almost impossible for them to maintain a job. If the time is up, and the project is not complete, your child should turn it in as is. When the grade is reduced for being an incomplete assignment, the lower grade will be the consequence. Don't run to the school and demand an extension. Accept it as a life lesson: If you want full credit for the work you do, you must complete the task. Are there ever extenuating circumstances that warrant asking for extended time? Yes. Examples of valid reasons for extending time to complete a project would be serious illness or a death in the family.

3. Parents call and make excuses when their high school child fails to show up for a final exam. If your child stayed up all night to study and then was too tired to go to school to take the test, this is another life lesson. Studying should be accomplished over time. Studying is a process, not a one-time event. A child who waits until the last minute to study is not developing good work habits.

How can I help my child study? If your child has a test on Friday, he needs to begin preparing early in the week. On Monday and Tuesday, he should read over the material, including all class notes. He may need to take additional detailed notes and make lists to ensure he understands all of the concepts. Include definitions, formulas, and procedures that will help him analyze the information during the test. On Wednesday and Thursday, he should memorize the notes that he has taken. On Friday, he will be ready for the test. The more he does this, the better he will get at test-taking.

During study time, don't forget to put away cell phones and any other electronic devices. Too many distractions will limit his ability to concentrate on his studies.

4. Parents give rewards for future good behavior. When parents say, "I will buy you this outfit today, if you will promise to behave at school all week," there is no incentive for the student to behave. The reward has already been given.

A second problem is inherent in this true scenario: Parents are teaching children to make promises they do not intend to keep or may be unable to keep. Either way, it is an integrity problem. Either way, it is sin. A promise is a commitment. It is wrong to promise, knowing you will not keep your word – this is a lie. It is better not to promise at all.

What does the Bible say about making promises?

> Lying lips are an abomination to the Lord, But those who deal truthfully are His delight (Proverbs 12:22, NKJ).

> It is better not to make a vow than to make a vow and not fulfill it. Do not let your mouth lead you into sin (Ecclesiastes 5:5-6, NIV).

In this case, no rewards should be given until behavior has improved. Give rewards sparingly and for specific results. Rewards given too easily lose their value. Later, a better reward will be required to achieve good results. Children need to know that good behavior and attitudes are expected because it is the right thing to do. Parents need to stress to their children that they are raising them to be caring, responsible adults. The reward is not the goal. The goal is a good, caring attitude with good behavior.

What about consequences? Consequences should be included in the package. When you only make goals with rewards, it will not be enough to correct behavior. Consequences need to be established for home and school.

What if my child's teachers do not like my child?

I have never known a teacher who did not like a well-behaved child who gave good effort. This is a reasonable expectation for all students. It is also reasonable for parents and teachers to work very hard to maintain a cooperative relationship where they give obvious support and effort to training and working with the child.

Know that your children behave differently at school than when they are at home. Remember, at home you probably have one or two adults working with one or two children. At school, it is probably one adult working with 20 or more children. Listen to the teacher if you are told that your child has attitude or behavior problems in class. Take the teacher seriously.

Is your child a bully?

We know that bullying is a serious problem in our nation. In school, we have rules designed to protect people from bullying. When parents dismiss rules as inconvenient obstacles to be ignored, the rules cannot do their job. Combine this attitude that ignores rules with the absence of consequences, and you have children who feel free to bully others with no worry of being punished. Now add parents who race to protect their out of control children, denying that their child has a problem. Yes, enabling is a root cause of bullying.

You may think that these children only bully students; that would be wrong. They bully their teachers and their parents. Some experts are sure it is a lack of self-esteem, but in reality, these bullies declare war on others because there is nothing to fear. They purposefully torment and harm others to demonstrate their prowess. They do not fear God nor man, knowing no one will stop them.

How does it end? Many bullies, thinking they are invincible, end up in prison for violent or drug related crimes. Others grow up to be spouse abusers. Still others increase their influence by joining organized gangs that will control them for the rest of their lives. All three paths lead to destruction.

How can all this be prevented? Stop the enabling. Parents who love their children recognize they must discipline their children from an early age. This ensures that rebellious attitudes and behaviors do not shape the person they become. They attend church with their children. They teach their children to care about others. By their words and actions, they teach their children to love and serve God.

The Church:

I would like to say all churches are equipped to help families with enabling issues, but that would be incorrect. I can say; however, all churches, even if they are not equipped to personally minister to these families, should have knowledge of available resources. These resources should include: ministries, counseling, and rehabilitation services that can help families break free and recover from the stronghold of enabling. God has not called each church to be an island unto itself, but an integral part of the Body of Christ. Today, the needs are great and many. No one church can do it all. Networking with others is vital to seeing families restored and serving God. I thank God for churches who work together.

God has placed within the Body of Christ, amazing churches and ministries that are experienced in delivering individuals from the deepest depths of sin. We need these ministries, if people held in bondage are going to be set free. Many times, the individuals God has called to these ministries have come from similar backgrounds to include alcohol and drug abuse. God has delivered them and anointed these mighty warriors to deliver others from the same sins that once held them captive.

Where codependency and substance abuse are involved, the person would benefit from a church that is not overwhelmed by their great need. Don't be confused – God is never overwhelmed by someone's great need. Our God is able and willing to deliver all who submit their sins and their lives to Him. The Salvation Army is a great example of a church that knows how to bring salvation, healing, and deliverance to people who are lost in the depths of sin. Complete deliverance, however, only works when individuals are willing to let go of their past and their sin, as they trust God with their future.

When God delivers those who have been enabled and exchanges their sin for His righteousness, they become a vital part of the Body

162

of Christ. The ones who have been set free from the prison of enabling can encourage others as they give testimony to what God has done in their lives. They are able to minister to others who desperately need God to deliver them from the same strongholds.

What happened in many Christian homes?

People got caught up in the American dream, their jobs, and an ever expanding lust for entertainment and things. Many families totally left God out of the picture or relegated Him to a Sunday only place. Worldly philosophies and distractions have bombarded our families. People are bored with everything and think that their opinions are more important than anything else in life. The examples set by too many leaders, the media, and even the lives of their own parents, have told them truth is non-existent and drugs, sexual promiscuity, and violence are the norm. In the midst of this pounding storm that is striving to destroy our children and grandchildren, codependency and enabling have only made it worse.

To the Church:

Our families desperately need to see God's power working in their lives today. If you have ever experienced the miraculous power of God in your life, you know exactly what I am talking about – your life was changed. That was not the end, but the beginning of a closer relationship with God.

Our families need to know that the Bible is not only our oldest written history book, but it is indeed – the Word of God. The Bible is God speaking to us.

In church, both the message and the music must provide hope. People need to know that God has the answer to every problem and question they have. They need to know that they can be forgiven and reconciled with Him. People need to hear words of conviction, repentance, restoration, and healing of broken hearts and lives. They need to know how to live lives that please God. They need to hear words that encourage them to trust God as their Savior, Lord, Healer, Counselor, Provider, and Deliverer. Then, their worship will be based on the reality of His love and His presence in their lives. Then, they will want to be in church to experience more of God and His plan for their lives. I thank God for churches like this.

Some churches settle for entertainment, clever quotations, and maybe a scripture or two. This will never be enough to satisfy the sin-sick soul. Too many people are desperate for real answers and hope. If all they find is entertainment with a brief word of encouragement, they may think they have tried God. When they see no change in their circumstances, it is easy to give up. They are sure that church just didn't work for them. They may never try God again. A multitude of families throughout our nation are dysfunctional to the point of destruction. They need straight talk and real answers. Does your church teach, believe, and live the truth that Jesus Christ is Lord? If not, then your church needs to repent – ask for forgiveness and trust God to help you change.

To the Enabled One:

Do you feel like you are rejected by both your family and the community? The rejection you feel has purpose. It is designed to cause you to bathe, dress, and behave appropriately. Yes, this rejection is painful, but it is designed to cause you to desire acceptance and relationships more than your stubborn will. This rejection is a consequence. God can use rejection to help you change, but only if you are willing.

Now, consider the eternal rejection awaiting you if you do not choose God over the things of this world. He wants to be your Savior and Lord. He wants you to trust and obey Him. He wants you to use the Bible as your standard for living and pleasing Him. You have a lot of changing to do, but God will help you. Submit yourself to Him, and you will be amazed at the person God helps you to

164

become. Your life can become a testimony of God's greatness, but only if you are willing.

Chapter 11:
Perspectives: A Time for Reflection

The following activity is a strategy you can use to help your family members recognize the far reaching influence of their behavior. You will need a large sheet of drawing paper or poster board to create a simple graphic organizer. Instead of just saying, "I'm sorry," the organizer requires time for reflection and analysis, while helping to direct change. Although this activity is created for children, it even works for adults. As you notice, God's perspective is in the center – right where it should be. This exercise is not meant to be a quick analysis, but should require thinking about how wrong behavior affects other people.

A sample of the graphic organizer is located on the last page of this chapter.

Directions:

- Select a behavior that needs changing.

- Create the chart. For a young child, the parent should draw the chart to make sure there is room for responses in each section. An older child may be able to effectively draw the chart on his own.

- Goals may be established by writing them outside the box.

167

- Have your child complete the chart by writing and/or drawing to show how your child perceives the reaction of others to the identified misbehavior.

- God's answer should include a Scripture that confirms His perspective, making this an excellent opportunity for Bible study.

- Discussion between parent and child should follow.

- Later, updates to indicate progress should be added, or a new chart can be created and compared for progress.

- Both large and small improvements can and should be celebrated.

- Other behaviors/goals may be added over time.

Example:

1. Parents help Sophia set the goal.

Goal: Sophia will use words that are appropriate and kind.

2. Sophia answers these questions and completes the chart with complete sentences:

- What do I think my mom would say about me using bad words at school?

- What do I think the family would say about me using bad words at school?

- What do I think my teacher would say about me using bad words at school?

- What do I think God would say about me using bad words at school? (Scripture)

- How do I feel about the fact that I used bad words at school?

(Or – When I use bad words at school, how does it harm me?)

Options: The choice of perspectives is flexible.
You may modify according to your situation.

This graphic organizer can provide amazing insights when the offender identifies problems, habits, strengths, weaknesses, and the person God wants him to become. While the offender is working on his chart, the parent and/or another family member (i.e. a sibling who was also involved in a fight) may be completing a chart as well.

This chart also provides a way to encourage accountability, especially when the entire family is involved in giving perspectives, setting goals, and recognizing improvement. When the graphic organizer is shared, it should be accomplished in a loving manner. It can be shared with no conversation. If participants are willing to talk about personal feelings with others, then a prior agreement for acceptable conversation and behavior is important.

Family Discussion:

Together, you can make your own rules or use some of these:

- Pray first.

- Only one person speaks at a time.

- You may use an object to pass to the person who speaks next.

- Voices should be moderate. No yelling.

- No obscenities, rude statements, or gestures are allowed.

- If the perspective of a person is not correct or inadequate, changes to the chart are appropriate.

- Everyone participates. Everyone shares something.

- Agree to meet in a week to review progress.

- Everyone watches for evidence of improvement.

The purpose is not to condemn, but to work together for family growth. Honesty is important, and disrespectful behavior should not be tolerated.

During follow-up meeting:

1. Sophia completes the chart with answers to the following questions:

- How does my mom feel when I use appropriate and kind words at school?

- How does my family feel when I use appropriate and kind words at school?

- How does my teacher feel when I use appropriate and kind words at school?

- How does God feel when I use appropriate and kind words at school?

- How do I feel when I use appropriate and kind words at school?

(Or – When I use kind words at school, how does it help me?)

2. Everyone shares evidence of improvement.

3. Did she improve? Did she meet her goal?

4. Areas that still need attention can be noted for the next meeting.

Goal:

Perspective of the Parent	Perspective Of the Offender	
God's Perspective		
Perspective of the Family	Perspective of the Community/Teacher	

Chapter 12:
Enablers are Energized by Purpose.

Enablers know they need purpose. They also know that God wants them to help others. When they seek God's purpose in their lives, God is pleased. Helping others is an awesome part of our Christian walk.

However, when their help allows others to avoid responsibility and live ungodly lifestyles, God is not pleased. Many enablers are motivated by the feelings of others. They allow these feelings to override all wise counsel, even the counsel of God's Word. They do not submit to God's leadership, but plow ahead thinking that they know what is best. They do not wait on God. When they see a problem, they just fix it. Sadly, it is usually a temporary fix with greater problems to follow. It is a cycle of sin for both the enabler and the one being enabled. Fixing problems becomes a compulsive habit that allows little or no place for God in their lives. It is time that Christian parents recognize even though they feel the distress of the situation, the sympathy of the parent is not more important than God's Word. True believers will bow to the truth and the authority of God and His Word.

God's perspective is different from ours.

Even basic logic tells us that quick decisions based on emotion, usually do not produce a successful end. Want frustration? Try to discuss a problem with someone who has already made a decision before they hear the facts. But even knowing all the facts, we do not have a full picture without consulting God. God's perspective is very different from our perspective. He sees the whole picture. He has plans for you and your family. When you fix the situation without consulting God, the problem is not solved; it usually gets worse. We need to hear from God and wait on Him before we plow ahead to a worse end.

With each answered prayer, God teaches us lessons about life – if we will listen to Him. He also teaches us lessons about Himself. God wants us to know Him. Yes, He wants us to know Him as Savior, accepting the sacrifice He made for us at Calvary as payment for our sins. He also wants us to know Him as Lord. Knowing Him as Lord is a life journey that builds our relationship with God. We can learn to trust Him to be our Healer, our Strength, our Hope, our Refuge in the midst of the storm, our Provider, our Peace, and oh, so much more. Through these experiences we learn we can and need to trust Him. It is not about our strength and the ability to fix our problems, but it is about trusting Him. God loves for us to trust Him. Through those experiences, He knows us, and we know Him. Our relationship is growing because we are learning to submit to Him, even in the most difficult of times. Trusting God, we have many opportunities to confirm His unfailing love and His faithfulness to His Word.

What about my family? God will teach your children and build a wonderful relationship with them, if you will let Him. When we run ahead of God, our children learn to rely on us instead of Him. God never meant for us to take His place in their lives. That would be impossible and only lead to disaster. God desires that each member of your family personally knows and trusts Him.

174

If all this sounds foreign to you, God is calling you to know Him in your own life. He wants a real relationship with you. As your relationship with God grows, your example will speak volumes to your family. Your testimony will grow exponentially as you submit yourself to God and learn to wait on Him.

To the Enabler:

You know you thrive on purpose, but what about your child? If the roles were reversed and you became the enabled one, would you tolerate someone robbing you of purpose? You know you would emotionally die without purpose. You know that purpose makes you feel happy, fulfilled, and productive. Consider your children. They may not know it, but they need purpose in their lives, too.

When you do everything for your unemployed son while he watches TV and hangs out with friends – you are robbing him of purpose. Are drugs or alcohol involved? You can do it faster, bigger, better, but you are robbing your child of his responsibility. Do you wash his clothes, wash his dishes, make his bed, pay his bills, mow the grass, and give him money? When you steal your son's purpose, he has no reason to develop or use basic living skills, to look for a job, or to do any work. Will you sacrifice your need for purpose, to allow your son to have purpose in his own life?

When you do everything for your daughter while she chooses a social life over taking care of her children, you are robbing her of purpose. Are drugs or alcohol involved? Does she treat you like a doormat, expecting Grandma to raise her kids? Does she endanger your grandchildren, exposing them to men who may be predators? She is making it obvious to your grandchildren that marriage is not important. Have you paid for her to have abortions? When you steal your child's purpose, she has no reason to live a morally responsible life. Will you sacrifice your need for purpose, to allow your daughter to have purpose in her own life?

175

To the Enabler and the Enabled One:

Are things so out of control and hopeless that you have come to the end of your rope, or worse, the end of yourself? When you are really ready for change, God will help you. You have to want it more than whatever pleasure you have found in being the enabler or the one who has been enabled. God will bring your situation to a successful end when you repent and actively trust Him to help you change. Don't be surprised when God requires all your energy and all your cooperation. You are to be a "living sacrifice, holy, acceptable to God, which is your reasonable service" (Romans 12:1, NKJ). It is worth the sacrifice to see God's victory and purpose fulfilled in your life and in the lives of your children.

Are you lonely?

Loneliness is a severe problem for both the enabler and the one enabled. When the situation is out of control, it is much easier for everyone if the enabler and the enabled one isolate themselves from those who disapprove of the arrangement. Loneliness is a cause of depression. Just like our sin separates us from God, our sin also separates us from other people. The enabled may think everyone should accept them just the way they are. Their refusal to bathe, unkempt hair and clothing, and constant smoking of cigarettes, are frequently accompanied by as much alcohol as they can acquire. These unhealthy and offensive behaviors are not conducive to building or maintaining relationships. The enabler may ignore or deny all this, but the reality still exists.

To the Enabled One:

Part of growing up and being a responsible adult is taking care of your own personal hygiene. You may have to force yourself at first, but develop a routine of getting out of bed, combing your hair, washing your face, brushing your teeth, and putting on clean clothes that are your size. Wash your clothes every week. Take a bath daily and put on deodorant, or loneliness will be the only one to accompany you all of your days.

To the Enabler:

Quit telling the one you enable that the way she looks is fine. Be honest. You desperately want your daughter to "fit in" with other people. Know this: If she continues to dress in an unacceptable way, the only type of people she will attract will look and dress the same as she does.

Does your adult daughter know how to wash her clothes? If yes, do not wash her laundry. If no, teach your daughter how to do the laundry and expect that responsibility to belong to her. You concentrate on taking care of your own laundry and keeping yourself clean and presentable. Too many enablers slide into depression from loneliness and give up on relationships outside the home. If they do it long enough, they get to where they can't take care of themselves, and dementia sets in.

Loneliness will destroy you. Develop relationships outside the home. Many people who have lost a spouse find volunteering a way to be productive and make friends. Volunteer where you can chat with others as part of your duties. You may enjoy volunteering at a school or local hospital. Let God use you to bring cheer into someone else's life. Did you ever think that while you have been enabling your child, you might have missed God's calling upon your life. You may say, "Taking care of my child is my calling." God is not calling anyone to enable someone else to sin or avoid responsibility.

You may argue that your child or spouse does not want to be left alone while you go out into the community to volunteer. Whether he is happy or not, you need to find some outside purpose or interest that allows you to have normal relationships with other people. He will get over it. When you return from volunteering, you may find that he has created a big mess – do not clean up after him.

Are you the only one who talks to your child? Have you allowed your relationship to be exclusive? Is he totally dependent upon you because he cannot get along with anyone else? Have you ever trained him in proper social skills? Have you set the example? Have you required civil conversation, or do the two of you constantly yell at each other? The rude, crude, perverse language and actions your family views on TV and in movies are not normal living. This is not the way God meant for you and your family to live. It does not please Him. Your child will need social skills if he is going to be accepted in the church and community. You will need to discuss this with the one you have enabled. If he has been taught better, then he knows better. This is a rebellion issue. He will only change if he wants to change, otherwise he is choosing to speak and act in ways that he knows will destroy relationships.

What does the Bible say about rebellion?

> For rebellion is as the sin of witchcraft, And stubbornness is as iniquity and idolatry (1 Samuel 15:23, NKJ).

If he has not been taught, teach him or buy him a book or video on social skills. If one of your children is missing social skills, it is possible you have other children who also need a social skill makeover. Make it a family project to practice and develop the skills they need. Set up different scenarios: phone manners, table manners, church manners, introduction manners, store manners, how to politely state and defend your opinion, etc. Be creative, but practice.

Does your child know how to cook? If yes, do not cook for her. If no, spend time cooking together. Train her to cook. Cook something you both like. Practice talking to each other in civil tones and polite conversation.

He needs a wife! When will I ever get that grandchild?

Do not be desperate for the son you have been enabling to find a spouse. Are you hoping this person will become his caregiver? If your son cannot take care of himself and is addicted to alcohol and/or drugs, he is not ready for a spouse. Unless your son radically changes, you are condemning that person to a life of torment. This home environment will ensure that any child who grows up under these circumstances will probably grow up to have the same problems. You don't need a grandchild that badly.

When you know you need to change.

Reading about God's purpose in your life will not cause you to change. Pray and then step out in faith to see God accomplish real change in your life. When someone tells you that you are doing so much better, give God the praise, honor, and glory for what He is doing in your life. God is the One who is making the change a reality.

Chapter 13:
When Does Compassion
Turn to Enabling?

Compassion is a Godly quality – it is not destructive. Compassion usually turns to enabling when a caring person gets caught up in someone else's problems. Lying in wait are two traps that easily ensnare the enabler and the one enabled. They both are called by the same name: Pride.

When compassion turns to enabling, it starts something like this:

- A caring person sees a loved one or someone with a need.

- Compassion rises up, and the soon to be enabler decides –
  I can help!

- Things go well for a while. She feels good about the help she is providing. She knows that God wants her to help others – Helping is good.

- She hardly notices that the person she is helping is changing. He is becoming increasingly dependent on her. She enjoys her role as helper so much that she is willing to sacrifice herself to benefit him. Helping, fixing, protecting, and/or rescuing all give her purpose. She diligently works to keep him happy, even though his attitude is not always the best. She is convinced: He needs me. I must help!

- She doesn't mind taking on more responsibilities while he does less and less. She makes everything easy, which enables him to avoid responsibility. He doesn't mind – it saves him work. It isn't long until he believes that he deserves this special treatment. She enjoys the role so much that she does not want any interference from others who may not understand or approve. Pride is gaining a foothold. She is now sure: No one can help like me! Compassion has now turned to enabling; it is now sin.

- Over time, rescuing and enabling become a habit and then a compulsion. The enabler becomes addicted to enabling, regardless of consequences to self or the one she enables. Both the enabler and the one enabled are entangled in a web of sin. The enabler is determined: No one can help, but me!

- Compulsive rescuing and enabling so overtake the enabler's life that there seems no way out. Family relationships are destroyed in the process.

Pride, the Great Destroyer

In being so careful not to hurt the feelings of her loved one and make him mad, the enabler "walks on eggshells," trying to make and keep him happy. Today, they call it self-esteem. Since the need for self-esteem has its roots in pride, it isn't long until the one enabled thinks the whole world revolves around him. He is deceived into thinking everything that is done to help him is either owed to him or he deserves it.

We were never meant to live on the "mountaintop" of happiness. God uses challenges and difficult times to develop character in us. Hard times teach us to trust Him. When we turn to God and place our trust in Him, we learn determination, endurance, persistence, and patience. We even learn compassion for others who are going through similar circumstances. In theory, these qualities can be taught, but true learning includes experience.

> Blessed be the God and Father of our Lord Jesus Christ, the Father of mercies and God of all comfort, who comforts us in all our tribulation, that we may be able to comfort those who are in any trouble, with the comfort with which we ourselves are comforted by God (2 Corinthians 1:3-4, NKJ).

Compassion in America is at an all-time low. People are focused on their personal opinions and their rights. To make things worse, parents make everything easy for their children. Children rarely experience times of struggle. Many young adults think good grades, financial prosperity, and successful living are owed to them. They become very angry when the reality of life does not meet their expectations. In America, many children and adults are angry. They want instant success. They want the prosperity of their parents as soon as they leave school. It just doesn't happen that way. In the past, parents who faced many struggles and challenges learned to appreciate the character qualities that helped them endure and press on until success came. They learned to appreciate the help and support of others, and above all, they learned to trust in God as their Provider and their source of strength. They were thankful. But today, those who demand instant success are not thankful. They are angry and filled with pride.

What are parents to do? Should they make everything difficult for their children to ensure positive character qualities are developed? Absolutely, not! There are enough real challenges in life. Instead, help your children face and overcome the challenges they do experience. Teach your children, by your words and by your example, to turn to God every time a difficulty arises. Teach them to

183

seek His will and His direction for their lives. Help them to see how God's Word applies to their real life situation. Teach them to maintain faith and a good attitude through difficult times. Overcoming challenges is an essential part of growing up to be a caring, responsible adult.

In difficult times, there are many lessons to be learned about trusting God. When we recognize God is teaching us through these experiences, our perspective is quite different from individuals who allow pride to control their attitudes and actions. Pride fights the process every step of the way and refuses to do things God's way. "Why is God doing this to me?" Then, pride claims ownership of any success. Pride is a deceiver that will steal, kill, and destroy. God desires we recognize His Lordship in all situations and willingly submit ourselves to His leadership.

Anytime pride is involved, God is not pleased. Self-confidence and self-esteem were never God's purpose for man. When man leans upon his own strength, God is not glorified. Our confidence is to be in God and God alone. Pride places us in direct opposition to God. No one can afford to live in direct opposition to God.

What does the Bible say about pride and self-confidence?

> For God sets Himself against the proud (the insolent, the overbearing, the disdainful, the presumptuous, the boastful) - [and He opposes, frustrates, and defeats them], but gives grace (favor, blessing) to the humble (1 Peter 5:5, AMP).

> God sets Himself against the proud and haughty, but gives grace [continually] to the lowly (those who are humble enough to receive it) (James 4:6, AMP).

184

The pride of your heart has deceived you (Obadiah 1:3, NKJ).

It is the "proud lock (the spirit that makes one overestimate himself and underestimate others)" that God "hates" (Proverbs 6:16-17, AMP).

God is not glorified when we walk in self-confidence. "Everyone proud in heart is an abomination to the Lord (Proverbs16:5, NKJ).

Pride goes before destruction, and a haughty spirit before a fall (Proverbs 16:18, AMP).

The Great Escape

Pride offers both the enabler and the one enabled a way to escape the intrusion of others into their relationship. Better described as codependency, this destructive relationship exists to meet the physical and emotional needs of both individuals. When addiction and enabling are involved, it is a codependent relationship. It can occur between family members, friends, and within romantic or work relationships. Any advice or intervention suggested to the enabler or the enabled one is usually met with rejection.

Pride destroys attitudes and relationships.

A self-confident and foolish man despises his mother and puts her to shame (Proverbs 15:20, AMP).

A self-confident and foolish son is a grief to his father and bitterness to her who bore him (Proverbs 17:25, AMP).

Pride refuses instruction and is easily offended by correction.

When the dependable one tries to help his parent understand that her enabling is destroying the entire family, he is sincerely seeking her help. The enabler appears to listen, but her pride prevents her from hearing the truth. Without another word, the parent continues on the enabling path of destruction, the path that says, "I'm doing this my way."

The ones who are enabled range in age from young children to the elderly. They choose their own opinions over wisdom and facts. Pride declares, "I will trust in my own knowledge and abilities to solve my problems. No one can tell me what to do."

Pride is a root cause for both children and adults who refuse to learn. They do not realize their futures will be filled with anger, heartache, and disappointment – all because they will not listen or learn.

What does the Bible say about those who refuse to learn?

(Note: In the Amplified Bible, the word "self-confident" frequently clarifies the meaning of the word "fool.")

> Now therefore, listen to me (Wisdom), my children, For blessed are those who keep my ways. Hear instruction and be wise, And do not disdain it.

> Blessed is the man who listens to me, Watching daily at my gates, Waiting at the posts of my doors. For whoever finds me finds life, And obtains favor from the Lord; But he who sins against me wrongs his own soul; All those who hate me love death (Proverbs 8:32-36, NKJ).

He who leans on, trusts in, and is confident of his own mind and heart is a [self-confident] fool, but He who walks in skillful and Godly Wisdom shall be delivered (Proverbs 28:26, AMP).

How I hated instruction and discipline, and my heart despised reproof! I have not obeyed the voice of my teachers nor submitted and consented to those who instructed me (Proverbs 5:12-13, AMP).

A [self-confident] fool has no delight in understanding, but only in revealing his personal opinions and himself (Proverbs 18:2, AMP).

A scoffer seeks Wisdom in vain [for his very attitude blinds and deafens him to it], but knowledge is easy to him who [being teachable] understands. Go from the presence of a foolish and self-confident man, for you will not find knowledge in his lips (Proverbs 14:6-7, AMP).

Speak not in the ears of a [self-confident] fool, for he will despise the [Godly] wisdom of your words (Proverbs 23:9, AMP).

The ear that hears the rebukes of life will abide among the wise. He who disdains instruction despises his own soul, but he who heeds rebuke gets understanding. The fear of the Lord is the instruction of wisdom, and before honor is humility (Proverbs 15:31, NKJ).

Poverty and shame will come to him who disdains correction, But he who regards a rebuke will be honored (Proverbs 13:18, NKJ).

What does the Bible say about those who listen and want to learn?

> Give instruction to a wise man, and he will be still wiser; Teach a just man, and he will increase in learning. (Proverbs 9:9, NKJ).

> Listen to counsel and receive instruction, That you may be wise in your latter days (Proverbs 19:20, NKJ).

Has pride prevented you from learning?

Have you become unteachable? Are you irritated when someone asks you to listen? When someone suggests that you are wrong, does your anger make it impossible for the conversation to continue? God will help you change, if you really want to be free from the pride that is destroying you and your relationships with others.

Another Escape: Denial

"I don't have a problem." Both the enabler and the one enabled find denial to be a place of comfort. It is easy to think everyone else is wrong. Examples: "My child would never bully someone else." "My spouse would never abuse my children." "I would never enable my son to avoid responsibility. He just has a few problems." If you deny the problem long enough, you may actually begin to believe you are right. To help you recognize denial, it is usually accompanied by excuses. Denial is an integrity issue. Denying our problems only multiplies our sins. We desperately need to acknowledge and confess our sin if we are ever going to be free of the entangled mess we have made of our lives.

Part of your daily prayer needs to be for discernment. It is very difficult for you to face your problems if you do not recognize your problems and the root causes of each. Mind you, knowing the root cause is no reason for blaming others. You are still responsible for your own sins. Recognizing the root cause and identifying the problem will help you to be specific when you ask God for forgiveness for denying and participating in the problem. You will also need to ask for God to deliver you from sin's stronghold – if you really want change in your family and want to please God.

Sadly, some enablers enjoy enabling so much that they do not want to let go of the role of rescuer. The enabler just wishes the one she is helping would act nicer to her. In many cases, where the spouse died or a divorce has taken place, the remaining parent clings to her child. This parent may even place herself under the authority of her child, allowing him to control her. She has replaced her missing spouse with her child. This is not a healthy relationship for either the child or the parent. If this is you, your child will not become a responsible adult unless you release your smothering grip and let go. I ask you again, do you really want change in your family? Do you really want to please God? If so, God will deliver you from this stronghold of sin.

To the Enabler and the Enabled One: PRAY WITH ME

Heavenly Father,

I come to you in the name of Jesus. I ask you to forgive me and free me from the pride that has controlled my life. I humble myself before you and submit myself to your Lordship. Change me, Lord and cause my desire to be focused on You and Your will in my life. Lord, make me teachable and able to learn. Teach me Your Word. Help me to be able to read and understand the Bible. Help me to be honest with You and with myself. Forgive me for living in denial. Help me to recognize when my motives are not pure, but polluted by greed or selfishness. Free me from these deceptions. Replace these strongholds with the fruit of Your Spirit: "love, joy, peace, longsuffering, kindness, goodness, faithfulness, gentleness, and self-control" (Galatians 5:22, NKJ). Lord, help me maintain a kind attitude that is pleasing to You. Help me to speak the truth in love,

189

instead of demanding others conform to my desires and opinions. As you change me, Lord, may my life glorify You in all I say and do. Thank you. Amen.

Chapter 14:
Can God Forgive
a Lifetime of Enabling?

Above all, God desires a relationship with you. Since our sins separate us from God, the only way that relationship can be restored is to trust Jesus as our Lord and Savior. His sacrifice at Calvary paid the price for our sins. Our debt was paid in full; however, this does not give us liberty to live any way we want.

If we sin after we a born again, does God give up on us? No.

God, by His Word, declares His willingness to forgive us when we repent – when we are sorry for our sins and trust Him to help us change. You cannot sin beyond God's ability to forgive you, but you have to be honest with God. He knows your heart. He knows if you are truly sorry, or if you are just saying words in an effort to escape consequences for your sin.

What does the Bible say about God forgiving us?

In a message to Christians, John the disciple wrote,

> "If we confess our sins, He is faithful and just to forgive us our sins, and to cleanse us from all unrighteousness" (1 John 1:9, NKJ).

Enabling is like any other sin; it is disobedience to God. When we ask God to forgive us, He will "forgive us our sins, and cleanse us from all unrighteousness."

We do not have to ask God over and over to forgive us for our sin. We ask Him, and then we receive His forgiveness by faith. If we continue to ask over and over for forgiveness for the same sin, we are not trusting God. He hears our prayer and forgives us.

What if I commit the same sin again?

Sin will keep you in bondage until you completely trust God to free you from it. Repentance includes being sorry for sin and changing. If you repeat the same sin, you need to ask God for forgiveness again. God expects you to trust Him enough to allow Him to help you change.

God removes our sins from us.

> For as the heavens are high above the earth, So great is His mercy toward those who fear Him; As far as the east is from the west, So far has He removed our transgressions from us (Psalm 103:11-12, NKJ).

Exactly, how does that work? (If you have a globe, use it to help you understand.) Place your finger on your current location. If you travel in a straight line to the north, you eventually will come to the North Pole. If you continue, you will then be travelling south. Now, travelling in a straight line to the south, you will reach the South Pole. If you continue, you will then be travelling north. North meets south at the Poles. However, you can journey east forever and never venture west. The same is true when you travel west. East and west never meet. When we ask God to forgive our sins, He removes our sins from us. Only God can separate us from our sins.

God remembers our sins no more.

> "This is the covenant that I will make with them after those days," says the Lord: "I will put My laws into their hearts, and in their minds, I will write them," then He adds, "Their sins and their lawless deeds I will remember no more" (Hebrews 10:16-17, NKJ).

God wants to restore your relationship with Him. Your life will change dramatically, because you are finally doing things God's way. It won't be easy, but He will help you.

When God forgives me, is that sin erased from my memory? No.

Now, when that sin comes to mind, let it be a reminder of the grief and hardship our disobedience caused us. Hopefully, it will be a lesson well learned. Let us rejoice for we are thankful that God forgave us. We give all the glory to God, for He is faithful to His Word.

Instead of forgiveness, can I work my way to heaven? No.

> For it is by grace you have been saved, through faith, and that not of yourselves; it is the gift of God, not of works, lest anyone should boast (Ephesians 2:8-9, NKJ).

To the Enabler: PRAY WITH ME

Heavenly Father,

I come to You in the name of Jesus. Forgive me for allowing my compassion to turn to enabling. I have set aside Your will and purpose in my own life. I have instead enabled others to avoid responsibility. Forgive me for not trusting you. I did not trust you with my life or the life of my loved one. I let my feelings control my actions. Help me to read Your Word every day so I will learn what pleases You. Help me to change and please You.

Father, forgive me for trying to take Your place in my loved one's life. You are God and You alone. I want and need to know You as my Healer, my Strength, my Provider, my Salvation, my Hope, and my Peace. You are the Great I Am. You are all I need. I want to know You and see Your will accomplished in my life every day that I live.

Forgive me for allowing my need to enable my loved one to cause my whole family to be dysfunctional and under extreme stress. Lord, restore my family to faith in You and love for each other.

I thank You and praise You for what you are doing in my life. I thank You for revealing all these things to me. Lord, I trust You to help me to change. I give you praise, honor, and glory for beginning and completing this work in me. Lord, help my life to become a testimony of Your faithfulness and Your greatness. I love You, Lord. Amen.

To the Enabled One: PRAY WITH ME

Heavenly Father,

I come to You in the name of Jesus. Forgive me for avoiding responsibility and not growing up to be the man/woman You desire me to be. I have chosen the easy path – giving in to sinful lusts. These sins only led to my destruction. I did not trust in You, but let my feelings control my actions. Help me to read Your Word every day so I will learn what pleases You. Help me to change and please You.

Father, forgive me for demanding that my parent/spouse take Your place in my life. You are God and You alone. I want and need to know You as my Healer, my Strength, my Provider, my Salvation, my Hope, and my Peace. You are the Great I Am. You are all I need. I want to know You and see Your will accomplished in my life every day that I live.

Forgive me for wasting so many years. Forgive me for my rebellious thoughts, attitudes, and actions that only made things worse. Forgive me for making demands of my family, causing my family to be dysfunctional and under extreme stress. Lord, restore my family to faith in You and love for each other.

I thank You and praise You for what you are doing in my life. I thank You for revealing all these things to me. Lord, I trust You to help me change. I give you praise, honor, and glory for beginning and completing this work in me. Lord, help my life to become a testimony of Your faithfulness and Your greatness. I love You, Lord. Amen.

Chapter 15:
Why Do I Need to Forgive?

Violent acts and ungodly lifestyles have separated many from family members and loved ones. You cannot demand that family members forgive each other. You can share with them what the Bible says about forgiveness, set the example by forgiving, and pray that their hearts will be made to understand how important forgiveness is to God.

What does the Bible say about forgiving others?

> Jesus said, "For if you forgive men their trespasses, your heavenly Father will also forgive you. But if you do not forgive men their trespasses, neither will your Father forgive your trespasses" (Matthew 6:14-15, NKJ).

> Therefore, as the elect of God, holy and beloved, put on tender mercies, kindness, humility, meekness, longsuffering; bearing with one another, and forgiving one another, if anyone has a complaint against another; even as Christ forgave you, so you also must do. But above all these things put on love, which is the bond of perfection (Colossians 3:12-14, NKJ).

What if you do not feel like forgiving them?

Do not check your feelings. Forgiveness is a choice, not a feeling. If you do not forgive others, God will not forgive you. We all need God's forgiveness in our lives every day.

If I forgive, won't I be saying that what they did to me is right?

Forgiveness is not saying the one who hurt you is right. It does not excuse their behavior. When you forgive, you are saying you trust God to deal with that person and their sin.

What if they do not deserve forgiveness?

No one deserves God's forgiveness. If you want God's forgiveness, you will forgive others.

Can I just get even with them first?

Then I will forgive them. This is not forgiving them. When you seek revenge for wrongdoings against you or your family, you are setting yourself up for similar treatment.

> Jesus said, "Judge not, that you be not judged. For with what judgment you judge, you will be judged; with the measure you use, it will be measured back to you" (Matthew 7:1-2, NKJ).

> Do not say, "I'll pay you back for this wrong!" Wait for the Lord, and He will save you (Proverbs 20:22, NIV).

Do I have to forgive them more than one time?

I forgave them last time, and they did it again. Thankfully, God does not limit the number of times He forgives us.

> Jesus said, "And even if he sins against you seven times in a day, and turns to you seven times and says, I repent (I am sorry), you must forgive him (give up resentment and consider the offense as recalled and annulled)" (Luke 17:4, AMP).

If I wait for a few months or years to pass, won't time heal all wounds?

Isn't that enough? Can I just walk away and never see them again? The hurts will still remain until you forgive those who have caused your pain. Bottom line: If you want God's forgiveness in your life, you will forgive others and allow God to heal your heart.

Apologize for any wrongdoing for which you are responsible.

This is part of the forgiveness process. Be sincere and take responsibility for any problems you have caused. Be specific and tell the whole truth. Avoid excuses.

What if you are a parent who doesn't like to admit your mistakes?

This is an integrity issue and a pride issue. Our children need to know that when we sin or make mistakes, we ask for forgiveness. We do whatever we can to correct the problem and then actively trust God to help us change. Thank God and praise Him for loving you enough to forgive you and help you change. Repeat this process often, maybe daily. Your child will learn from the attitude, effort, and changes they see in you.

What if after you apologize, they do not forgive you?

That is between them and God. You have done what God wanted you to do, and that was to confess your wrongdoing and forgive.

I don't like to be corrected. What if someone corrects you?

When others correct you, do not respond in anger. Listen. Humble yourself. Have a teachable spirit. Ask God for further clarification. We all need constructive criticism now and again.

What if the criticism is not constructive?

Forgive them. The criticism may or may not be constructive, but God can still use it to benefit you. Sometimes, this kind of criticism is offered when the person does not know the whole situation. Pray and ask God to reveal the truth to you. He sees the whole picture and knows what has transpired from beginning to end. Seek to please Him, then forgive and move on. Don't dwell on past failures – learn from them.

Finally, demonstrate the love of God.

Be kind to one another, tenderhearted, forgiving one another, even as God in Christ forgave you (Ephesians 4:32, NKJ).

Therefore be imitators of God as dear children. And walk in love, as Christ also has loved us and given Himself for us, an offering and a sacrifice to God for a sweet-smelling aroma (Ephesians 5:1-2, NKJ).

How can we get past the past?

- Allow God to heal your relationships.
- Forget the past.
- Encourage any positive changes.
- Express real needs or concerns.
- Set clear boundaries.
- Be honest with each other.
- Expect improved relationships.

What if you do all this and the relationship does not improve?

By forgiving, you have pleased God. You do not have to continue in an abusive, dysfunctional relationship just because the other person lives that way.

In your heart, you know that the one who hurt you needs God. Only God can save and change that person. By continuing to pray for that person, you demonstrate God's love and the reality of your forgiveness.

Forgive yourself:

In forgiving others, don't forget that you need to forgive yourself. You will not experience complete deliverance from the addiction to enabling or peace of mind unless you forgive yourself.

You are not alone.

There were many dysfunctional families in the Bible. By studying God's Word, we can learn from others and not have to repeat their mistakes. His Word is true unto all generations.

What can we learn from the father of the prodigal son? (Luke Chapter 15)

A father had two sons. The younger son asked his father for his portion of his inheritance and then traveled to a far country. There he squandered his wealth in wild living. He was rebellious and immature, wanting to be free to live as he pleased. When he had nothing left, there arose a famine in the land and he hired himself out to feed pigs. It was not until he was at the point of starvation that he came to his senses. He determined it would be better to return home and work for his father, than to die from hunger. The prodigal son left for home, but when he came within view, his father saw him and ran to welcome him home.

It is interesting to note that the father did not go to the city to rescue his son, nor did he force his son to return home. He waited for him to come to his senses. When his son hit rock bottom, the son returned home. He was humbled, repentant, and changed.

Today, too many parents run to rescue their children from the sin and degradation in which they have chosen to live. These children return home unchanged, full of pride and rebellion. God used the time the prodigal son lived in squalor and poverty to humble him. He learned the value of his father's love and the wonderful life he had forsaken. He was humbled and broken. God used that brokenness to restore the prodigal son's relationship with his father.

When parents run ahead of God and try to rescue and fix their prodigal child's life, the child is not humbled. There is no repentance or change. The prodigal child returns with the same rebellious baggage with which he originally left.

What about the other son? He was jealous and angry at the return of his younger brother. Just as sin separates us from God (Isaiah 59:2), sin also separates us from family and people in the community. You may argue that attitudes like that are wrong, but they are reality. The father consoled his dependable son, telling him all that he had was his. The dependable son could have had a party any time he wanted.

It would have been nice if the dependable son had welcomed his long lost brother home, but he didn't. We really don't know much about the relationship of the two brothers, but in our humanness, we can understand the dependable son's concern when his younger brother returned home. He was uncomfortable welcoming the one who squandered the family's wealth on harlots and riotous living. Immediately, the father-son relationship was restored. Now, according to Scripture, both his earthly father and heavenly Father expected the dependable son to forgive.

Chapter 16:
Are You Ready to Reclaim Your Life?

To the Enabled One:

Now is the time to step out in faith and start reclaiming your life. First, due to past irresponsible behavior, you will need to rebuild trust. Trust is not owed to you. When you were young, your parents just naturally trusted you. Once trust is broken, it needs to be restored. Demanding trust will not restore it. Trust must be rebuilt. I believe that as you read this book, God is removing deceptions and teaching you to be honest with yourself. If you really want change, you will be patient and build trust over time. Trust built too quickly will seem of little value to you. Trust built over time will teach you much about its worth. Trust is a precious treasure. Being trustworthy is one of the building blocks necessary to prepare you for responsible adulthood.

What should you do first? Start doing things that build trust.

Can you start with managing your own finances? No. That would be doing too much, too fast. Whether you live in a room, apartment, or house, start by cleaning it up and keeping it clean. Do not ask for help. If you really do not know how to clean something – learn. Read directions or listen to someone who can teach you. Listening demonstrates a respectful attitude. If the person who is teaching you is the former enabler, that person may be very anxious to help. Help may sound really good to you. This is an important moment: You must decide if you really want change. Do you want to be enabled forever? Do you want to develop life skills of your own? Right now, you may think, "I already know how to clean my house." Knowing how to clean your house does not demonstrate responsibility. Cleaning up and keeping the area clean demonstrates that you are starting to build trust and can move on to other tasks. This demonstrates that you are finally taking basic life responsibilities seriously. Later, when you have shown that you are maturing, finances may be entrusted to you. If you are not working and earning money, then your efforts need to be focused on fixing, cleaning, maintaining your own living area, and looking for work.

When you do find a way to earn money, contribute to your living expenses. Tithe, pay bills, save some, and spend only a small portion – the portion you have previously designated as spending money. You need to be working toward the day you will return to independent living. To accomplish this goal, the saving component is very important.

What will destroy trust? Procrastination.

When you have an agreement, commitment, or responsibility to do something and there is no visible evidence that you are going to accomplish it in a timely manner, you are procrastinating. It is very difficult for others to trust that you will actually fulfill what you said you would do. You may protest, "I'm going to get it done." However, thinking about washing the laundry is not the same as washing the laundry. There must be effort and results. How can someone trust you if you do not keep your word? This becomes an integrity issue. Procrastination is sin. Procrastination produces much fruit in our lives – none of it good.

Procrastination:

- Is caused by pride, placing self-interest first.

- Is an integrity issue – what you say you will do, you need to do.

- Allows feelings to rob you of your motivation.

- Frustrates others.

- Prevents you from returning something you borrowed, in a timely manner.

- Demonstrates a lack of respect for others who are depending on you.

- Demonstrates a lack of respect for the urgency of the situation.

- Causes you to be late for just about everything.

- Causes you to miss many important appointments.

- Causes the need for a rushed job in the end, frequently with substandard results.

- Limits your future and your ability to plan.

- Limits others in their ability to plan.

- Destroys relationships.

- Prevents you from being organized.

- Invites an enabling situation, leaving others feeling compelled to finish the job or fix the problem – just to get it done.

- Limits your ability to maintain a good job or be promoted.

- Robs you of the joy of a job well done.

Even though you "know" that you will get the job done, others cannot trust that you will and that the results will be satisfactory. In order for you to rebuild trust, you will refuse to allow procrastination to control your life. This is a very important step in becoming the dependable person God has called you to be.

Procrastination and pride are frequent companions.

Both are hoping to damage the trust you are working to rebuild. How can you overcome them? Do something to help someone else. A good place to begin is to help the one who is providing your living area and finances. Perhaps you could mow the lawn, fix things, or help with other chores. You may complain, "I'm and adult. I shouldn't have to do these things." At this point, pride is rearing its ugly head. For you to be a winner in this battle, you will need to humble yourself. We all have to drastically humble ourselves at different times in our lives. You are no different.

You may think, "Instead of helping others, I'll just take some time to rest." Too much time spent resting will rob you of ambition. You need 7-8 hours of sleep each night; that should be sufficient rest. Too much rest will make it almost impossible for you to sleep the next night. Then you will wake up tired. Many people who have been enabled get their days and nights mixed up because they are idle all day. They frequently require rest for any minimal amount of effort. Work is part of life. Even if you don't have a paying job, you still need to find productive ways to spend your time.

Pray and ask God for opportunities to help others, ways to fulfill His purpose in your life. Don't think about what you can get out of it. Think about how you can please God, by helping others. Ask your pastor if there are any people in your church who need help. Many times the elderly or disabled can no longer take care of themselves or their homes. What skills do you have to offer the elderly or disabled? Use the carpentry, painting, mechanical, or cleaning skills you already have. Add a generous helping of friendly talk. You will be so glad you were able to help someone and add a little cheer to a life that may be very lonely.

To the Enabler:

Now is the time to step out in faith and start reclaiming your life. You have been held in a prison – thinking there is no way out – no way to stop enabling your child. You have been deceived. There is a way out, but you will have to trust God.

Now is the time for you to look beyond your child's immediate needs and look down the road to his future. Be honest, your child really needs to grow up into responsible adulthood. For so long, pride has told you that you are the only one who can help your son. You have become compulsive, not really thinking about how bad the future will get if you don't stop enabling him. (If you have forgotten, go back and reread the initial list of questions in Chapter One that foretell of impending disaster if you do not quit enabling.)

God will deliver you from your pride, but you will need to humble yourself and reach out to others who can and will help. Yes, you may be embarrassed that your enabling has been going on for so long, and you have not told anyone. Tell your pastor, but be sure to listen to his advice. Find a Christian counselor. There are also many social service agencies that offer help. Know this: Listening to wise counsel will never be enough. You must step out in faith to see real change. It will be difficult, probably very difficult, but God will help you.

Or are you one of those enablers who find it easy to collect a lot of advice from everyone? Perhaps you play the victim, knowing that you have no plans to accept help. Playing the victim can be very rewarding. You do so much for your son, and this is how you are treated! The sympathy and attention feel so good, but in the end, your son is incrementally being destroyed. You are not allowing him to grow up. He remains dependent on you. You have made everything easy for him and have protected him from consequences.

Just in case you think that the prayer for deliverance from pride is only for the one enabled, it is also for you, the enabler. In all things, pray. If God does not deliver you from your addiction to enabling, it will not happen. Do you really want change? Perhaps you are thinking, "Well it isn't so bad. I can tolerate my son's behavior. I can keep him happy, if I try hard enough. I know he manipulates me, but I'm OK. Besides, he gives my life purpose." These are real comments from real enablers. Know this: You will never be able to make and keep your son happy. You probably feel like you have a tiger by the tail! If you let go, someone or something is going to get hurt. According to the seriousness of your enabling and depths of dysfunction and depravity your son has reached, things can get even worse. His insatiable desire to have you supply his every want and need will not end well, unless you take action.

Now is the time for you to be honest with the son you have been enabling. Set boundaries. If you say you will not clean up after your son again, don't do it. Speak in a kind, but firm voice. When you yell, he will not listen to you or take you seriously. If you say you are going to call the police the next time he is abusive to you, do it. File a police report. Are you going to wait until your son becomes violent and someone is hurt or killed? And then, what will his future look like? If you truly love your son, you will be honest with him. Your son will learn – what you say, you will do. God desires honesty in your life.

What will you do with your newfound time?

How will you spend all the free time you will have, now that you are not enabling your son? It is time for you to take care of your own health and clean your own house. Too many enablers clean up after the one they have been enabling, but do not have sufficient energy left to clean their own homes.

Find other worthwhile things to do. Pray and ask God for His direction. Since you probably have spent an inordinate amount of time on your enabled son, spend some time with the rest of your family. While you are with other family members, don't spend all your time thinking or talking about the son you enabled. Focus on the rest of your family. Build some memories with them.

Find areas for ministry at your church. Ask your pastor or church leaders where help is needed. When they tell you, don't procrastinate. Show them you are serious about serving God, by helping others. Be faithful to the position the Lord entrusts to you.

Volunteer in your community or at local charities. Check out your local newspaper's classified advertisements in the volunteer section or try networking to discover volunteer opportunities. You may have to humble yourself when you are asked to help people who are living in extreme poverty or are victims of abuse. God will help you. Just be very careful that your enabling skills do not overcome your sense of reasonable help.

As you volunteer, you may find specific areas of ministry God is calling you to do. Since you have been caught up in enabling before, don't try to do everything yourself. You will be on the way to a quick burn-out if you try to do it all. Leave something for other church or community members to do. Work together. You need the fellowship. Pray and ask God for His leadership, wisdom, and direction.

Pride was never God's plan for you. In our daily lives and in the midst of overwhelming circumstances, God wants us to humbly seek His help. Rejoice, for by refusing to allow Satan to control you through pride, you are making great steps in restoring your family to right relationship with each other and with God.

It is Time to do Things God's Way: God's Purpose for Our Lives

> "For I know the plans I have for you," declares the Lord, "Plans to prosper you and not to harm you, plans to give you hope and a future" (Jeremiah 29:11, NIV).

To the Enabled One:

God has called us to live our lives with purpose, His purpose. Whether you know it or not, you desperately need purpose for each and every day of your life. You also need purpose that keeps you grounded and supports God's plan for your future.

We are going to compare Proverbs 29:18 from the King James Bible and the New International Version. You will get a better view of what happens when we do not seek God's purpose in our lives:

King James Bible:

> Where there is no vision, the people perish: but he that keepeth the law, happy is he (Proverbs 29:18, KJV).

There are many types of death. Physical death often pales in comparison to emotional and spiritual death. In today's terms, we call it depression. There is an epidemic of depression in our country today. It is an epidemic of emotional and spiritual dying and death.

Enabled One,

You may have already given up on any purpose or plans for your life, thinking everything is hopeless. Without God's purpose, you will "perish." You will remain in deep depression. You know depression well. It is a miserable existence. God does not want you to live this way. Through Jesus Christ, there is hope for you.

I will first address the enabled since childhood:

The vision, the revelation of God's purpose in our lives, makes our lives worth the living. With no vision or purpose, everything is dependent upon feelings. The world appears to revolve around the one being enabled. Everything is done for him: Every need met. Every want is supplied. There is no reason for the enabled one to do anything but become lethargic, lazy, and demanding. While the muscles atrophy, the mind becomes numb, and there is nothing to pursue. It is the ultimate easy life – or is it? You can always put off plans until tomorrow, but when tomorrow comes, why bother? Success is only a day or month or year away, but rarely a reality. The mind revolves around the question, "How do I feel?" Know this: Laziness leads to depression. Laziness leads to emotional and spiritual death (Proverbs 19:15).

What else does the Bible say about laziness?

The desire of the lazy man kills him, for his hands refuse to labor. He covets greedily all day long, but the righteous gives and does not spare (Proverbs 21:25-26, NKJ).

He who is slothful (lazy) in his work is a brother to him who is a great destroyer (Proverbs 18:9, NKJ).

The soul of a lazy man desires, and has nothing; But the soul of the diligent shall be made rich (Proverbs 13:4, NKJ).

To the Newly Enabled or the Soon to be Enabled:

Loss of jobs, homes, and marriages has caused multitudes to lose hope. You very likely will encounter a family member or friend who, for a time, will help you. Whatever the reason for your loss, your focus must be on God, seeking Him and His will in your life. Will it be easy? No. Giving up only leads to laziness, which leads to depression (Proverbs 19:15, NKJ). You cannot afford to embrace depression. Depression will destroy you. Get up! Help the one who is helping you. Do work around the house, repair something, or cut the grass. Clean up, fix the car, or help at church. Use your skills to help others and maintain a thankful attitude.

To the Enabled One:

God has called us to press on even when life is hard, especially when life is hard. He has called us to repent for wrong choices and to trust Him to work things out for our good. Depression seeks to destroy all that we are, but God has other plans for us.

> "And we know that all things work together for good
> to those who love God, to those who are the called
> according to His purpose" (Romans 8:28, NKJ).

Every mature Christian clings to this promise. Each one of us needs God's purpose to give our lives meaning and hope.

Now, let's read from the New International Version:

> Where there is no revelation, the people cast off
> restraint; but blessed is he who keeps the law
> (Proverbs 29:18, NIV).

When people are controlled by their feelings, they do not use self-control. They "cast off restraint." They do not think about the consequences of their actions – they just act. For the enabled, consequences have no meaning. No one has ever required them to admit responsibility and make restitution for their misdeeds. Because they act by their feelings, many isolate themselves from the community.

> A man who isolates himself seeks his own desire; He
> rages against all wise judgment (Proverbs 18:1, NKJ).

To the Enabler:

What is happening to the one you enable? His mind is constantly bombarded as television gives him a perverted view of the world. The more TV he watches, the more anger and lust rule his mind. His mind truly is a battlefield. We know that TV and movies are not the real world, and yet it is reality to him. Violent video games only serve to intensify his anger and lust. Then comes the tipping point, and he acts on his anger. He "casts off restraint." Why not? He has no purpose, no God given reason to rise above his circumstances. He satisfies his feelings and pleases self. What starts as a small thought, takes root and become an action. It isn't long until his actions take control as habits and shape his character. When a person has been allowed, or even encouraged, to react to every disappointment by their feelings, stubborn disregard for authority and anger filled tantrums are usually the norm. This storm of emotions does not just stop when the enabled one runs out of energy, but can become an internal fire that rages as he fantasizes about doing harm to others.

To the Enabled One:

If you recognize yourself in this description, you need to know that God loves you just the way you are – but He loves you too much to leave you in that condition.

- First, admit the problem: You have been enabled. This is step one in accepting responsibility for your life.

- Then, pray and ask God to help you change. Expect change. Will it be easy? No. But God will faithfully supply your need for change when your prayer is sincere.

- Next, accept that God has a purpose for your life. Turn your focus to Him. Those who truly trust God choose His will over emotional feelings or logic. We need God's purpose in our lives to direct our paths, paths that please Him.

- This is important: Do not check your feelings. How you feel usually does not really matter. You just need to get started doing the right thing for your situation. Many times, getting started is the hardest part.

- The following may seem so simple, but know this, it is effective. Make a list of the steps you need to take – the steps as you currently know them. The list can always be adjusted when God gives you additional information. Not only will making a list get you started, making a list will also help keep you focused and accountable until the job is completed.

- Do not expect constant praise or rewards for doing what is right. Work to please God. Keep your eyes on your goal: Becoming a caring, responsible adult.

- Accept criticism as an opportunity to learn and improve.

- Keep a thankful attitude and give God praise for what He is doing in your life and family.

To the Enabler:

First, recognize the problem: You are an enabler. Don't ask the enabled one how he feels. If you ask him this question, he will probably not be able to focus on anything else. And you will have caused it! When you ask how he feels, you open the door to complaining. He will expect sympathy for every ache and pain. He may feel too tired to continue today. The truth is, if he gets out of bed or off the sofa and gets moving, he will feel so much better. Don't ask your child or spouse how they feel. And don't ask yourself that question either.

Encourage the enabled one, but do not give him money for future projects until this one is finished. Since you, the enabler, probably pay for the materials, it does not cost your son anything. Therefore, he does not value or take care of the product after it arrives. When it is delivered to the house, does it lie in the middle of the floor for weeks? Do you finally pick it up and put it away – so it doesn't get ruined? When it costs him nothing, it means nothing. He can always demand that you purchase more. Be the responsible parent. You are the one who pays for the materials. Use wisdom. The first project, and perhaps a multitude of projects already waiting completion, needs to be finished before more money is spent.

Encourage your son, but do not give him too much praise for effort or completion. Rewards that are the most effective are intrinsically motivated. Constant praise from you may actually slow him down, as he relaxes and takes time to bask in the praise you lavish on him. The best reward is completion of a job well done.

Too much praise can also become an integrity problem. If you overly praise every effort and product your son has completed, regardless of amount of effort or quality of work, your son does not learn what is good effort or good work. He may begin to think that any effort is good work.

Children need to hear praise, but they also need to hear constructive criticism. Parents, who do not correct their children and make constructive suggestions, allow their children to become lazy and poor workers. As adults, they will expect praise for poor work and wonder why they got fired. After all, they did the work; it just wasn't up to company standards. Yes, offer honest praise and honest constructive criticism along the way. Everybody makes mistakes, and everybody can improve. Learning to accept constructive criticism, with a cooperative attitude, is part of growing up.

The best praise comes from knowing you are pleasing God. You are doing the right thing. Jesus set the example as He said to His Father, *"I have glorified You on the earth. I have finished the work which You have given Me to do" (John 17:4, NKJ).* And finally, as Christians we look forward to hearing the Lord say, *"Well done thou good and faithful servant."* Hmm, seems like all these examples have something to do with completion of a job well done. Yes, we

217

actually glorify God when we are faithful to complete the tasks and the calling He has placed upon our lives.

Anyone can start a project, but not everyone will complete it. Enabler, do not jump in and complete it or fix it. Many of life's projects require us to intensively trust God. God planned it that way. Pray, trust God, and trust the list to help your son get organized and finished with the current project. No, do not make the list for your son. What if you never trained your son to make a list? If absolutely necessary, sit with your son to start the first list. Demonstrate how to break large tasks into smaller tasks. Prioritize the list to create a logical order. Oh, and if you have been negligent to make your own lists, it is time for you to set the example by organizing what you need to do. God will help you, too, if you will ask Him.

What about spending? Credit Card Fever is fueled by feelings!

Some parents, wanting to trust their adult children, allow them to use their credit cards. Again, anything purchased has no value. Your daughter won't feel the sting of paying the bill if it doesn't come out of her money. Shopping is motivated by feelings, though sprinkled with a liberal dose of twisted logic. "I really needed that new expensive outfit. When I looked in the mirror, I looked so good in it. I knew it was meant for me." Or your son dives into the latest video game that just arrived with the other electronics he ordered. He won't feel the discomfort of having to pay for his purchases either. Although deemed as needed by the ones who hold your credit cards, we know these are wants and not needs. Too many times our children have not had to learn the difference because the cost was not coming out of their pockets. While Mom is struggling to pay the bills, Credit Card Fever may be overtaking her children.

Perhaps your adult child has a big emergency debt to pay. Thinking, "This is an easy fix. I'll just put it on my credit card." You give your daughter your credit card for this one purchase and maybe allow her to take care of a couple of her other household expenses. You wait for the card to be returned and wonder when you will get it back. You then discover she is adding restaurant bills, shopping, and theme parks to your ever-increasing credit card debt. The amount owed rises to over $30,000 and is still growing. Your daughter has made no effort to return your credit card.

How can you get control of this situation? First, pray and ask God for help. Next, call the credit card company and request that your credit card number be changed. They will issue a new card in your name and cancel the old card. If you unwisely allowed your daughter to have a card in her name, assigned to your account, call and tell the credit card company to cancel her card. If she wants her own card, one she will be responsible for, she can apply for one.

Now you have a decision to make. Are you going to speak with the fraud and theft division of the credit card company? If you gave your child the credit card, you are probably liable for all charges. If your child used your card without your permission, you can report your card as stolen. If this was a first time offense, you may inform her that this is theft. (Believe me; she already knows that it is theft.) You will expect her to pay you back for charges she incurred at a weekly or monthly agreed upon amount. You may give her a warning. Inform her that next time you will report this to the credit card company and file a police report. Sound harsh? If you don't protect yourself, things will get worse. When you give the warning, your child will be checking your integrity. Will Mom really do anything – or am I getting away with another big financial score?

Does your adult child have a Durable Power of Attorney? Has your primary physician declared that you are no longer able to administer your own finances? If not, your adult child has no business having or using your credit cards. It is your responsibility to make sure all of your credit cards are secure. God never told you to trust the untrustworthy. Instead, He wants you to use wisdom and common sense.

Chapter 17:
Violence in America,
Root Cause: Enabling!

The Bible says that in the last days, people will cry out for "peace and safety" (1 Thessalonians 5:3, NKJ). While the secular experts try to determine why there is so much violence in America, I would like to weigh in on that topic from a Christian perspective.

I believe violence in America has root causes based in enabling. Although I have already written about many of the following issues, this compilation focuses on the increasing presence of violence caused by enabling.

Through the years, I have been abundantly blessed to teach many children from Christian homes. They were polite, hard workers focused on learning and being a positive influence in the classroom. I thank God for parents who have diligently lived Godly lives and maintained Godly expectations for their children. Their reward is to see their children to grow up to be caring, responsible adults. Also numbered among the excellent students were many who were not from Christian backgrounds. The parents of these students were also determined that by their example and expectations, their children would grow up to be caring, responsible adults.

What about the students with severe behavioral issues? Although I taught for many years, I did not understand until I began asking God what was going on at home in the severe cases I personally encountered. In my classroom, I had a student whose use of profanity and poor behavior were some of the worst I had experienced. After trying many strategies to correct and encourage a change in behavior, without success, I asked the parents to come to school for a conference. Only one parent attended the conference. She freely shared with me that they were Christians. I was shocked. How did a child coming from a Christian home develop such out of control behavior? The family appeared to be stable. Both Mom and Dad were living in the home. As the conference continued, I learned much about the home environment. Both the Godly example and the Godly expectations were missing from the picture. The mother and I had a long talk that day about the reality of her home. She did not think that her husband could or would change. She said that she would work with her son, but little change followed.

Through the years, I have had many opportunities to teach children from homes where Christianity was tried and then abandoned. I also taught many students from families who attended church, but whose involvement in Christian teaching and living was minimal. The latter was the case in this family. They went to church on Sundays; however, there was no additional talk or teaching about God's love and His very real expectations for Christians in their everyday lives.

From that time on, whenever I had a student who was consistently rebellious and out of control, I looked for evidence confirming that church attendance was a part of the family's current or past history. The evidence was always there, and I was always saddened. At this point, you may think I am making too much of church attendance. Being a Christian is much more than being present at church on Sunday. Parents and children who have tried church, but have fallen away, or even still attend church, but live lives that are self-serving and ungodly, have a similar impact on their children: When parents live sinful lifestyles in front of their children, their children notice. Even if their children don't say anything – they notice. Their children have heard the Bible teachings and know right from wrong. When their parents rebel in their choice of sin, the children learn to do the same. The children may or may not duplicate the same sin as their parents, but they will choose their own rebellion and sin. By living an ungodly lifestyle in front of their children, parents have declared that you can pick and choose the parts of the Bible you like and ignore the rest. This is not acceptable to God. Parents experience their own consequences in broken marriages, loss of careers, loss of finances, or loss of something else they hold dear. It is likely that their children will follow in their footsteps.

Violence in America:

What happens when we enable our children by giving them too much?

- Too much attention focused on pleasing our children destroys any compassion or understanding of real life they might have developed. Everything is based on how they feel. Their feelings have been warped by their parents – avoiding tantrums to keep them happy. Now, when circumstances don't please them, they don't care how their actions may impact the lives of others. Their anger may convince them to take matters into their own hands, resulting in violence at home or in the community.

- Too much time to "hang-out" allows too much time for complaining and spewing feelings and opinions that will eventually demand an outlet. These "friends" may join forces with your child to fuel a fire that will explode in acts of violence. Violence may be against those who disagree with them or against innocent ones who just happen to be in the location targeted for attack.

223

- Too much spending money may be used for drugs and alcohol, changing our children's ability to think in a rational, reasonable way. Violence becomes the answer for problems that overwhelm them. Drugs and alcohol give them the courage to do what they have been planning. And when they run out of money – that only angers them more!

- Too much money may be spent on violent music with pounding rhythms that brainwash our children. Children are programmed to think that sexual immorality, perverse language, and gross violence are cool, acceptable, and part of a normal life. This plugged in generation tunes out to real life and tunes in to an atmosphere which produces emotional and spiritual death.

- Too many library and book club books encourage our youth to read stories where rebellion is the norm. Books that introduce children to the occult, sexual activity, and violence only serve to stimulate interest in these subjects.

- Too many late-night violent and/or sexually explicit TV shows, reality shows, movies, and video games consume their nights. When the morning comes, they are easily angered due to lack of sleep. Too many days are lost to catching up on sleep. They get their days and nights confused. Late night becomes primetime for doing something productive. However, bored with nothing else to do, they vicariously exchange real productivity for the ever addictive seduction of explicit sexuality and violence.

- Too much trust allows parents to ignore or deny the existence of family problems. Many parents dismiss angry statements. They do not take their children seriously. Without active parenting, which includes training, correction, and punishment, small problems escalate into big problems. If not stopped early, wrong attitudes and rebellious behaviors become strongholds that severely shape who they become as adults.

- Too many rewards for too little effort distort our children's ability to understand what is considered acceptable effort. If the reward is not big enough or quick enough in coming, it is easy to quit. They become angry and blame others when they do not reach their goal. Seeing themselves as failures, nothing matters. Violence gives them an outlet for their increasing anger. In reality, diligence, patience, and endurance would have earned them the reward they wanted.

- Too much time spent is spent in isolation. Too many activities that do not require personal interaction rob children of learning how to communicate without technology. Children are given TVs, video games, cell phones, and computers with Internet access that encourage time spent alone. Technology creates an atmosphere where normal social interaction and communication become foreign. Conversations with parents are almost non-existent or end up in an argument. Listening to the teacher is rare. Nothing seems as important as the latest text-message or phone call. Online social media replaces real relationships, leaving children open to connections with adults who are sexual predators. Online recruiters provide religious indoctrination to encourage, train, and equip children to commit violent acts. Finally, in search of friends, lonely teens post personal information and sexy photos of themselves – just hoping to connect with another person. Parents rarely monitor cell phones, TV, or the Internet until it is too late. A dangerous connection has been made.

- Too much involvement in sports and entertainment activities may indicate to children that school and church are not important. When children miss school, learning is lost. When children miss church, learning is lost. Parents who want their children to be successful in life make sure their children attend school. And they attend church with their children. Consistently attending school and church brings stability and purpose in life. Godly purpose causes people to focus on what is important – trusting God to direct our paths. When our focus is on God and doing the right things, we are not focused on violence and hate. God provides us knowledge, understanding, and discernment to know the difference between what is right and wrong. He gives us the courage and the ability to do what is right.

- Too much help weakens our children. When a child starts out needing just a little help, there is probably a simple problem or weakness that parents are trying to correct. Over time, as the child becomes enabled, he demands more and more help to manage his life. He doesn't recognize the slippery slope that will soon place him in a position of utter helplessness. To him, it just seems easy and comfortable, with no stress. Don't get me wrong, the enabled one wants to feel strong and confident. Trapped in the prison of enabling, he becomes physically, emotionally, and spiritually weak. The way out requires great courage and energy. He may view violence as a reasonable way to show himself strong.

- As the parents recognize their increasing struggle to help their child, they also see an arising need that declares, "Protect yourselves." Anytime the parents step back and require their child to do for himself, anger and self-entitlement rage against his providers. The anger often leads to violence. Oh, if the parents had simply required their child do for himself at an early age, things would be so much better. Now, the demands continue, as does the threat of violence. Sadly, too many parents rest in their comfort zone of denial and do not protect themselves.

- Too many excuses allow children to think that rules do not apply to them. If you think long enough and hard enough, you can always find someone else to blame for your child's wrongdoing. If you can't find someone else to blame, personal guilt will take over. You can always site self as a reason for your child's out of control behavior. The enabled one learns that blaming others is an effective strategy for reaching personal goals. Manipulation becomes a faithful friend; it activates the sympathy of others who will help him.

226

If not stopped, simple misbehavior escalates until actions are extreme. The law must step in to protect the family or community from violence.

Violence in America (continued)

What happens when we enable ourselves to avoid personal responsibilities?

Personal enabling includes: excuses, denial, stubbornness, laziness, depression, pride, negligence, and apathy. All are sin. Almost all could be factors in the following situations:

- Too many homes are divided by unnecessary divorces. Too many children are growing up without benefit of two parents who teach them right from wrong, set limits, and impose consequences.

- Too many children are not disciplined from an early age, making it almost impossible to discipline them later. Ever increasing rebellious attitudes and behaviors lead down a path of lawlessness.

- Too many children are from homes where they are verbally and physically abused. Children, following their parent's example, learn to bully others. When abuse is all you know – violence follows.

- Too many children go home to an empty house after school. Too many have no adult supervision or support until almost bedtime. They cook their own meals and take care of younger siblings. Too many parents are too busy to parent their children and expect them to grow up on their own.

- Too many children are not required to suffer the consequences for wrong behavior. It may be parents protecting their children or laws that are not enforced. Children who are protected from consequences have no reason to believe their ever escalating involvement in sinful or lawless deeds will negatively impact them. Threats of punishment soon fall on deaf ears. Children have no reason to fear the possibility of consequences. Courts need to enforce our laws with consequences that deter repeat offenses. Even if the law does not fulfill its responsibility to punish the offender, parents still have the responsibility to provide consequences for wrong behavior.

- Too many who have mental health problems do not take their medicine. Medicine plus counseling plus active parenting may be able to turn this situation around. The medicine can help, but only if it is taken as prescribed.

- Too many parents are too busy to be consistent. They are so busy they hardly notice the changes in their children that are leading them to act out in violence.

- Too many parents give up on their children. God has called parents to teach, train, guide, nurture, discipline, and pray for their children. There will be times when parents have to step back and trust God to change and restore their children, but giving up is not an option.

- Too many parents do not secure and monitor the guns they have in their homes.

Enabling breeds violence:

Now, when violence seems the perfect solution to a problem, the enabled one has no sense of guilt. Right and wrong do not matter, as long as he is able to execute his plan. Over time, the one who initially needed a little help becomes a psychopath with no remorse or shame. He plots and plans until he puts into action an explosion of violence that will impact both family and community.

Call the Police!

When the enabler finally realizes that she is no longer in control of the situation, the logical source of protection is the police. She makes the call, but when the officers arrive, her sympathy has had time to set in. She refuses to file a police report. After a few calls like this, the police recognize her as an enabler and give little credence to her complaint. This only serves to further liberate the enabled one. Violence is ever in his mind. No one can or will stop him. He does what he wants. He knows that the enabler will "fix it."

Who is responsible?

After reviewing the effects of enabling, you may think that the enabled one should not be held responsible for the violent acts he commits. This thinking is absolutely wrong. The enabled one is responsible and must be held accountable for his behavior. If not held responsible and accountable, then abusive or violent behavior will be dismissed. The courts may declare him incompetent to stand trial or not guilty by reason of insanity. He will eventually be returned home – unchanged and ready to continue making demands, abusing others, and planning his next reign of terror.

Stop the Violence? Stop the Enabling!

The best advice for the protection of parents and family is: Never enable your child. If you are currently enabling your child – Stop! Use the information in this book to help you. If the situation is out of control, seek professional help. Your safety, the safety of your family, and the safety of your community depend on you.

Chapter 18:
Anything You Value, You Will Fight For!

You are in a battle of enormous proportion. You are fighting for the survival of yourself and your family. It is a battle for your earthly and eternal futures. This is not a battle you can win on your own. You might try to convince others and comfort yourself by saying, "I've done my best." Know this: Your best was never meant to be enough to overcome life's battles. Your best united with God's best, is the combination that honors God and empowers you to be the victor, not the victim, in every situation.

> For it is God who commanded light to shine out of darkness, who has shone in our hearts to give the light of the knowledge of the glory of God in the face of Jesus Christ. But we have this treasure in earthen vessels, that the excellence of the power may be of God and not of us. We are hard-pressed on every side, yet not crushed; we are perplexed, but not in despair; persecuted, but not forsaken; struck down, but not destroyed (2 Corinthians 4:6-9, NKJ).

> Therefore we do not lose heart. Even though our outward man is perishing, yet the inward man is being renewed day by day. For our light affliction, which is but for a moment, is working for us a far more exceeding and eternal weight of glory, while we do

231

> not look at the things which are seen, but at the things which are not seen. For the things which are seen are temporary, but the things which are not seen are eternal (2 Corinthians 4:16-18, NKJ).

We recognize physical warfare.

In physical warfare, armies use weapons to destroy the enemy. The earth has a long history of physical warfare where nations call upon their people to defend home and country. In America, men and women have given their lives in defense of freedom.

As Christians, we know that we are also called to Spiritual warfare.

> For though we walk in the flesh, we do not war according to the flesh. For the weapons of our warfare are not carnal but mighty in God for pulling down strongholds, casting down arguments and every high thing that exalts itself against the knowledge of God, bringing every thought into captivity to the obedience of Christ (2 Corinthians 10:3-5, NKJ).

The Spiritual battle is in your mind.

Satan causes a constant warring of logic and emotions in an attempt to defeat us in every area of our lives. The tactics include attempts to enflame us with anger, greed, pride, and lust. He wants to cause us to quit in apathy, rejection, and fear. He wants to bury us in poverty, hopelessness, and depression. All cause death. All are sin. We can deny the presence of the battle in our lives, but that does not alter its existence. Denial is an open door to deception that can only be destroyed by the truth.

Why is there so much deception today?

> The coming of the lawless one is according to the working of Satan, with all power, signs, and lying

> wonders, and with all unrighteous deception among those who perish, because they did not receive the love of the truth, that they might be saved. And for this reason God will send them strong delusion, that they should believe the lie, that they all may be condemned who did not believe the truth but had pleasure in unrighteousness (2 Thessalonians 2:9-12, NKJ).

God has created us to be seekers of the truth. His Word is truth. Settling for opinions, myths, legends, and traditions of men will neither save us nor protect us from the evil that is to come. As part of the army of God, we cannot afford to be ignorant and unprepared for the battle.

How do we fight?

> The Word of God is living and powerful, and sharper than any two-edged sword, piercing even to the division of soul and spirit, and of joints and marrow, and is a discerner of the thoughts and intents of the heart (Hebrews 4:12, NKJ).

The Word of God is a two-edged sword that slices between our logic and emotions. His Word is not dependent upon our feelings or our logic. His Word is the standard that settles the issue, gives us purpose, and calms the raging storm of confusion within us. His Word reveals our true motives, brings conviction and reconciles us to God. We can be confident in God, because He is faithful to His Word.

What weapons will pull down strongholds in my family?

Your Weapon is Prayer:

Constantly giving God authority over your problems and trusting Him for His answers will produce much good fruit in your life. Our prayers must be in faith and not in fear, expecting to receive from God.

> Do not be anxious about anything, but in everything, by prayer and petition, with thanksgiving, present your requests to God. And the peace of God which transcends all understanding, will guard your hearts and your minds in Christ Jesus (Philippians 4:6-7, NIV).

Your Weapon is Fasting:

Most people think about refraining from eating food as fasting. It is a way to deny self and focus on God. Prayer and fasting should be done with a humble attitude, seeking God and His will, and in the name of Jesus. Then, even the most difficult of strongholds will come down (Matthew 17:21, NKJ).

Fasting is about more than food. Read Isaiah 58:6-12.

> 6. "Is this not the fast that I have chosen: To loose the bonds of wickedness, To undo the heavy burdens, To let the oppressed go free, And that you break every yoke

> 7. Is it not to share your bread with the hungry, And that you bring to your house the poor who are cast out; When you see the naked, that you cover him, And not hide yourself from your own flesh?

8. Then your light shall break forth like the morning, Your healing shall spring forth speedily, And your righteousness shall go before you; The glory of the Lord shall be your rear guard.

9. Then you shall call, and the Lord will answer; You shall cry, and He will say, 'Here I am.'

If you take away the yoke from your midst, The pointing of the finger, and speaking wickedness,

10. If you extend your soul to the hungry And satisfy the afflicted soul, Then your light shall dawn in the darkness, And your darkness shall be as the noonday.

11. The Lord will guide you continually, And satisfy your soul in drought, And strengthen your bones; You shall be like a watered garden, And like a spring of water, whose waters do not fail.

12. Those from among you Shall build the old waste places; You shall raise up the foundations of many generations; And you shall be called the Repairer of the Breach, The Restorer of Streets to Dwell In" (Isaiah 58:6-12, NKJ).

Fasting from the wickedness of this world produces healing, deliverance from depression, answers to prayers, abundance, and a legacy that restores and encourages many generations.

Your Weapon is Praise and Worship:

It is easy to praise God when everything is going well in your life, but when you find yourself in the heat of the battle, you may not feel like praising Him. Praise is an expression of your faith and an act of your will. As Christians who worship Him in "Spirit and Truth" (John 4:23-24, NKJ), we set aside our logic and emotions.

We trust Him in all circumstances, especially those that are beyond our control. This is the "sacrifice of praise" God desires (Hebrews 13:15, NKJ). True believers know that as they lay their "sacrifice of praise" on the altar, they are giving themselves to trust God, and only God, for His provision in their lives. Whether spoken or sung, your praise and worship are spiritual warfare.

Your Weapon is Tithing and Giving Offerings:

Choosing to trust God with your finances is Spiritual warfare. God wants you to prove Him as you prepare for battle and in the midst of the conflict.

> Bring all the tithes (the whole tenth of your income) into the storehouse, that there may be food in My house, and prove Me now by it, says the Lord of hosts, if I will not open the windows of heaven for you and pour you out a blessing, that there shall not be room enough to receive it (Malachi 3:10, AMP).

Your Weapon is Giving Thanks:

Is giving thanks a way of life for you and your family, or have your lives become a constant stream of bitter complaining? Everything you say produces fruit. Giving thanks brings blessings – constant complaining results in destruction. God has called us to guard our attitudes and guard what we say.

> All these curses shall come upon you and shall pursue you and overtake you – They shall be upon you for a sign [of warning to other nations] and for a wonder, and upon your descendants forever. Because you did not serve the Lord your God with joyfulness of [mind and] heart [in gratitude] for the abundance of all [with which He had blessed you], Therefore you shall serve your enemies whom the Lord shall send against you,

> in hunger and thirst, in nakedness and in want of all
> things; and He will put a yoke of iron upon your neck
> until He has destroyed you (Deuteronomy 28:45-48,
> AMP).

An attitude of praise and thanksgiving is best learned by example. For your children or your spouse to willingly change, they need to see those attitudes in you. In the midst of good times, do your children see and hear you praising God? Do you thank Him for what He has already done and for what He is currently doing in your lives? You may already do this during prayer time, but what are you saying throughout the day and in general conversations? In the midst of difficult times, are you complaining and crumbling under the weight of the situation? Or in faith, are you standing firm, believing that God is going to bring you through to a successful end? What do your children and your spouse see and hear? They will learn to acknowledge and trust God when you do the same.

Your Weapon is Forgiving:

> Forgive them, even if they don't deserve it. Jesus
> said, "For if you forgive men their trespasses, your
> heavenly Father will also forgive you. But if you do
> not forgive men their trespasses, neither will your
> Father forgive your trespasses" (Matthew 6:14-15,
> NKJ).

When the enabling is finally over, your family may draw closer together. Some family members may need a fresh start and choose to move to a different location. It is obvious that a family that remains living together needs forgiveness to be a part of the healing and restoration God has planned for your family. However, those who choose to move to a new location need forgiveness, too. Forgiveness frees all involved and allows them to receive God's forgiveness in their lives. Forgiveness allows closure, healing, and peace. What if someone does not forgive you? By asking for forgiveness and forgiving others, at least you will have been obedient to what God desires you to do.

Your Weapon is Obeying God:

Obey Him even when it is not the comfortable or popular thing to do. When you demonstrate your love for your family, many times tough love will be necessary for the one who has long avoided responsibility. Tough love is not easy and will require faith in God. As you trust God and do the right thing, He is working in the heart and life of the one who has been enabled. Only God can change him. Then, as he learns to trust in the Lord, he will finally be able to learn to act in a caring, responsible manner.

Your Weapon is Casting Down Imaginations:

Will there be temptation to return to a former sin? When your flesh says, "This won't really hurt you," do not listen. Declare, "In the name of Jesus, I am not going back there!" God does not want your life controlled by an addiction to any earthly thing. This is true for the enabler who was addicted to enabling and the enabled one who was addicted to substance abuse or sexual immorality. Instead, focus on God, His will for your life, His Word, and consistently count your blessings.

> Finally, brethren, whatever things are true, whatever things are noble, whatever things are just, whatever things are pure, whatever things are lovely, whatever things are of good report, if there is any virtue and if there is anything praise worthy-meditate on these things (Philippians 4:8, NKJ).

Fear Not! Stand on His Word!

Do you need strength?

> Jesus said, "My grace (My favor and loving-kindness and mercy) is enough for you, [sufficient against any danger and enables you to bear the trouble manfully]; for My strength and power are made perfect (fulfilled and completed) and show themselves most effective in [your] weakness (2 Corinthians 12:9, AMP).

Do you need courage?

When you find yourself in the heat of the battle, one of the enemy's tactics is to tell you, "Sure, God helped you last time. This time it is different. He won't help you now." Satan's goal is to make you so afraid that you will not even attempt to follow God and do what is right. Satan "is a liar and the father of lies" (John 8:44, NIV). Do not listen to him. For it is Jesus, "who is the Author and Finisher of our faith." He endured the shame and the agony of the cross, "lest you become weary and discouraged in your souls" (Hebrews 12:2-3, NKJ). God will help you.

> "Be strong and of good courage, do not fear nor be afraid of them; for the Lord your God, He is the One who goes with you. He will not leave you nor forsake you" (Deuteronomy 31:6, NKJ).

> "Fear not, for I am with you; Be not dismayed, for I am your God. I will strengthen you, Yes, I will help you, I will uphold you with My righteous right hand" (Isaiah 41:10, NKJ).

Even when the battle is long and the odds seemingly impossible, God can take what the enemy means for your harm and use it for your good (Genesis 50:20, NKJ). So it was for Joseph, and so it will be for those who trust in Him, today.

Do you need endurance?

When you feel like you can't go on – endure. Don't check your feelings; they will deceive you into thinking that you should give up or quit. Don't check your logic. God is not limited by the logic of this world. Know this: God has good things planned for your life. Have faith and endure to the end. He will reward you for choosing to trust Him.

> Finally, my brethren, be strong in the Lord and in the power of His might.Put on the whole armor of God, that you may be able to stand against the wiles of the devil. For we do not wrestle against flesh and blood, but against principalities, against powers, against the rulers of the darkness of this age, against spiritual hosts of wickedness in the heavenly places. Therefore take up the whole armor of God, that you may be able to withstand in the evil day, and having done all, to stand (Ephesians 6:10-13, NKJ).

Don't settle for peace at any price.

Some people are afraid of any kind of battle. They will sacrifice everything for peace. Many enablers are like that. Even though the battle may be long and difficult, it will not overtake you if your trust is in the Lord.

Enabler, consider this:

You have sacrificed many things to enable your loved one, and it has only entangled you in his sin. So many times you wanted to speak up, but your silence has made you complicit in it. God wants to free both you and the one you have enabled from the bondage of sin. God is calling you to trust Him in the battle. There may be new sacrifices along the way. This time you know – in the name of Jesus – victory is coming! Use Spiritual warfare every day. Do not try to understand everything that is going on, just fight the good fight. Do not stop with small victories when there are greater victories needed. Do not give up until complete victory is a reality in your family! The battle is great, but so is the prize! Finish strong! Fight to win!

> Let us not become weary in doing good, for at the proper time we will reap a harvest if we do not give up (Galatians 6:9, NIV).

> I have fought the good fight, I have finished the race, I have kept the faith. (2 Timothy 4:7, NKJ).

What will the victory look like?
What will my family see?

Our families need to see an unrelenting passion in us to know and serve God. We are to live His Word and share it with others. They have been with us through the good times and the bad times. They have seen the sin of enabling almost destroy their family. If, in any way, it has not been made very clear to them, they need to know – it was God who delivered your family from this stronghold. With thankful hearts, we give God the glory for He alone is worthy of praise.

You see, for too long, families have attended church, enjoyed youth activities, and even participated in helping others. All this was good, but it was not enough. Our families need to know that God is still the Miracle Worker and Way-Maker that He was in Bible times. He sees the deep need in our lives, and He cleanses and restores individuals and families who will seek Him with their whole hearts. He is our victory! Let there be no more time wasted playing church. Our lives must reflect our love for God and His Word. Our spouses and our children need to see the reality of God in their lives, too. He wants His people to know Him as Savior, Healer, Deliverer, Wonderful Counselor, Mighty God, Everlasting Father, and the Prince of peace. We must not settle for less!

Chapter 19:
The Responsibility is Yours!

To the Enabler:

Only God knows how or why each one of us has enabled someone else, making it possible for them to avoid responsibility. I ask you, do you really want your family free from the destruction of enabling? If your only motivation is to stop the insanity and get some peace in your life – it is not enough. If your motivation is to see loved ones saved and walking in the Word, growing up, fulfilling their responsibilities, and pursuing God's will in their lives, then you will trust God enough to step back and let Him change them.

When you began reading this book, some of you were not aware of the destructive power of enabling. You started out to help your loved one, and it has not turned out as you had hoped. You now have the knowledge and understanding that will equip you to stop enabling. God will help you, if you will trust Him.

Some of you knew that your enabling was harming your family, but you could not see any way to stop yourself. Enabling became a habit, a compulsion that demanded you continue. In the name of Jesus, be set free from those destructive addictions and compulsions. God will give you the courage and ability to stop the enabling, if you will trust Him.

Some of you need permission to stop the enabling. Is it really the right thing to do? Although God has called you to help others, He has never called you to help others avoid responsibility. The right thing to do is stop the enabling and allow God to work in the enabled one's life. God will strengthen you and stand by you when it seems impossible. Not only will God help you, He will help your whole family, if you will trust Him.

Finally, as you step aside and let God work in your life and in your family's lives, you are removing the roadblock that has kept God from being able to restore and heal your family. Equipped with many new revelations from God's Word and this book, you can no longer live in denial. Now that you have been taught what is right, you are responsible to do what is right. God will help you become the person/parent/spouse He wants you to be. There is hope for your future because your trust is in the Lord.

To the Enabled One:

The responsibility is also yours. No longer can you be satisfied with saying, "I didn't know. I didn't mean it. Give me another chance." You have learned much as you read this book. Just as with the enabler, once you have been taught what is right, you are responsible to do what is right. Being enabled has held you in the bondage of sin. No longer will you be satisfied when you see others try to fix your problems, make excuses for you, or desperately try to keep you happy. You know what kind of life is behind you. It is a life of depression and failure. Your life isn't over – it is just beginning. From now on, you will choose being productive over being lazy, and you will choose listening and learning over arguing and rebelling. You know that learning new things will help you do more to responsibly manage your own life. As God gives you the discernment to know what is really happening in your life, you will remember that if you give in to the easy way, you will never become the man or woman God created you to be. If you falter or fail, get right back up and get to work. Manage the basic living skills you know you are capable of doing and keep a good attitude. There is hope for your future because your trust is in the Lord.

And therefore the Lord [earnestly] waits

[expecting, looking, longing]

to be gracious to you;

and therefore He lifts Himself up,

that He may have mercy on you

and show loving-kindness to you.

For the Lord is a God of justice.

Blessed (happy, fortunate, to be envied)

are all those who[earnestly] wait for Him,

who expect and look and long for Him

[for His victory, His favor, His love,

His peace, His joy, and

His matchless, unbroken companionship]!

(Isaiah 30:18, AMP)

When Enabling and Alzheimer's Collide

When Enabling and Alzheimer's Collide

Dr. Mary Willock

ABUNDANT LIFE PRESS
Port Saint Lucie, Florida

When Enabling and Alzheimer's Collide
Dr. Mary L. Willock

All quoted Scriptures indicate the Bible translation. Scripture quotations marked:

KJV are from the King James Version, The Scofield Reference Bible, Oxford University Press, 1945, 1937, 1917, 1909. Used by permission.

NKJ are from The Holy Bible, New King James Version, Thomas Nelson, Inc., 1992, 1982, 1980, 1979. Used by permission.

AMP are from The Amplified Bible, Zondervan Bible Publishers and the Lockman Foundation, 1987, 1965, 1964, 1962, 1958, 1954. Used by permission.

NIV are from The Life Application Bible, New International Version by Tyndale House Publishers, Inc./Zondervan Publishing House, 1991, 1990, 1989, 1988. Used by permission.

ISBN: Softcover - 978-0692302484
          0692302484
ASIN: eBook - B00N1BXL4C

To order additional paperback or Kindle copies of this book, visit Amazon.com.

To learn more about Mary Willock Ministries or to invite Dr. Mary Willock to be a guest speaker on enabling or many other life-changing topics, you can reach her through www.marywillock.net.

Acknowledgements:

I thank God for His amazing faithfulness, loving kindness, and constant provision in my life. Time and time again, He has taken what the enemy meant for harm and has worked it for my good. Above all, I thank God for Jesus, my Savior and Lord.

I thank God for my husband and daughter who have lovingly supported me all the years I taught school and as we experienced my family's journey through enabling and Alzheimer's.

I thank God for Vicki Baird, Linda Brabble, and Barbara Forgus who are precious sisters in Christ. We have prayed together, wept together, rejoiced together, and seen God work in miraculous ways to help our families as they are growing up to become caring, responsible adults. They have shared their time and talents in many ways to see the enabling books finished. They have also ministered through music with me for many wonderful years.

I thank God for my Church and Pastors who have prayed for me a multitude of times and shared the joys of seeing God amazingly provide hope and answers in every situation.

When Enabling and Alzheimer's Collide

When Enabling and Alzheimer's Collide

Contents

Preface

Introduction

When Enabling and Alzheimer's Collide

Preface
Two book set:
When Compassion Turns to Enabling

Compassionate people enjoy helping others, but when compassion turns to enabling, that help becomes destructive. Enabling prevents others from acting in a caring, responsible manner. Compulsive rescuing and enabling can so overtake an enabler's life that there seems no way out. Families become dysfunctional. Relationships are destroyed in the process.

Information in this book will help you identify enabling and recognize the effects and root causes of enabling. Whether you are an enabler, the one who is being enabled, or the one dealing with family members who are out of control, you will learn how and why unacceptable thinking, attitudes, and behaviors must be changed. This book provides easy to understand, practical Bible-based answers and strategies to heal and restore your family. Your lives are about to change!

When Enabling and Alzheimer's Collide

Both Alzheimer's disease and enabling are destructive forces, but when they collide, the results are overwhelming. Both problems are experienced by thousands of people every day. After reading this true story, you will understand: Enabling must be stopped while the enabler still has clarity of mind. Once dementia or Alzheimer's disease is present, there will be no way to protect the enabler from the one who has been enabled.

This narrative is not a composite of many families; it is the true story of one family. The names have been changed to protect the identity of the individuals. As you read this amazing story, you will clearly understand God's desire and willingness to free your family from the bondage of enabling. Your family's situation may seem hopeless, but with God, all things are possible (Luke 1:37). This book provides help for desperate families who are caught between Alzheimer's and the dysfunction of enabling.

Introduction
Frances and Andrew: A True Story

Two weeks after I retired from teaching school, I discovered my mother and brother were living in extreme dysfunction. Through the years, Mom's constant enabling and Andrew's endless taking advantage of her had been bothersome. Now, I had time to take an up-close view of their lives. I was shocked. Their finances were out of control. I hoped if I made some strategic changes, they could survive financially. The closer I got and the more I learned it became obvious: It was so much more than finances. As you read this book, you will learn what can happen when Enabling and Alzheimer's Collide.

In the months that followed, I tried to secure their finances. Each time I made changes, I kept hoping to have corrected every financially dangerous situation – only to find things were getting worse. As of late, Frances' mental clarity continues to deteriorate, and Andrew's verbal abuse and attacks on her finances have escalated. Although I suspected dementia, it would be a full year before Frances would be diagnosed with Alzheimer's disease. As you read this, you will recognize increasing evidence of dementia/Alzheimer's disease throughout many situations in her life. Frances was almost ninety years old, and Andrew was in his late fifties. Francis built a home across the street from Andrew to enable her to take care of him, a move that almost destroyed them both.

I did not start to keep a journal until after many months of trying to intervene. The situation was so overwhelming that I realized I must write to accurately document the seriousness of their dysfunction. They both desperately needed help. Without documentation, the police, the courts, and other agencies did not take me seriously. After months of writing, God spoke to my heart to share what I learned through this process. It is a simple message: Enabling must be stopped while the enabler still has clarity of mind. Once dementia or Alzheimer's disease is present, there will be no way to protect the enabler from the one who has been enabled.

Why didn't I immediately bring Mom home to live with me? She always adamantly refused. She insisted she wanted to live in her own house – and she must take care of Andrew. Over a period of time, however, she was no longer able to take care of him. And as you will see, the system did not take care of him either. Their lives could be a movie entitled something like, "The System is Broken" or "Fear This: Right in Your Neighborhood" or "Won't Anyone Help Us?"

Since many of the individuals mentioned in this book are alive today, all of the names have been changed to protect their identity. The person writing the narrative will be identified as Sarah. As Sarah tells her story, whether you are the enabler, the enabled, or the person who lives responsibly, think about your situation and consider what your future may be like if the enabling in your family is not stopped.

Chapter 1:
The Early Years

My brother, Andrew, has been in and out of mental institutions all of his life. Our parents always experienced problems disciplining him. As a young boy, he was frequently in trouble at school. He had great difficulty making friends, and therefore became a loner. What about Andrew and me? We really didn't get along very well. Our parents excused our behavior as normal sibling rivalry.

My mother was quick to excuse Andrew's angry tirades, saying he was just like Grandpa. Grandpa had red hair and a terrible temper. Andrew had a terrible temper, too. Once, when we were young, I remember my brother chasing me through the house with a baseball bat. Thankfully, he was not fast enough to catch me. I escaped into my bedroom, where Andrew slammed his bat against the door. In his anger, Andrew left a deep gouge in the wood. Andrew was excused, not punished. Mom's attitude was, "Boys will be boys."

It wasn't long until Dad found a nighttime job, leaving the three of us home alone most evenings. Andrew really needed tough love and a father who was home to make sure he behaved. But with Mom's constant enabling, Dad found it less frustrating to be busy at work. We did attend church on Sundays, but Dad stayed home.

As with most families, Mom and Dad loved us very much. They wanted the best for our family, and they both worked very hard to provide for us. I don't know when Mom's compassion turned to enabling, but I do know that as far back as I can remember Mom's desire to help and rescue was an ever present force in our lives. I was strong enough to resist her constant suggestions to rest and take it easy. By my teen years, I realized that if I gave into the comfort of her sympathy, I would find myself unable to face and overcome any of life's challenges. Sadly, Andrew was not that strong. He enjoyed her sympathy and willingness to excuse and fix every aspect of his life. He didn't have to behave in a responsible manner. It was always Mom to the rescue.

Not too long after I graduated from high school, I married and moved away. The information I have concerning Andrew's teen years is minimal. I do know, however, during those teen years, things got much worse. Andrew became involved in illegal drugs, black magic, and promiscuous sex. He was arrested several times. Mom was always quick to make sure he returned home as soon as possible, so she could take care of him.

The physical violence started in 1988. Andrew severely beat our father, striking him many times in the face and body. Again, Andrew was sent to a mental health facility. As usual, Mom diligently worked to secure his release. She was successful, and Andrew returned home – unchanged. His relationship with Dad was marked by constant arguing and disagreement. My husband, Sam, and I first learned about the beating months later, when my parents came to visit. It was November, and I was recovering from surgery. Mom and Dad arrived to take care of me. During their visit, Dad took us aside and revealed he was upset about Andrew's violent attack. We were shocked. He was very distressed that Mom insisted upon Andrew's release. Mom and Dad returned home the Friday after Thanksgiving. Two days later, Sunday, November 27, 1988, Andrew used a knife to brutally murder our father. Andrew was 33 years old.

Later we learned that Andrew spent a lot of time listening to heavy metal rock music. The lyrics called for a "blood sacrifice." The pounding music added intensity to Andrew's continual anger that was focused on Dad. Andrew was sure Dad had millions of dollars that he wouldn't share with him. My father was a retired Air Force Sergeant. He was not a rich man. (FYI – Dad became a Christian in his later years. Even in the midst of this great horror, I have peace knowing that my father is with the Lord.)

Andrew, found incompetent to stand trial, spent many years in a mental institution in northern Florida. Mom visited him as often as possible. She always arrived with a carload of delicious treats and desserts. I am sure the facility loved dealing with the sugar highs and lows caused by those treats. As time went on, Mom wearied of the long drive to north Florida. She requested he be moved to a mental health institution closer to home. It wasn't long until Andrew relocated to a facility within a two hour drive of her house. Again, Mom lavished him with treats and desserts, but Andrew's requests now included expensive electronic equipment. Andrew found he could use those items to establish favor with girlfriends at the institution. Mom bought many presents for his "harem," as he called it. Electronics, food, and cigarettes made him "Big Man on Campus."

Andrew was confined in the mental health institution for a few years until the government decided to repurpose the facility. The institution, no longer used for adults, then housed juveniles. As part of the efforts to accomplish this transition, in September 2000, the court determined Andrew needed to be placed in a "less restrictive" setting. They attempted to move him to a half-way house, but his violent history and poor cooperation at the state hospital made that move impossible. No half-way house accepted him. With nowhere else for Andrew to go, my mother volunteered to oversee his medication and a place to live. He was free to live in the community, and yet his diagnosis continued to be, "chronic, paranoid schizophrenia." I read the doctor's statement. Andrew never showed remorse for the heinous crime he committed. Andrew was not the only patient released into unsuspecting communities. By court order, a multitude of mental patients were released during the decades that passed.

Note: A few months after my dad's murder, I saved an article from the Palm Beach Post Newspaper, knowing one day it would be important. According to the article dated July 30, 1989, by balancing the patients' medications and giving them enough mental clarity to stand trial, the patients could be declared "no longer a danger to society." They called it, "competency by drugs." I believe that is just what happened to Andrew. During his time at the Florida institution, evaluation after evaluation declared that Andrew needed to remain in the facility under involuntary placement.

Upon Andrew's release, it wasn't long until he quit taking his medication. He was supposed to receive ongoing counseling from a support agency, but Andrew's ugly sexual threats to the social worker abruptly ended the home visits. I asked about psychiatric counseling. Shouldn't he have undergone intensive outpatient follow-up? Andrew's doctor told me that the patients who were released from the mental hospital were not required to have psychiatric counseling; it was optional. I cannot tell you how sickened I was to think about all of those wasted years. Would Andrew have been helped and be all better by now had he received counseling? I don't know, but what I do know is that leaving it up to the mental health patient, especially one with a violent history, to determine if he wanted counseling or medication, is insane. From the 1989 Post Newspaper article, it was also noted, "Some patients will be a danger forever." Over twenty years later, Andrew's current doctor provided me with a report stating Andrew is an "uncontrolled schizophrenic." Andrew continues to be very dangerous.

But wait, you may say your child would never behave that way. You just have a little trouble with enabling. You know if you could fix everything one more time, things would be better. I pray your loved one does not fall into this "forever dangerous" category. But you must remember – Andrew did not start out that way. It was a combination of continually risky behavior, coupled with a mother who just had to fix things for her son, which led to great sorrow in my family.

So how did Mom feel when Andrew was released? Of course, Mom was glad to have him home. Her enabling was about to go into overdrive. Right away, Mom arranged for him to have a subsidized home. She borrowed five thousand dollars for the down payment, which took her years to pay off. To secure the subsidized home, physical labor was required as part of Andrew's investment in the house. Andrew and Mom decided they would work to clear the overgrown yard for their part of the investment. It was a great idea, but it didn't last long. It was too hot outside for Andrew to work in the yard, so his eighty year old mother did it for him.

Then it was time to furnish his home. With many trips to thrift stores, Mom quickly found furniture and decorated the entire house. His home was lovely. Andrew wanted for nothing. Mom, having an expensive water system on her house, bought one for Andrew as well. It wasn't long until Andrew dismantled much of it, leaving her with a useless collection of parts and thousands more in debt. Since the house and beautiful décor came so easily to Andrew, he did not really appreciate it. Oh, he said he loved the house, but words have always been easy for Andrew. Over the few years he has lived there, any remnants of decorating have been replaced by filthy stains on the furniture and carpets. A Halloween grim reaper shrieks out at anyone who dares to walk through his dimly lit living room. Trash and dirty clothes are strewn throughout his house, accompanied by stacks of dirty dishes, a multitude of empty beer cans and liquor bottles, and a stench that reeks of tobacco and marijuana. Any cleaning was done by Mom. She always said, "Men cannot be expected to do housework." How quickly she forgot Dad bought the groceries, cooked, washed the dishes, washed the clothes, and mowed the lawn. He also fixed anything and everything, including the cars.

Andrew's house was reflective of his mental state. His constant anger and verbal abuse made visits with Mom intolerable. She rarely visited with any other family members, to include her granddaughter and great grandchildren. Over time, Mom's visits to my house became less and less as her inability to trust Andrew increased. Every visit was cut short, with Mom having to hurry home. Andrew saw her absence as freedom and immediately headed for trouble, usually with the law. When that happened, she rushed to bail him out.

Chapter 2:
Fast Forward about Twenty Years.

Summer through the End of Year

Twice in one month, my mother was transported to the hospital. First event: She was very dizzy and feeling faint. She was not taking her medication, eating well, nor drinking enough water. To save money, she kept her household temperature at ninety degrees. A neighbor saw Mom in distress and called 911. The ambulance quickly responded, and within minutes, she arrived at the hospital. Doctors addressed the above mentioned factors, and released her within a couple of days. A few more days passed. Second event: A repeat of the first event, but this time, her stay in the hospital was a little more than a week. Sam and I hurriedly drove across the state, very concerned about her condition. When we arrived, we found her sitting up, cheerfully enjoying a visit with the nurses. They loved her. We were relieved to see she was not at death's door, but the doctor's did express concern about possible heart problems. From her two visits to the hospital, we learned she needed to take better care of herself. Upon her release, her doctors directed her to schedule follow-up visits with her own physicians.

After visiting Mom in the hospital, we spent the night at her house. Of course, our visit was unexpected. She did not have time to clean her house or prepare for our arrival. We were shocked with what we found. Mail, newspapers, and magazines were everywhere.

7

Papers covered every table surface and were stuffed into every nook and cranny. We visited Mom during the day, but between visits and in the evening, we sorted papers and washed a lot of laundry. For more than eight hours each day of our week-long stay, we diligently worked to clean her house and organize her papers. We threw out nine large, black yard bags filled with sweepstakes offers, old bills, flyers, advertisements, magazines, and donation requests from charities. At the end of the week, Mom remained in the hospital. The doctors wanted to observe her for a few more days. Since Sam and I had responsibilities at church on Sunday, we decided to return home. We gathered up and took home two very large boxes of papers still needing to be sorted. Bright and early Monday morning, we traveled back across state, retrieved Mom from the hospital, and drove her to her home.

Cleaning Mom's house was a real eye-opener. I learned she was spending money on sweepstakes when she didn't have money for food. She promised to quit sending them money, but she didn't. Sam and I drove over to Mom's every week, to help her get her bill paying straightened out. We worked a multitude of hours to get both Andrew's bills and her bills signed up for automatic payment. Mom and Andrew were present during the phone calls, giving permission for me to arrange each autopay. My husband set up a budget for Mom. We explained how much money she could have for spending, food, and all other basic essentials. We showed her how much she needed to pay her bills. She seemed to understand and agreed to work to make sure she and Andrew did not indulge in too much personal spending. Keep in mind, throughout my mother's working years she was in charge of Civilian Pay at an Air Force Base. She understood finance. She assured us she would go back to using her bill book to keep track of her bills and money. But she didn't.

The following week, Mom requested to meet with an attorney to confirm her Trust and Will were up to date. Mom wanted to make sure my Durable Power of Attorney was correct, in case the need ever arose. She selected a lawyer out of a phone book. At first, Mom and I met with the lawyer to work on the documents. When summer was over, I returned to my job teaching school. Mom and my husband continued to meet with the lawyer to complete the Durable Power of Attorney. Copies of the final documents were given to us for safekeeping.

With me in school, I was no longer available for weekday travel. Sam, however, was free for weekday visits with Mom. This made it possible for them to take care of any business or banking issues. He continued to visit Mom a couple of times a month. His visits seemed to be productive, with hopes of everything improving. Andrew was very clever. Each time my husband returned home, Andrew hovered over Mom's finances, actively attempting and succeeding in getting her money. We did not know how aggressively he was hitting her charge cards until later.

Sam's final visit to work on finances ended very abruptly. Andrew and Mom requested my husband drive them to a store located some distance away. Just as they got into the car, Andrew arrived with a very large tumbler filled with vodka and gin, which he proceeded to drink throughout the trip. For four long hours, Andrew ranted and raved about "his delusional fantasies" of working for the government in the CIA and declaring he invented the stealth bomber. Tiring of that, he dramatically proclaimed his belief system. He insisted his spiritual position was in the following hierarchal order: Baal, Andrew, Jehovah God, and Jesus. Finally, they returned to Mom's house. Since my husband and Mom planned to go to dinner, it was quite a surprise when Mom invited Andrew to join them. Sam, still reeling from the constant stream of insanity, hurried out of the car and into the house. Mom followed close behind him. When Sam questioned her about Andrew's delusional ranting and raving, Mom said she never heard any of it. Sam could not, and would not, take any more of Andrew's insanity at dinner. He drove three hours to arrive at our home. My husband did not return to assist with Mom's finances.

From this, I learned whenever Mom was stressed she escaped to her mental happy place. She did not hear what was happening around her. As I listened to Sam relay the events of that day, I remembered how Mom told me years ago, when she was a child, she was quite the daydreamer. I don't know if this current escape was daydreaming about being down on the old creek bank where she played as a child, or if she was just blanking out. But I do know that escaping from reality was easier than facing reality. She was totally unaware of what was going on around her. From experience, I knew Andrew was both a verbal and financial abuser. When he started on one of his tirades, she told me she did not hear it. I was concerned for her safety. And yet she remained resolute as she declared, "Everything is fine. I am not leaving my home."

Chapter 3:
Fast Forward to Spring.

It was four months since my husband gave up trying to rescue Mom's finances. He started a new job in February and focused on getting back to work. We were very thankful for his new position since very few people were finding jobs after being laid-off. Besides, Mom's bills were on autopay and everything seemed to be moving along – not perfect, but better.

During the intervening months, I called Mom every day. I could not reach her every day, but I diligently called and attempted to check how things were going. One day, I was having great difficulty reaching Mom on the phone. I was concerned for her health and safety. This went on for two more days. I called Andrew and asked him to walk across the street to Mom's house to see if she was OK. I asked him to call me back and let me know what he found out. He never called back. Finally, after phoning many times, I reached him. He told me that she was OK. Relieved, I then suspected it was a problem with the phone. For some unknown reason, Mom's phone started working again. Everything seemed to be OK until a day or so later when I could not reach Mom again. Again, I phoned Andrew and asked him to go over to Mom's house to check on her. He insisted he was too busy and hung up. Since I couldn't just jump in the car and drive three hours to find out what happened, I called the phone company. It turned out to be a problem with the phone. Ants were invading the phone box and nesting in the warmth of the wires. The phone company van arrived, and the phone was easily repaired.

So what kept Andrew from being able to walk across the street to check on Mom, for the second time this week? Andrew was a man of habit. He was usually very busy – very busy sitting, lying around, eating, and resting. I didn't ask him to check on Mom very often. It was a small request, but he was too tired and too busy. It just didn't sound like something he wanted to do. With Mom living three hours away from me, this created a frightening situation. What if Mom had fallen or was hurt? Andrew was satisfied with his response to my request. Mom did everything for him, but he couldn't walk across the street for her. Her constant enabling robbed him of any motivation to help someone in need. He wouldn't even help her – the one who did so much for him. Mom easily dismissed Andrew's behavior, as if everything was fine. And to both of them, it was fine. Andrew was focused on Andrew, just like Mom.

In May, my mother tearfully called and told me she was out of money. It was the 25th of the month. She just needed a little to get her to the end of the month. I immediately sent her some money. Now, keep in mind, Mom received retirement income from four sources. Living in moderation, she should have had sufficient funds. I found the emergency to be troubling, but it had only happened once, so I wasn't overly concerned.

In June, again my mother tearfully called and told me she was out of money. This time, it was the 22nd of the month. I told her she needed to go to the bank and take money out of her CD. At that point, she and I had a long discussion about money management. I suggested she save some of her regular income for the end of the month. This way, she would have enough to last until she received her next month's checks. She assured me everything was fine and was determined to manage her money more carefully in the future.

The following month, reality hit. My mother frantically called to tell me she was out of money and had no food in the house. It was the 15th of the month. Her finances were out of control. I instructed Mom to take money out of her CD and to buy some food. I let her know that I would drive over to her house as soon as possible, but due to other obligations, it would not be until the first of August.

When I arrived in August, the house was again littered with sweepstakes papers, old bills, donation requests, newspapers, advertisements, and magazines that arrived in the mail. In order to find her current bills and attempt to get everything in order, I started by throwing away anything I was sure was trash. Mom just sat there and watched me. I told her that because she let the papers pile up, she needed to help clean up. Together, we sorted the trash from the important papers. We opened every envelope. I found two hundred dollars in cash and checks that were on their way to the sweepstakes. She was thrilled. Now, she had money for food. We threw away nine tall, white kitchen bags full of papers. The money management strategies Sam and I attempted to put in place the year before were obviously ignored or forgotten. I determined I would have to get seriously involved to rescue her from her careless money management. I traveled to Mom's house every week, sometimes multiple times a week, for many months.

Now, you may picture us at the kitchen table cheerfully resolving all those paperwork issues that only accountants truly enjoy. But that wasn't the way it was. As soon as I started to organize her finances, Andrew appeared at Mom's front door demanding to be part of the process. Immediately, he plopped himself down at the table, pulled out a pack of cigarettes, and proceeded to smoke. I requested he put the cigarettes away. He ignored me and continued to chain smoke. I insisted he either put the cigarettes away or go home. He no longer ignored me, but ranted and raved in a constant stream of obscenities – making it impossible for us to work. Andrew continued railing obscenities at me for more than thirty minutes, declaring he would "get me." I called the police.

They arrived quickly. All of the officers in that county were well acquainted with Andrew. As the patrol car drove up to the house, Andrew stepped outside on the front lawn. The police accompanied Andrew to his house. The officers were able to deescalate the situation and finally visited with Mom and me before they left.

The police made it abundantly clear on that day, and on subsequent visits, verbal abuse is not a reason to make an arrest. Instead, the police recommended that Mom and I sit at a table in a restaurant to pay her bills and take care of her financial matters. That way, Andrew wouldn't be a problem. So we tried, but having to give personal information on a cell phone within earshot of other customers proved that paying bills in the restaurant just didn't work. On other occasions, we attempted to sit in the car to pay bills. It was exasperating. Each time, we worked more than four hours in the excessive Florida heat, surrounded by street noises and confusion. We used my cell phone to try to address and correct a multitude of financial problems Mom and Andrew created. This solution was obviously unbearable, but the bills had to be paid. We desperately needed to be able to work at Mom's house where we had a safe environment and all of the bill-paying information and supplies at hand.

I didn't have a moment of relief until the day Andrew was arrested for repeatedly calling and cussing out the 911 operators. He went to jail, and I was able to spend three full days helping Mom pay her bills and straighten out her finances in the comfort of her home. As soon as I left for my house, she immediately bailed him out, making it impossible for me to return.

How did I rescue Mom's finances?

If you or your family is entangled in out-of-control financial issues, you may need the following information:

Each time Mom and I met to rescue her finances, we prayed first. We prayed in the name of Jesus (John 14:14). Without God's faithfulness to reveal problems and provide solutions, we could not have secured her finances (Matthew 10:26). In retrospect, without God's intervention, at the rate she was going, she would have depleted her entire savings within ten months and still owed thousands in credit card debt. I thank God for His faithfulness to rescue and provide amazing answers and help (Philippians 4:19).

> "If you ask anything in My name, I will do it" (John 14:14, NKJ).

> "Therefore do not fear them. For there is nothing covered that will not be revealed, and hidden that will not be known (Matthew 10:26, NKJ).

> And my God shall supply all your need according to His riches in glory by Christ Jesus (Philippians 4:19, NKJ).

The steps to rescue Mom's finances:

1. I reviewed all of Mom's bills, making sure they were still on autopay. Insufficient funds at the time payment was due, cancelled the autopay. Some automatic payments had to be reestablished.

2. I reviewed Mom's bank accounts. I discovered Mom's daily withdrawal from the bank – for spending – was an average of one hundred dollars per day!

Andrew's constant demand for money, alcohol, and cigarettes was insatiable. When I visited Mom at her house, I experienced his tirades. He constantly called her, screaming for cigarettes and money. Every time we hung up, he called back again – Screaming! Screaming! Screaming! Mom never learned to read the Caller ID. She always answered the phone. The verbal abuse was horrific. This was not an isolated event. Since Mom always enabled Andrew to have money for all of his addictions, he knew if he just kept calling, she would eventually give in and give him whatever he wanted.

3. Something had to separate Andrew from Mom's money. He was bleeding her dry. With the help of the bank, we created the following plan. I placed my mom, with her permission, on a 3 account system:

a. Bill paying account – All regular bills were placed on autopay.

b. Intermediate Management Account – Monthly, the bank transferred $808 from the bill paying account into an account in my name. The bank made weekly transfers to her spending account. This made sure she had money every week. If I had left the $808 in her bill paying account, she would have confused spending money with bill paying money. She would have spent it all in a brief time. It worked. I only needed to add money in months where there was a fifth Saturday. I used money from the bill paying account to accommodate this extra pay date.

c. Spending account – This was the only account Mom was supposed to be able to access. $202 moved to her account every Saturday. She took $200 out for church, food, gas, etc. The essentials were to be bought before she drove home, to protect her food money from Andrew. Too many times, she went home first. He got the money.

d. The $2 accumulated in the spending account during the month and was used for bank fees. I also kept a ten dollar cushion in the account, but I did not tell Mom it was there.

4. Mom's income was directly deposited into her bill paying account at the beginning of each month. As soon as the money was in the account, I visited Mom and made sure the lawn service was paid. Any necessary items not covered by the food budget were also purchased.

5. Andrew was considered disabled; Mom was Andrew's Social Security Representative Payee. (Andrew received funding from my dad's Social Security. Ironic, isn't it?)

a. Mom requested that I show her how to set up a similar plan to control Andrew's spending money. He had a 2 account system. Since he did not have access to his bill paying account, money moved from his bill paying account to his spending account on the 5th and 20th of the month. It was a good plan, nice and organized.

b. Then there was the enabling issue. Mom did not require Andrew to pay basic living costs. His bill paying account covered his mortgage and phone. She paid for all of his food, snacks, alcohol, and cigarettes. She paid almost $300 per month for his electric bill, while her bill was $87 per month. Andrew kept his house at 60 degrees and then covered up with a heavy blanket. The electricity didn't cost him anything. This meant he received $200 spending money every month. Neighbors told me drug dealers and prostitutes frequented his house. When Andrew wanted to buy drugs, he ordered Mom to go home so he could "buy weed." Mom denied knowledge of any wrong doing on Andrew's part. When told or reminded this was happening, she was always shocked. She couldn't stop him. She enabled him to have excessive spending money, but had no idea what he spent it on. She always said it was his money. I believe she was afraid of him and what he might do, if he didn't have spending money. Only once have I ever heard her say she was afraid of him, but that soon faded from her memory.

c. I couldn't figure out how my Mom had so many cash advances on her credit card statement. I discovered that every time my mom overdrew at the bank, the bank's overdraft protection moved the overdraft amount to her credit card. This greatly increased her credit card debt. When I received each online statement declaring an overdraft, I sent Mom to the bank, directing her to move money to cover the account. She tried to do just that, but when she told the teller, the teller looked at the account and saw there was still money in the account. The overdraft "fixed the problem." This left Mom thousands of dollars in debt. With the bank's help, I stopped the overdrafts on all accounts. When there were insufficient funds in the future, the check would be returned to the company, unpaid. I worked very hard to ensure sufficient funds were always available for all regular transactions.

d. With her permission, I took all of Mom's checks and credit cards into my possession. They would now be used responsibly for bill paying, emergencies, and serious needs. When the credit cards were in her possession, she let Andrew use them. She frequently drove Andrew to town for shopping trips. He also used credit cards to purchase items advertised in magazines and catalogues. She shared with me that she enabled his lavish shopping sprees because she felt he did not have much of a life. She was trying to make up for the fact he did not have a family or a job. Due to his excessive spending, she owed more than she had in the bank. I also consolidated Mom's credit cards to eliminate multiple late fees that were occurring on a regular basis. Placing the bills on autopay eliminated the possibility of late payments. Every month we paid extra until all credit cards were paid in full.

e. Andrew was very angry with me for removing Mom's credit cards. He no longer possessed cards of his own. Andrew had already experienced one judgment against him for not paying his credit card bills. Once I took control of Mom's finances, every time I found that Andrew charged without permission, I filed a legal complaint with the credit card company.

f. In the midst of the big sister takeover, Andrew charged an array of TV and satellite equipment. He also ordered a large TV package which included many pornography channels. Of course, Andrew was not paying for this. All services were stopped. Mom was not going to be paying for pornography.

g. In the fall, Andrew knew he was going to court. The week prior to the court date, Andrew charged $400 worth of electronics. (Andrew had a history of excessive charges when he knew he was going to court/jail, thus leaving the bills for Mom.) My mother told me she stood next to him in the store while he charged the equipment, but declared later she did not want him to charge the items. This time, when Andrew went to jail, Mom and I took the unopened electronics back to the store and closed the account.

h. When I thought I had all of the credit cards under my control, I discovered many businesses retained Mom's credit cards on "file." Stores could easily resurrect those accounts for new charges. I closed every account as soon as I was aware of its existence. The remaining credit charges were part of the credit card consolidation.

6. Mom's mail was redirected to my house. Let me explain why this was necessary. After we threw away the last nine trash bags of garbage mail, I gave Mom a fancy container and instructed her to place all of her bills in it. This way, when I came to visit, I could easily pay her bills and organize her papers. I arrived the following month to find: There were no bills – anywhere! I asked Mom where the bills were. She said she did not get any bills that month. No bills? She threw them all away! That is when we changed the mail delivery to my address. Initially, I requested a temporary change of address. I learned I should have skipped the temporary change and just applied for a permanent change of address. This situation would not be improving. One by one, I completed a change of address for all of her bills. Since many of them required Mom to be present to execute the change, it turned out to be a very long process.

7. Mom and Andrew liked to enter sweepstakes. Mom continued to send money to the sweepstakes scam artists, even when she did not have money for food. She admitted to sending a gold chain. And when she didn't have money or gold to send, she pawned a $2000 keyboard for $100 to enter the next phase of the contest. She was sure she would win – this time.

One group of scam artists was from Jamaica. They called Mom every fifteen minutes throughout the day. This went on for months before she told me about the calls. The constant ringing of the phone tormented her. And yet when she answered, she believed everything they said to her. One day, I arrived at her house to find her dressed up and waiting in the front yard. She said Mr. Brown, from the sweepstakes company, told her he was bringing her a new car. He directed her to dress up and be ready for pictures. Neither the car nor Mr. Brown arrived that day. The next day, he called and apologized that the car delivery was postponed for two days. He encouraged her, "But be ready and dressed for the next visit."

Andrew's phone record showed that he phoned the Jamaican scam group often. I never knew his full involvement with the scam artists, but one day, something very revealing happened. When I arrived at Mom's house, she was on the phone. Excitedly she announced, "It's Mr. Brown, with the sweepstakes money!" I picked up the phone – surprise! It was her son, Andrew, attempting to get money. She refused to believe Andrew would do such a thing, but he did. And it was confirmed by Caller I.D.

Mom ordered expensive magazines to learn about more sweepstakes. I found many envelopes with cash or checks ready to be mailed. It is no wonder that I started having Mom's mail sent to my house. As per my agreement with Mom, the sweepstakes mail went straight to the trash. I eliminated the temptation. I also stopped the Jamaican scam artists from calling her. I worked with the phone company to get her number changed and unlisted.

8. Andrew also believed he would be a sweepstakes winner. Frequently, he convinced Mom to take him to a local drugstore to buy prepaid money cards. Mom loaded hundreds of dollars on the gift cards to send to enter the sweepstakes. How do I know? Sometime later, when Mom and I visited the drugstore, the clerk came out to the car and informed me about the frequent purchases. She also told me that Andrew verbally abused Mom in the store on a regular basis. His demands were ugly and loud. The store workers were very concerned about her safety. Without hesitating, I declared, "Next time, call the police." And they did.

Chapter 4:
The Perfect Storm

How did I feel about all this craziness? My life was dramatically changed. I spent a lot of time on the road to Mom's house, trying to resolve a multitude of problems. Neither Mom nor Andrew provided me with much information. Many times, I asked God to reveal to me what was going on in their lives. And I can tell you, He did. There were so many factors that I would have had no knowledge of, but God faithfully placed just the right person with the right information in my path. I thank God for those revelations, His wisdom, and the diligence to see each challenge through to completion.

You wanted to know how I felt. The movie, The Perfect Storm, comes to mind. I felt like I was in the center of two raging storms, converging toward me as I attempted to sail my boat between them. I focused on trusting God and doing what was right for all involved, while maintaining a course of safety.

When I began to write this narrative from the notes in my journal, I searched for fictitious names to protect the identity of the real people involved. I asked God for names, and He made it clear. I glanced down at the newspaper sitting in my lap and noticed an article about Florida hurricanes. Two storms that wreaked havoc in Florida were Hurricane Andrew and Hurricane Frances. With this information, the symbolism should be obvious. Through the years,

Andrew and Frances formed a super-hurricane called Enabling. Their ongoing turbulence collided with Alzheimer's disease, which left Frances vulnerable to total destruction. I thank God for sending me on a rescue mission only He could make successful. I thank God for His amazing presence and faithful provision in my life as He confirmed, once again, the Anchor still holds!

> [Now] we have this [hope] as a sure and steadfast anchor of the soul – it cannot slip and it cannot break down under whoever steps out upon it – [a hope] that reaches farther and enters into [the very certainty of the Presence] within the veil, (Hebrews 6:19, Amp.).

Chapter 5:
Andrew and Frances

What else do you need to know about Andrew and Frances? Frances was a Christian who loved God and her family. She had a good sense of humor that is still very active today. She had a practical side, but memory issues interfered with her ability to do what she knew was right. She liked to shop and get bargains, paint pictures, arrange flowers, do arts and crafts, sing, dance, play the piano, travel, and chat with people. Mom told me she desperately wanted to live in her own house, but she was extremely lonely. She interacted with neighbors, but not frequently. She told me Andrew did not talk to her; mostly, he slept. When he did talk to her, it was to get something he wanted – money. Since she was very lonely, I took Mom to visit the senior center in her home town. She had a great time and signed up for a membership. However, when I asked later if she visited the senior center on her own, she said that she didn't want to go there.

My mother valued honesty. One spring day, Mom and I went to lunch. It was one of my weekly visits. I asked Mom if she would like to pray. She very nicely thanked God for the food, but then she said, "And forgive us for our sins, but I know I didn't commit any." She completed the prayer. I decided not to say anything until a more opportune time. I wanted to enjoy lunch with Mom, and there was no point in disturbing the peaceful moment. Later, while we were driving to complete one of her many errands, I asked her if she knew lying was wrong. She acknowledged that she did, but insisted, "I don't lie. I am a Christian." I reminded her, on many occasions that she told me one thing and the police something different. That was a lie. She needed to tell the truth.

I believe Mom learned to lie as a defense mechanism to protect Andrew. Years of simple lies in his defense became a habit of lying that was very difficult to break. She still complained to me about the atrocities of her son, but then told the police everything was fine. Then again, she may have found that lying about Andrew protected her from him. Whatever the case, I needed Mom to be honest with me and the police. I talked to her, and she seemed to listen until the obsessive compulsive behavior that declared she must protect her son at all costs intervened. She lamented the fact that Andrew "had a bad life." Who would help him when she died? So, she determined not to die. At this point, what I observed as increasing dementia indicated she was losing ground, even if she was still physically alive.

Frances never liked to read. Now, in her desperate need to know and understand, reading dominated her attention. Each time I placed a written document in front of her, she appeared to read it, but was simply pronouncing the words without comprehension. When asked about what she read, she did not have a clue. And yet she read it over and over again, ignoring anyone trying to talk to her. If I wanted her attention, I had to withhold the reading material until I was through telling her everything she needed to know.

Neither Andrew nor Frances took their medicine. This had been going on for decades. Every day, I called and reminded Mom to take her meds, but she didn't always get the job done. Sometimes she insisted that she had taken them, and then I found out later, she hadn't. What about Andrew? He refused to take his meds.

Mom allowed lots of food to accumulate in the refrigerator and then smelled the food to see if it was still fresh. When I warned her that the sandwiches were almost two weeks old, she still wanted to smell them. I threw the sandwiches away. Many seniors allow food to accumulate in their refrigerators. They don't like to waste food. Although this is not uncommon, we know it is not normal or safe.

Mom was having difficulty solving even simple issues and problems. At Thanksgiving dinner, she repeatedly asked me if there was anything she could do to help. Since she no longer cooked, I wanted her to feel useful and a part of the dinner preparation. I looked for something simple, yet important for her to do. I asked her to set the table. Placemats were already on the table, and we were only setting the table with two pieces of flatware – a fork and a knife. Stressed and confused, she could not figure out where to place the napkins and the flatware. Finally, we all worked together to complete the setting of our table. We were thankful she was with us.

Mom could not use her debit card or set her security alarm system. She could not remember the code, even though it was the same code she always used. When the bank insisted she use a debit card, I knew she was not going to be successful. I asked her to demonstrate to the customer service representative her ability to remember the code. "Tell me your birthday," I prompted. (That was the code.) After a full ten minutes of hints and repeatedly telling her the answer, she still could not repeat it. She gave up using the debit card and went to the teller for all banking transactions. The alarm system, from day one of installation, remained unused.

Let's talk about Andrew. As a youth, Andrew had a very difficult time making friends. His elementary school called Mom many times to discuss Andrew's out of control behavior. Things would settle down, but not for long. He displayed an interest in music and mechanics. Andrew was never required to complete anything. Through the years he totally dismantled a Fiat Spyder sports car, a Datsun, a Rambler Javelin, a Kawasaki Motorcycle, and now, his older model Jaguar – all purchased by our parents. Andrew always said he was going to make his vehicles the "fastest and most efficient on the planet." But in a very short time, all of his automobiles and his motorcycle lay in pieces, never to be assembled again. He coerced Mom and Dad into funding expensive, top of the line, parts which also littered the garage. He was smart, but a multitude of LSD trips in his teens destroyed any possibility of a productive life. Mom kept it very simple as she responded to all of his destructive behaviors by saying, "He has problems." And of course, with any issue, it was Mom to the rescue. Sadly, at my wedding reception, Dad announced that they were through having to parent kids. Andrew was thirteen years old and ready for freedom; freedom that eventually destroyed him.

Andrew was a financial predator, and Frances was obsessed with taking care of him. He did nothing for himself, except get into trouble. She revealed to me years ago that she liked doing everything for him. It gave her life purpose; it destroyed Andrew. At fifty-seven years old, he still called her Mommy.

My mom viewed my relationship issues with Andrew as brother and sister rivalry. She was wrong. She tried to fix all confrontations between us, stating that she loved us both the same. I heard that phrase all of my life, but the more I labored to help her, and the more I was aware of Andrew's verbal abuse and even stealing her food money, I just couldn't take it any longer. I let Mom know it did not give me any comfort to hear she loved us both the same. She was surprised and reiterated, "But I do love you both just the same." After all the months I tried to help her, and the multitude of times Andrew was verbally and financially abusive to her, I did not want to hear that statement again. I asked her how she would feel if her brother treated her mother the way Andrew treated her. She appeared very upset with the idea. I told her I was upset, too. Did that resolve anything? Not too much, but she did quit telling me she loved us both the same.

On one occasion, she did have Andrew Baker Acted. (The Baker Act allows for involuntary examination and confinement of a person who may do harm to self or others.) His response to Mom was, "I'm going to burn your house down!" Since I had no doubt he was totally capable of fulfilling his threat, I no longer felt safe spending the night at Mom's house. There were no hotels or motels nearby; therefore, every trip became a day trip requiring six hours of driving plus all the banking, bill paying, doctors' visits, and grocery shopping we needed to accomplish. It was exhausting, but God consistently gave me the strength and mental alertness to make those drives and finish each week's long list of necessary errands, appointments, and paperwork. Andrew's behavior and attitudes, combined with Mom's enabling, made family time together almost nonexistent. How destructive. How sad.

Andrew's verbal abuse was constant. When asked if she was afraid of him, she always said, "No." I believe the truth was – she was afraid to say, "Yes." Neighbors notified me that Andrew frequently yelled at her in the front yard. She just stood there and took it while visibly trembling from the verbal blast. One day when she and Andrew were in the bank, an Elder Abuse Investigator observed Andrew's verbal abuse of Mom. Andrew demanded that Mom either get more credit cards or change banks. When the bank alerted me about the incident, they gave me the officer's phone number. I was ecstatic! I had a witness, and I would finally get help! I called the officer multiple times. I left messages – with no return call. The bank even placed a call for me and requested he call me. Still, no return call.

Andrew loved to watch the news on TV, even though much of it made him very angry. I was told by the police that the FBI visited Andrew's house when he threatened to kill the President. He was sent to a south Florida mental health facility where they actually put him in charge of teaching a class! He was allowed to teach job skills to other patients. Andrew never worked! This only served to feed his delusional state. Why did they let him teach a class? I can only guess. Andrew probably informed them about his "fantasy" work history with the CIA. For more than ten years, Andrew insisted he was in the CIA, and the government owed him millions of dollars for designing the stealth bomber. He called both the government and police several times requesting assistance with his monetary claim. I personally heard Andrew declare this tale many times. Several police officers also confirmed that Andrew shared the same story with them on multiple occasions.

Andrew also loved the telephone. Mom informed me that Andrew received a letter from a national news channel requesting he quit calling. He logged over 6,000 calls to this channel, trying to tell them what to do. When I next saw Andrew, I asked him if he quit calling the news channel. He said, "No," and smiled.

Andrew made multiple 911 calls because he was angry. His phone was not working. The police warned him to stop, or he would go to jail. Obviously, 911 is not responsible for phone repairs. The next day, Andrew was arrested for continuing to jam the 911 phone lines. The officer told me that Andrew repeatedly used profanity with the 911 workers. He was also arrested for not showing up in court for this offense.

Chapter 6:
Peace in the Midst of the Storm

By this time, there were so many problems going on with Andrew and Mom that I started having physical problems, trying to cope with the ever escalating "storms." With the weekly trips and the constant stress, I found myself suffering severe pain in my shoulders and neck. I made an appointment with my chiropractor, who I rarely see, and began some serious massage therapy. It was either get help, or I needed to stop driving. When I attempted to change lanes, make turns, or back the car up, turning my head was excruciating. The sharp pain sent me into instant tears. Months of massage therapy helped immensely. The therapist told me she prayed every day that her hands would be healing hands.

For many months, my stress level was more than I could handle. I felt like I had to keep so much information ever present in my mind. When I finally found someone who could help my family, I wanted to be ready to share the information they needed to hear. It was during this time, God impressed me to keep a journal. The journal gave me almost instant relief. I no longer needed to keep this craziness at the forefront of my mind, but would have a well-documented reference when the time was right.

April through September

From this point on, I will be writing from unfolding events. There will, however, continue to be reflections and information from past history, when needed.

Chapter 7:

April, Safe Harbor was Not Enough.

In April, Andrew was arrested for disturbing the peace at Mom's church. After that incident, Andrew was not allowed to return. Mom's pastor later informed me that in all of his years in ministry, he had never before made such a decision. Andrew went to jail for a few weeks, so Mom agreed to come and stay with me.

While at my house, I was determined to get Mom back on her medication. I set her medicine bottles on the table and reminded her to take her medicine. She needed one pill from each of three bottles. (We already tried pill organizers, and they didn't work.) She walked over to the bottles and handled them for some time. I thought she had taken her pills. About an hour later she told she needed to take her meds. I reminded her she had already taken them. We discussed this for about an hour. Finally, I recommended that since she had not taken her meds for months, waiting one more day wouldn't hurt. I didn't want her to harm herself. She remained quiet until lunch. As we sat down to eat, she emphatically declared, "I'll have you know I am going to take my medicine after lunch." After a morning of arguing with her about meds, I looked at her and replied, "Well, you do just that." She looked at me and did not take her medicine until the next day. I don't remember Mom as stubborn, but as the

31

Alzheimer's has progressed, I have seen a determination in her to prove she is managing her life just fine. That stubborn attitude could be very harmful.

When she came to my house, she brought a suitcase full of clothes. She told me she didn't have to pack. They were the same clothes she brought the last time she stayed with me. I remembered how she refused to wash them before she left to go home. So, when she arrived at my house, I suggested that we wash her clothes. She became very upset. I explained that her clothes were dirty. She was quick to argue, telling me that she would smell them to see if they were dirty. I let her know that I had already smelled them, and they were indeed dirty. As she continued to disagree, I simply picked up her clothes and placed them in the washer. Even though Mom didn't wash her own laundry very often, she had been taking care of Andrew's laundry for years; she left hers mostly undone. Andrew owned his own washer and dryer; he even knew how to use them. But with Mom taking care of his every need, she was forgetting to take care of even the basics for herself. By now, Andrew just expected it to happen. He had no reason to take responsibility for his basic living needs. It was the way it had always been.

During the month of April, Mom lost her wallet two different times. The first time, she immediately went to the Department of Motor Vehicles to try to find out what to do about her lost driver's license. That would have been fine, but she panicked and visited the DMV office seven times in two days, desperate and confused. (I had already noticed Mom's problem solving ability had greatly diminished in the last few months.) The DMV checked her contact list and called me. They wanted her to take a test to determine her ability to continue driving. I agreed it would be a good idea. I had been concerned about her ability to drive for some time. Had I insisted she take the driving test, she would have been upset with me. It would have been my fault if she failed. This way, because she lost her wallet and acted erratically at the DMV, I could let the DMV take the blame for this one.

To show Mom I supported her and wanted her to be successful, I took her to get a driver's study book. We discussed how important it was for her to study. While I was cooking dinner, she studied for a few minutes and then declared that she was tired. I encouraged her to try to study just a little bit more. She studied for an additional ten minutes and insisted that she had been studying for at least an hour. She was too exhausted to continue. She never studied again. On my next visit to Mom's, I found her wallet in her garage. It was sitting on top of a cardboard box, two feet from where she always parked her car. The wallet was in plain sight. She must have walked past it for days as she got in and out of her car. She did learn from this experience. She removed most of her ID cards from her wallet and placed them in her change purse. I also made copies of her important papers and placed them in my file for safekeeping. One week later, Mom lost her wallet again. I suggested a few places for her to look. She became aggravated with my suggestion; even though she admitted she had not checked those places. When I arrived at her house, I searched for her wallet and could not find it. She never found it.

When Mom stayed with me, she ate well and even gained some weight, which she really needed. However, as soon as Andrew was released from jail, nothing could keep her from him. At my house, she was safe and had people to talk to. She didn't think about the chaos and confusion awaiting her at home. No, the safe harbor of my home was not enough.

Chapter 8: May
The Storms Intensify.

During the first week of May, Andrew's friend, Jeanne, called. She cried that her boyfriend had beaten her up. She wanted Andrew to send her money so she could come to Florida. (FYI – When Jeanne visited in the past, she always stole from Andrew and then hopped on a bus to head home to Georgia. Jeanne was never Andrew's girlfriend. He met Jeanne through her former boyfriend.) Jeanne's phone call gave Andrew ideas. He considered this a prime opportunity to "get a woman." Since my mom always wondered who would take care of Andrew after she died, this may have sounded reasonable to her. She wasn't thinking about the fact that Andrew did not have enough income to feed, let alone support, a wife. And what if there were kids from this joyous union? I shudder to think of the possibilities.

Immediately, Andrew insisted that he and Mom take a trip to Georgia. Mom did not want to travel. A neighbor observed Mom to be visibly shaking as Andrew forcibly convinced her to go with him to rescue Jeanne. Mom's car had a full tank of gas, and Andrew had twenty-five dollars in his pocket. On a Friday in May, they drove north. They took no change of clothes, food, or anything else they might need. I had no clue any of this was happening. I became suspicious when it had been hours since I talked with Mom on the phone. Concerned, I phoned some of her neighbors. They filled me in on the details. Andrew and Frances were headed for Georgia.

Twice Andrew and Mom called looking for money. The first time was from a store in Rome, Georgia. I sent one hundred dollars, enough to get them back home. When I spoke with Andrew on the phone, I reminded him not to bring Jeanne home with him because he would lose his house. (Andrew's home was subsidized by the government. If an additional person moved in to live with Andrew, his mortgage holder required a substantial increase in the monthly payments. This was something Andrew could not afford.) A store clerk overheard Andrew as he angrily threatened me, "I'm going to come over there and kill you!" I later asked Mom about the threat. She said she never heard it. When Andrew talked on the phone, she didn't listen because it was Andrew's business. However, this time, it was her business, too. They were stranded with no money. Mom was the responsible adult, and now she did as she always had done: She gave in to whatever Andrew wanted.

The second day Andrew and Mom called, I sent another hundred dollars to a store in Ashburn, Georgia. I didn't speak to Andrew this time. I sent the money because I wanted my mother to be safe and come home. Instead, they continued on their way to rescue Jeanne in northern Georgia. When they reached her house, all of his expectations came to an abrupt halt. Jeanne screamed at Andrew and demanded he leave. She slammed the door.

Rejected, Andrew and Mom headed toward home in Florida. The Tifton police arrested him for speeding and driving without a license. Mom revealed that he was also swerving in and out between the cars. (Andrew's driving history: Andrew received many speeding tickets and caused many accidents throughout the years. He did not have a valid Florida driver's license, and was told by the DMV that he needed a mental exam to prove his ability to drive. Without passing the exam, the state of Florida would not issue him a driver's license.)

The Tifton police officer called and informed me that Andrew would be in jail for sixty days. However, the time could be reduced to thirty days if Andrew would do hard labor. Andrew was in jail about two days when the judge released him. The officer advised me that Georgia was not going to pay for Andrew's serious mental issues. Andrew and Andrew's problems belonged to Florida. The officer drove him forty-five miles south and left him there.

I called to make bus arrangements for Andrew's return to Florida. The arrangements turned out to be very complicated. It took him almost a week to finally arrive home. Did Andrew thank my husband or me? No. He was angry because he had to walk a mile to pick up the tickets. He then shouted, "I hate you!" and hung up the phone. I charged the travel costs on my credit card to get him home. Total cost for the trip was nine hundred dollars. My mother reimbursed me for the expenses. If she hadn't, I would have been enabling them both.

When Andrew was locked up in the Georgia jail, a kind police officer directed Mom to a nearby motel where she could spend the night. He gave her clear printed directions to make sure she arrived at home. "Drive south, straight down the Interstate," he instructed her. The next morning, she mistakenly headed west instead of south. She traveled about one hundred miles when a police officer from another county called to tell us that he found her driving the wrong direction on a one-way street. She was lost and confused. The officer arranged for Mom to spend the night with his sister; his sister was a nurse. She needed to be at work by nine the next morning. Sam did not arrive home from work until 11:00 p.m. We then woke up at 2 a.m. and drove a total of fifteen hours to retrieve my mom and her car, transport her to her home, and return my husband back to our house – ready for work the next morning. When we arrived at the nurse's house, Mom was entertaining the officer's sister by playing the piano and singing. She was happy to see us and promised she would never run off like that again.

That promise was short lived. Two days later, we called the police and requested a Silver Alert for Mom. She disclosed to her neighbors that she was heading for Georgia to get Andrew. Mom, of course, had no idea where Andrew was in Georgia. At least, she took money and food with her this time. She drove to northern Florida before she realized she did not know how to find Andrew. She had no idea where he was. Mom drove hundreds of miles back to her hometown and stopped at the police station. I believe she may have seen the Silver Alert on an overhead Interstate sign. When she spoke with the police, she insisted that Andrew had been in the car with her. She didn't know where he was. She was sure he disappeared. Mom was very confused. Her neighbors made sure she arrived safely home. They phoned me, and then I spoke with Mom. After a long discussion, once more, she promised she would never run off like that again.

A couple of days later, I called Mom early in the morning, like I do every morning. She was not home. I called again a little later, and she told me that she drove to the store to buy a map of north Florida and Georgia. Busted! Thankfully she didn't try to go again. From beginning to end, the multiple trips for Frances and Andrew extended over three weeks.

Why didn't I leave Andrew in Georgia to fend for himself? Mom's compulsive behavior, ever focused on fixing things for Andrew, meant she would not end her frantic pursuit until he was safe at home.

Chapter 9: June

Gale Force Winds

AKA: Mom's Money, Gone with the Wind

Andrew had taken money out of Mom's purse for years. Every time, she told me that all he left her was change. A day later, he took the change. Since I have been managing her finances, I instructed Mom to withdraw her money from the bank on Saturday, set aside her tithe for church, get gas for the car, and buy groceries before she went home. At least she would have the basics bought for the week – if she followed the plan. This time, Andrew went to the bank with her. During the first week of June, Andrew stole a total of $450 from Mom.

Saturday - Andrew asked Mom to drive him to the bank. When she received her money from the teller, she placed it into an envelope and slid it into her purse, as she always did. In the car, she placed her purse on the floor on the passenger's side, as she always did. By the time Mom and Andrew reached Walmart, the envelope and the money were gone. HE STOLE HER FOOD MONEY! She had just received her weekly spending money, and he took it all – before she could buy food. I was outraged! She tried to console me by saying she still had plenty of food at home.

I asked her who she thought took the money. She didn't know. Mom insisted that she didn't see Andrew take it. There were only two of them in the car. I asked her if she took it, and of course, she told me she didn't. So, that only left Andrew. She didn't want to believe Andrew was the thief.

When they arrived at Walmart, she went in and bought a six-pack of Ensure. I asked her where she got the money to buy the Ensure. She said she found a few dollars in her change purse. The envelope with two hundred dollars was still missing. She did tell me that Andrew drank one of her bottles of Ensure. I wanted to race right over and pursue the mystery, but I was out of town and unable to return until Tuesday afternoon. At least, she had food.

Tuesday - I drove to Mom's house and arranged for her to have an additional one hundred dollars. Since she frequently used a sandwich card at a local restaurant, I added one hundred-fifty dollars to her sandwich card. I also bought her 3 six-packs of Ensure. She was half-way through the week, and it was only a few days until she could go to the bank and withdraw her next two hundred dollars.

Thursday - Andrew asked her to drive him to the grocery store. He filled a cart with junk food and drinks. When they walked to the register to pay, he ran out of money and verbally abused Mom until she gave him the one hundred dollars I had just given her. The grocery store manager demanded that Andrew never to return to his store again.

Friday - How could it get worse? Andrew insisted that Mom drive him to the bank. He wanted to get twenty-five dollars out of his account. (FYI – For months, every time Andrew went into the bank, he verbally abused my mother and the tellers. He even threw things at the tellers – as disclosed to me by the bank manager. To avoid Andrew's traumatizing behavior inside the bank, the bank manager directed Andrew to get his money outside at the ATM.) This day, not only did Andrew get his twenty-five dollars from the ATM, he went into the bank and demanded money from my mother, leaving her in tears. The teller took the money from Mom's bill paying account. (Not good.) I was not there, but as Mom told me, "Andrew took the money and declared he was going to buy weed with it." I was very concerned. Now, he knew how to get into Mom's bill paying account. Just stand there and demand it. There would be no stopping him!

Why didn't we contact the police? We did. My mother went to the police station on Saturday, when the first theft took place. As she started to report the incident, the officers immediately asked if she wanted him home or in jail. She said, "Home." To me, this was an inappropriate question. When I arrived on Tuesday, I took Mom back to the police department, where the officers insisted that the question was appropriate. If Mom wouldn't file a police report, they could do nothing. They also described how jail would not provide help. And for Mom, that was all she wanted – help for her boy.

Reluctantly, since there was no safe place for me to spend the night, I returned home. There was nothing to stop Andrew from stealing from Mom. After the two incidents on Thursday and Friday, I called the police and was directed to call the Economics Investigator. Surprise! The officer who previously was the Elder Abuse Investigator was transferred to the Economics Department. Though in a new job, he was consistent. I called and left a message. Again, I received no return call.

I then called the police station and relayed what happened. They wanted to know if she would file a report. I assured them she was very upset, and I believed she would file the report this time. They said that they would send an officer to her house to do a wellness check. The officer called me, and we talked for a very long time. He had personally been dealing with Andrew for ten years and knew him very well. I told him that I believed Mom would file the police report. She was very upset. I asked him to let me know, after he spoke with her, if she did indeed file the report. He agreed. When the officer arrived, Mom was standing at Andrew's front door. He asked Mom if Andrew took any money from her. She said, "None that I didn't want him to have." No police report was filed that day. When I questioned my mother about her response, she denied ever making the statement. I couldn't protect her from Andrew. I needed help.

The next day, the driving issue reappeared. The DMV required she take a test to prove she was still able to drive. Mom thought she could just ignore the requirement, and it would go away. But it didn't. We finally received the paperwork from the DMV. There was a medical requirement before she could take the test. Since I knew I would not be able to be present for her actual appointment, I made a point of driving to Mom's house, taking her to her doctor's office, making the appointment, and having the office staff place the paperwork in her file to prevent it from being lost. Everything was in place for Mom's appointment the following Friday.

When Mom arrived at the doctor's office, the physician's assistant called me. She informed me that Mom had no idea why she was there. I assured the assistant that I called Mom daily, and for a full week, we talked about her upcoming doctor's appointment. No, Mom didn't remember why she was there, but at least she was present for her appointment.

During the office visit, the doctor filled out part of the DMV form, but refused to sign it until Mom attended a special Driver's Clinic for seniors who are in danger of losing driving privileges. Problem: The DMV gave Mom forty-five days to complete the test. With this new requirement, she would not be able to complete the medical requirement and the driving test in the time stated. The doctor returned the paperwork to Mom, and Mom promptly lost it. I called and asked the DMV what to do. They instructed me not to intervene. It was Mom's responsibility. I did not intervene.

What other challenges occurred in June? Within the week, Mom's dishwasher started gushing water all over the kitchen floor.

The house was only three years old, but things were already wearing out. Mom no longer had the where-with-all to call a repair person. I called a plumber, and thank God, the plumber happened to attend her church. He explained that her dishwasher needed to be replaced. Since his company did not sell dishwashers, we needed to go to a store and buy one. The store would provide workers to correctly install her new appliance. In the meantime, I told Mom to wash dishes by hand until we could purchase a new dishwasher. That was no problem. She had been stacking up her dishes for a long time; she just continued to do so.

On my next trip over to Mom's, we purchased a dishwasher. I called and scheduled the installation. I instructed Mom to write the date on her calendar, and I reminded her daily about the upcoming appointment. The morning the installers were scheduled to arrive, I phoned Mom. No response. After multiple attempts, about ten in the morning, I finally reached her. She was at Andrew's house fixing coffee for him. She forgot about the dishwasher. I insisted, "Stay Home!" I called Mom again when I found out the delivery was scheduled between 10:30 a.m. and 2:30 p.m. That day, they partially installed the dishwasher. Additional plumbers had to be scheduled, so we hoped for completion the next day.

The same day, Mom locked herself out of her house. She had no idea why her purse was in the house. Her front door couldn't be locked without a key. Her garage had a number pad, and she rarely locked the inside door. She knew how to use the garage door opener. Apparently, that day she locked the inside door. Thankfully, a neighbor was able to help her get back into her house.

The next day, I phoned Mom. She said she would stay in the house and wait for the second plumber. Again, when the plumber called, she was at Andrew's house making coffee for him. Andrew did nothing for himself. Mom almost missed the plumber. I phoned again later to find out if the installation was successful. No answer. It took three days to find out the installation was complete, and the dishwasher was working.

It was Saturday again. I reminded her not to take Andrew to the bank. She didn't know why he couldn't go with her. I reminded her that he stole her food money two weeks prior. No longer having free use of her total income for spending, Andrew was still demanding money from her. She had a new strategy; she spent very little on groceries so she had money to bring home to him. I tried to arrange for Meals-on-Wheels, but as long as she could drive, I could not trust she would be home when the meals arrived. Every month, I put a substantial amount of money on her sandwich card to pay for submarine sandwiches. At least she had food.

In the middle of June, Andrew renewed his determination to get Jeanne to come to Florida to live with him. Here we go again. He was back to the idea that cost Mom nine hundred dollars and my family much grief. Mom, concerned about Andrew's plan, repeatedly insisted that she would not leave Florida again. Andrew, however, could be very assertive. He knew how forgetful she was and purposefully used her forgetfulness as a weapon against her. Thankfully, for some reason, this trip did not take place.

A couple of days later, Mom drove Andrew to the drugstore. He wanted soft drinks. When she pulled out a twenty dollar bill and placed it on the counter, he grabbed another twenty from her wallet and refused to give it to back to her. The cashier at the drugstore witnessed the theft. Mom was very angry and drove straight to the police station. It was late in the day, and the station was closed. She returned home. A neighbor called and let me know two police cars arrived near Mom's house at 6:30 p.m. Although I did not get all of the details of the visit, I did learn some information from the neighbor. When the police tried to leave, she followed them down the street on foot. She hurried past three houses to tell the officers again – Andrew stole her money. The officers had heard it all before and did not take her seriously. Later, Mom explained to me that the police officer said there was nothing they could do because she gave the money to Andrew. She did give the first twenty to him, but not the second. She was very angry and upset. She assured the police she wanted Andrew to go to jail. Andrew told the police she gave him the entire forty dollars. He lied. The police were satisfied with Andrew's answer.

Over the last few months, I have spoken with many officers who visited Andrew's house on a regular basis. They did not take my mother seriously because they knew she was a compulsive enabler. They also disclosed to me that Andrew could instantly change his mood 180 degrees; he was dangerous. They really didn't want to deal with him. He weighed almost three hundred pounds, and it took many officers to subdue him. First Andrew was cooperative, next enraged. If Mom filed a police report but then bailed him out, changed her mind, or forgot what Andrew did to her, the officers' time and energy were wasted. It was easier for them to calm Andrew than to address the problems and do the paperwork. Neighbors reported to me they actually saw police officers sitting in the patrol car, laughing hilariously after returning from a visit with Andrew and Mom.

If Mom had filed police reports and followed through years ago, perhaps Andrew would be a different person today. Regardless, she would be the better for it. Instead, she was drowning with no one to rescue her. Oh, I could have taken her by force to live with me, but she was adamant. She was not leaving her house! She was not leaving Andrew! One police officer informed me – if I took her by force – I would be charged with kidnapping. I had no interest in being arrested; it would not help Mom or me. Andrew should never have been set free from the mental institution that first housed him after he brutally murdered my dad. He tormented his family and his community, with no one who could or would stop him.

In the third week of June, Mom could not start her car. Her car battery died. I asked her to see if Andrew could charge it for her.

Even though he said that he would, he never did. She was also low on gasoline. She forgot to get gas on Saturday. I called AAA for assistance. They informed me that they could charge her car battery and provide some gas. Mom called me from Andrew's house to tell me not to send AAA. Andrew decided he would charge the battery. Andrew, however, insisted that she could get a much better battery through the mail. Mom thought this was a reasonable idea. She wanted a good battery. (As her dementia progressed, she deferred more and more to Andrew's instructions, which only created more problems.) I informed them that I had already ordered a battery at Walmart. Andrew then accused me of not caring about Mom's well-being. I reminded him of his theft of almost five hundred dollars from her that month. He could not possibly care about Mom's well-being and steal her food money. Andrew continued to complain about the possibility of an inferior battery.

When Mom was at Andrew's house, he never let me talk to Mom alone. He always used the speakerphone. The conversation changed to what Andrew really wanted to talk about. He demanded Mom's credit cards. I told him that she and I already decided it would be best for me to keep them. His blaring TV and continuous raving made it almost impossible to talk to Mom. In the end, we bought the battery at Walmart.

During the battery crisis, Andrew struck again, helping himself to an extra hundred dollars of Mom's food money. He knew that in times of stress, she became more confused. It was easy for him to extract money from her purse.

In the midst of all of this chaos, Mom locked her keys in her house – again. The neighbor who helped her last time was out of town. I let her know that Sam and I would be over the next day. She could sleep at Andrew's house, which she already did on occasion. In the meantime, I asked Mom to check the garage to see if she left her keys in the car. Both Andrew and Mom declared that checking the garage was too much work. In light of their refusal to help themselves, I changed my mind and advised them that I would not be over the following day. If they wouldn't walk across the street to look in the car for her keys, I would not drive six hours to open her door. The following morning, they still refused. Good news: The neighbor returned home and helped Mom get into her house. Surprise! Her purse and keys were in the car in the garage. If Mom or Andrew had listened, they could have accessed the house by opening the garage door.

So many times I could have helped Mom, if only she would have listened. With her dementia, I could see she was becoming very stubborn and demanded things be done her way. She did not want to admit needing help. In her confusion during this last episode, however, Mom did admit to her neighbor – she thought she was "losing her grip." As the dementia gained more control, she was starting to recognize something was not right. But she wouldn't admit it to me.

It was time for Mom to visit the Memory Clinic. I had previously scheduled an appointment for her, but Mom became ill and was unable to keep the appointment. I called to reschedule. There was a waiting list, and we had to wait for someone to cancel their appointment. After a few days, there was a cancellation. The morning of the appointment, Mom was unreachable. I needed to leave my home by 7:30 a.m. in order to drive across state, pick her up at her home, and be on time for the 1:30 p.m. appointment. That morning, I could not reach her by phone. I repeatedly called, finally reaching her at 10:00 a.m. Thank God for cell phones. I left my house, trusting God would somehow help me connect with her in time to keep the appointment. I did not have a plan B. We arrived at her appointment on time.

At the Memory Clinic, Mom and I met with the psychologist for an initial interview. I thought everything went well. Mom answered most of the questions, stating she did not have problems or many problems in each area. I then filled in the blanks with specific details, each time looking to Mom for confirmation. Next, Mom went into the other office for testing. I met with the psychologist to allow time for me to provide additional information or ask questions. I informed her that I wanted an honest evaluation. She appreciated my concern and confirmed that evaluations completed at the clinic were done with integrity. When we were finished talking, I waited in the seating area for Mom. The examiner told me that she was a lot of fun to test. Sadly, Mom received a similar response almost everywhere she went – she was a lot of fun. And yet because of Andrew, she was isolated and rarely had an opportunity for socializing. After the tests, we drove to Mom's house. She always invited me to stay, but I couldn't, not after the recent death threat. She said that she understood.

Chapter 10: July
Diagnosis: Alzheimer's Disease

It was the first Sunday in July. I called Mom after church and finally reached her in the afternoon. I was surprised to find her furious, since she rarely became angry. It all started the previous night. Mom, constantly trying to find ways to please Andrew, invited him to dinner at Perkins. She bought him a carton of cigarettes and planned to pay for their dinners. She should have had plenty of money, but Andrew added two additional entrees to her bill without permission. He liked to play host, and requested that she give him the cash so he could pay for their food. He pocketed the remaining money. She didn't realize what happened until the following morning when she arrived at church. Her wallet was empty! She discovered she didn't have any money to give in the offering. That really made her angry!

This was only Sunday, and Andrew cleverly took her money, again. I asked her if she had hidden any of her spending money. Frustrated, she admitted that she had not. Yes, she was angry, but before I spoke to her again Sunday afternoon, Mom had already driven to town to buy Andrew's lunch with her sandwich card. Was he thankful for the lunch? No. He refused to open the front door. She stood on his porch for a very long time, in the extremely hot Florida sun. When she relayed all of this to me, I called him. He immediately made some rude remarks, demanded more money, and shouted, "Burn in Hell!"

49

Feeling the dramatic pounding of hurricane winds that constantly threatened to overtake me, this day, I received a new revelation from God: Although Mom needed protection from Andrew, more than that, she needed protection from herself. She was obsessed with taking care of him, when she desperately needed to step back from him and take care of herself. But she wouldn't. She couldn't. So the storms raged on, but now, my perspective was changed.

I drove over to Mom's house on Tuesday to take her to a follow-up appointment at the Memory Clinic. Mom's initial visit to the Memory Clinic was six years ago. At that time, they were able to establish a baseline for memory and function. She scored very well, with a minimal amount of dementia. Three years later, she showed additional loss of memory, but was still able to live on her own and drive her car. Now, in her third evaluation, her tests revealed substantial loss of memory, problem solving, and ability to function. The final diagnosis was Alzheimer's disease.

That day, Mom and I talked about a lot of things. I was concerned about her reaction to the diagnosis, but most distressing to her was the fact she could no longer drive. She had made it abundantly clear through the years and even recently, she did not want to live with me. So, I suggested she come and live near me. I had already done my research and located a beautiful senior living facility. It was a lovely place near me with activities, church, meals provided, trips to town, and nice apartments. There was hope, but in order for her to be safe and near me, she needed to leave Andrew. All she could think about was driving. She repeatedly asked, "Does this mean I can't drive?" The doctor made several suggestions, fully recommending that Mom come home with me. I asked Mom if she would willingly give me her keys. She said, "No." The psychologist informed me that Mom's primary care physician would provide me with a report I could take to a lawyer to complete requirements for the Durable Power of Attorney. Sounded easy enough, but it wasn't.

As we left the Memory Clinic, Mom and I stopped by the grocery store to buy food and supplies for the week. I left Mom with some money and even gave her additional cash for her birthday. We were taking things one step at a time. She would be without transportation, but I would return the next week. Right before I left for my home, I determined to try one more time. I asked Mom if she would willingly give me her keys. She exclaimed, "Not my house keys!" I assured her that I only wanted the key to the car. She took the car key off the ring and gave it to me. I hugged her and left for home. She took some of the food to Andrew.

The next day when I phoned, she immediately informed me she was going to sell her car to Andrew. (Keep in mind he was instructed by the DMV he would not be able to get a driver's license until he passed a mental evaluation. Not only was he without insurance or money to pay for it, he had no money to buy gas, and for that matter, no money to pay for the car – unless he stole it from her.) I shared all this with her and let her know selling the car to Andrew would not work. Mom still owed $9,100 on the car.

Then she told me that not being able to drive was very hard. She sounded very depressed. I assured her I knew it was difficult, but I had an open door for her. She needed to come over and live near me. I reminded her about all of the wonderful qualities of the facility. I asked if she would be interested in seeing one of the models. She said she might be interested.

Later that evening, Andrew discovered one of the catalogues he previously used, still maintained Mom's credit card on file. He went shopping. Only God could reveal this to me. Up to that time, I had never checked her credit cards online. But that evening, I did. When I saw a new charge on the statement, I called the bank the next morning and filed a fraud report. The purchase was stopped, and the credit card account numbers changed. Andrew took every opportunity to steal from Mom. When I explained to her what Andrew did, she was upset. That too, quickly faded from memory.

Since Mom was no longer allowed to drive, I called her Sunday School teacher, who also happened to be her cousin, and let her know Mom would not be attending her church anymore. The church was located more than thirty minutes away, making it too far for someone to come by and drive her to services. I suggested that perhaps one day, if I could get someone to fill in for me at my church, Mom and I would visit and see her Sunday School friends one more time. That seemed to satisfy everyone.

Mom's cousin was very concerned about never being able to reach Mom on the phone. She frequently called Mom, but Mom was never home. I knew the reason for that problem; Mom was probably at Andrew's house. This revelation only made her cousin more concerned. She knew Andrew's violent history. But Mom was not concerned or afraid. Two things drove Mom to Andrew's house: the compulsive need to help Andrew and loneliness. On many occasions, Mom shared with me that she was very lonely. I believe it. She was always so friendly, never knowing a stranger. By limiting her contact to Andrew, she shut herself off from the rest of the world. It was very sad.

The next day was Wednesday. I repeatedly called my mom, with no answer. Finally, I reached her at Andrew's house. The music was blaring. Thankfully, he was not in the room. Mom decided she wanted another memory test because she was, "Fine – fine as ever." I could tell right away she was getting advice from Andrew. Next, she announced she was going to let Andrew drive her car. I repeated the list of reasons why Andrew must not drive her car.

While I had her on the phone, I asked her if she had any money. She checked her purse. It was the same amount she had the other day, just a little change. I reminded her that when I left yesterday, she had almost fifty dollars. Part of the money was birthday money from me. She had no idea where the money went. She questioned, "I had birthday money?" I confirmed that she did. Andrew was very quick to access her purse. He loved the fact she couldn't remember. I could not protect her from him, when she was constantly in his house.

Finally, things were changing. Now, with the diagnosis of Alzheimer's disease, I knew we were going to get some help. I was sure the authorities would finally pay attention when I next reported elder abuse of an 88 year old woman with Alzheimer's disease. Dream on. Because Mom had been a constant enabler, no one took anything she said seriously. After all, with a lifetime of dismissing Andrew's behavior, protecting him from the consequences, and fixing everything for him, nothing changed. As the dementia increased, the enabling increased. I felt like no one took the magnitude of this situation seriously, except me.

I called the local police and informed them that Frances could no longer drive due to a diagnosis of Alzheimer's disease. I alerted the police that Andrew would be out of control and was already looking for money. They politely listened and informed me they could give me an ID bracelet for Mom. A bracelet was nice, but I needed real help. When I called the Department of Children and Families (DCF), I was told elder abuse was not considered a serious crime unless, the victim was disabled. Since she was not physically disabled, the police were not likely to become involved.

I refused to allow myself to be defeated by these latest revelations. Undaunted, I pressed on. I trusted God to help me do what I needed to do. What was next on my list? I knew I needed a statement from two doctors to complete the Durable Power of Attorney. The psychologist at the Memory Clinic informed me she could not provide a statement. The Statement needed to be from medical doctors. She instructed me to request a statement from Mom's primary care physician and use the psychologist's report as supporting evidence for a diagnosis of Alzheimer's. I left word for Mom's primary doctor stating, that in order to complete the Durable Power of Attorney, according to Florida Statute, the statement must be from her primary care physician. The doctor's office called back and insisted they wanted the Memory Clinic to make the statement. I informed them about the Florida Statute stating that it must be the primary physician. I read the statute to them. Reluctantly, the doctor agreed to provide the documentation I needed.

Next, I called and requested the updated report from the Memory Clinic be sent to Mom's physician. The reports were faxed. But when the final report from Mom's primary care physician arrived in my mail, the local bank would not accept the statement. They required a notarized original statement declaring Mom could no longer manage herself, her finances, or her property. What should have been an easy process required multiple trips. But God was with me, and step-by-step, I was making progress.

In the midst of this, I tried to find help for Andrew. I called every agency I could think of to get assistance. Andrew was getting worse and the situation with Mom was deteriorating. I called phone numbers to find them not in service. I called and left messages with no return calls, but I did not give up. I tried again, later.

In Mom's county, all seniors are required to take a driving test to prove competency in order to continue driving. After the Memory Clinic's report, I called the Driver's Clinic and cancelled Mom's appointment. The psychologist stated that Mom was not to drive. I called again and asked if that meant she shouldn't take the driving test at the other clinic. The psychologist said it would be a waste of money – upwards of four hundred dollars. The psychologist confirmed that the Driver's Clinic gave the same initial tests Mom had already taken at the Memory Clinic. Mom did not pass them before, and Mom would not pass them if retested. Leaving no stone unturned, I called and spoke to the gentleman who gave the driving tests. He confirmed what the psychologist said. Surprise! Even though I told the primary care physician what I have just relayed to you, she scheduled the tests for Mom and informed her of the date for her appointment.

It was the first Saturday in July. Hurricane Frances and Hurricane Andrew were brooding over the driving issue. They were converging, joining forces, to take control of the situation. How did I find out? The teller from Mom's bank called and let me know that Frances and Andrew used the drive-through teller – twice. They withdrew money on Friday, not Saturday. Mom's spending money was not due in her account until Saturday. Something was up. Mom wasn't even supposed to be able to drive. I had her key! Cleverly, Mom and Andrew out-foxed me. When I went to check their online banking statement, I discovered that Mom picked up her two hundred dollars for the week from Andrew's bill paying account! Andrew also picked up two hundred and eighty-five dollars from the same account! The phone bill was first on autopay, meaning there would be insufficient funds to cover his mortgage payment.

I tried to call Mom about 20 times, with no success. I planned to go over to her house on Monday, but since she was driving and able to get food, I could not stop her. There was no point in me traveling for six hours. Obviously, there was another key to the car. I finally reached Mom in the afternoon. When I questioned her, she admitted she was driving and had another key in her purse. Come to find out, she and Andrew called the car dealer and arranged for a driver to pick them up. Mom and Andrew rented a car while they waited for the new key to be created. I reminded her she should not be driving. At the Memory Clinic, the psychologist informed us that if she had a wreck, with a diagnosis of Alzheimer's disease, she would be responsible – even if the accident was not her fault. She advised us the courts are now ruling this way. Mom should not be driving.

Since I knew Mom and Andrew withdrew almost five hundred dollars from the bank, I asked Mom how much money she had in her purse. She found less than two dollars in her change purse. I called the police and requested a wellness check. I notified the police about Andrew taking money from Mom. I also reminded the police she had Alzheimer's disease. The operator said the officer would call me back, when he was on the scene.

While I was waiting for the officer's call, I received another call from the Police Station. (It's a small town.) I was warned that Andrew phoned the station and told them I was stealing Mom's money. (Andrew loved to accuse me of whatever he was doing.) I thanked her for the call. She also recommended some resources to help Mom.

When I finally reached Mom on the phone, she let me know that the police visited the house and then left. "Everything was fine." I could hear Mom repeatedly asking Andrew to confirm that everything was fine. I did not get a call back from the police officer who went to Mom's house.

Andrew was sure he was finally taking charge. The following Monday, I received another call from Mom's bank. I was alerted that Frances and Andrew were requesting a statement for all accounts that belonged to Frances. I talked to Mom on the phone. She told me Andrew wanted money, but she didn't know for what purpose. I instructed the bank to provide Frances with her spending account information and Andrew with his spending account information. Andrew and Mom must not be allowed to think bill paying money was available for spending. Although the bill paying accounts had some money in them, there was nothing extra at the end of the month. The accounts were sufficient to pay incoming bills, nothing else.

When Andrew discovered he was unable to access additional cash at the bank, he focused on another possibility – Mom's safe. It took a few calls, but I finally reached Mom in the afternoon. She told me Andrew was trying to get into her safe. He was searching through all her papers, but she did not know what he was hoping to find. She thought – possibly money.

During this whole stormy season with Frances and Andrew, I attempted to learn as much as I could learn. I wanted to correct everything I could correct and to get information to make the next change. It was step by step, many times having to back track to call agencies and people who promised help. They either forgot or were too busy to actually provide the help we desperately needed. It took many weeks from the time of the diagnosis of Alzheimer's until I could secure all of the documentation to complete the requirements for the Durable Power of Attorney. The Power of Attorney not only provided help in securing Mom's finances, her lawyer told me that I could move Mom from her home to other living arrangements. Somewhat hesitantly, he added, "She does not have to agree with the move." I preferred she did agree, but in order to protect her, I understood it may come to that.

You see, if it was just the disease and she was cooperative, I would have already moved her. But she was not cooperative, and this was just a continuation of a lifetime of enabling and protecting Andrew. When I spoke with the police, they advised me I would have to have her declared incompetent in order to move her without her consent. I considered the decision, and weighing the possibility of violent confrontation with Andrew, I continued to pray and look for God's protection and provision. For now, I waited on Him and maintained my strategy of rescuing her finances. I hoped by reducing the number of her bills and the amount of her credit card debt, her monthly income would eventually be enough to pay for assisted living.

Again, I contacted many social service agencies, attempting to get help for either Mom or Andrew. I finally reached one case worker who helped me locate Andrew's doctor. I needed the doctor's help to have Andrew's SSD Representative Payee changed from Mom to someone else, anyone else. Since Mom could no longer manage her own finances, she had no business trying to manage Andrew's finances. The case worker provided me copies of the paperwork I needed to accomplish the change. I immediately made a trip across state to visit with the doctor. He gladly helped me. He had worked with Andrew for years. Curiously, he was an internist, not a psychologist. When I asked why Andrew was not seeing a psychologist or psychiatrist, the doctor informed me counseling was optional for Andrew. In desperation, I took what help I could get. The form I needed filled out required a diagnosis. The diagnosis: "uncontrolled schizophrenic." It was just two simple words, but enough to free my mom from trying to manage Andrew's finances. The doctor signed the form indicating a change of Rep. Payee as appropriate and necessary.

I then called Social Security, and they instructed me to contact the local office; the local office would provide a new Rep. Payee. I immediately made an appointment and met with the local Social Security office. They told me that they did not have any Rep. Payees to appoint, since they did not have resources for such services. My only options were to hire a lawyer, for which there were no funds, or to become Andrew's new Rep. Payee. I chose the latter. If I did not become his Rep. Payee, he would lose his house and therefore be homeless. I recognized at that moment, after a lifetime of watching my mom enable Andrew, I was placed in a position where I had responsibility for him – something I declared I would not do. It was one of those times when I used the word "never." I do know better than that. So humbling myself before God, I agreed to take the role required in order for Andrew to continue receiving his SSD funds. Since Andrew had a consistent history of verbally abusing me, I asked what would happen if, in the future, I determined I no longer could continue in that role. I was told Andrew would lose his SSD benefits until he either hired a lawyer or found a person to take over those responsibilities.

Due to the Alzheimer's, I was also required to become Mom's Representative Payee for her Social Security income. The timing was good. At least this would prevent Mom and Andrew from being able to access their bill paying accounts for reckless spending.

The following day Andrew called me. He and Mom were on the speakerphone, as usual. He blurted out a stream of obscenities directed toward me and then hung up. I phoned his house. He made me wait a long time, with lots of noise on his part, before acknowledging I was on the phone. As soon as he spoke to me, I declared that I wanted to say something to Mom. At first he wouldn't allow it, but I kept insisting that I wanted to talk to Mom. Finally, when I was allowed to speak with her, I told her I loved her and warned her to be very careful. She said she loved me, too. Again, Andrew hung up the phone.

The next Monday, when I drove back to Mom's house, I took her to the bank. The bank manager privately informed me that Andrew threatened him during the previous week. He warned that if Mom brought Andrew back to the bank, the family would not be allowed to bank at that branch. Andrew frightened the tellers, and this could not happen again. I let Mom know. First, she said she would change banks. I informed her that Andrew was the problem. The bank had worked very hard to take care of her. I also declared if she changed banks, I would not reset the autopay for her bills. Her bills would go unpaid. The right thing to do was to keep Andrew away from the bank. She agreed.

Mom consistently had a difficult time protecting her money from Andrew. Twice that month she ended up with nothing but change in her purse. The first time she started with eighty dollars, the second time, about seventy-five dollars. Each time she told me that she did not know where the money went. It usually happened after she visited Andrew. For months, I repeatedly instructed her not to take her purse to his house. While she made coffee for him, he stole her money. And then again, if Andrew wanted something, and she had money, she was quick to give it to him. That was nothing new.

During this time, Mom was still driving with her very expensive, newly purchased key. When I talked to the DMV, they said that her driver's test would be scheduled very soon. It had been more than six weeks since they originally informed her she would have to take the test. In the meantime, she could continue to drive.

Oh yes, the psychologist insisted she was not to drive, but the DMV refused to restrict her driving because she had not yet taken the test.

On Sunday, Mom's Sunday School teacher/cousin called to tell me that Mom had driven to church. They were all surprised to see her. Mom's cousin had already let her class know that Mom was no longer allowed to drive. Her class was happy to see her, but concerned. Mom started crying, but finally composed herself. At the end of Sunday School, Mom announced that she was not staying for church. She felt dizzy, like she might faint. Her cousin offered to drive Mom home, while another church member followed. After they dropped Mom off at her house, the two of them rode back to the church together.

During the drive to Mom's house, her cousin advised her it was time to quit driving. She made Mom promise she would stay home. She told Mom to expect a call from her as soon as she returned to her own house. Mom promised three times she would not leave her house. When her cousin called, Mom did not answer the phone. I called Mom a couple of times. She was not home. She was at Andrew's house.

While Mom's cousin was with her in the car, she also tried to comfort Mom by telling her Andrew was not responsible for his behavior. She told Mom that he was like a little child; he didn't know right from wrong. She tried to comfort Mom by saying Andrew would go to heaven. When I spoke with Mom's cousin, I let her know that nothing could be further from the truth. Andrew was responsible. From an early age, Andrew chose to get involved in drugs, black magic, and promiscuous behavior. He did know right from wrong. He did not have limited intelligence. He was not like a child, but purposefully chose to be wicked. Andrew was ever running to evil. Out of the abundance of his heart, his mouth constantly spewed vile words and names. Was there any hope for him? Yes. God could still save him and change him. It was up to Andrew.

A few days later, it was Mom's birthday. I called Mom about 9 a.m. and reached her at her house. I wished her a Happy Birthday. I reminded her I had already given her a birthday present during my last visit. As soon as I took her home, Andrew stole her birthday money from her. Mom sounded sad.

About 5 p.m., I called Mom. There was no answer. I called Andrew's house. When he answered the phone, I asked to speak to Mom. Again, I wished Mom a Happy Birthday. I hoped that he would acknowledge her birthday in some way, but he didn't.

Next, I directed my conversation to Andrew. Since I now managed his finances, I asked him if he had applied for Food Stamps. Had he actually sent the required information to receive his Food Stamp card? He became very angry and shouted that he had it under control. He then started screaming a very long tirade of obscenities aimed at me. I told him that God still loved him and would forgive him, if he would fall on the mercy of God and ask for forgiveness. I explained to him there was still hope. Andrew continued his tirade.

I had a last word with Mom. She positioned herself near the speakerphone and said in a quiet voice, "I'm still here." How could she sit there and listen to all that? Whenever she was stressed, she escaped to her mental happy place and did not listen to anything going on around her. I was always concerned for her safety, but she always insisted she was fine. When I finally hung up, Andrew was still screaming obscenities.

The last Sunday in July, Mom was very upset. When she finished preparing lunch for Andrew and herself, he stood behind her and demanded that she get out of his house. He then called her a "bitch" and shoved her with both hands. She left his house and drove to the drugstore. Still upset, she promptly recounted what happened. The store manager called the police. Four police officers arrived at the drugstore and talked to Mom. The police instructed her that she could "sign some papers if she wanted to," but she didn't bother. They also asked her if she wanted them to take Andrew to jail. She said, "No." So they didn't. I had already notified the police that Mom had Alzheimer's, and was outraged that they were not protecting her from elder abuse. If I had been informed at the time this was occurring, perhaps I could have done something. Since I did not find out about the events of this incident until late in the evening, and since I knew Mom was already safe at home, I waited until the next morning to drive across state to take Mom to the Police Station.

The next morning when I arrived at her house, I decided to try a new strategy. I knew Mom easily forgot the details of Andrew's abusive behavior. I asked her to tell me what she remembered from the previous day, while I wrote it down on paper. When she finished telling me all she could remember, I read the statement to her. She confirmed it was accurate. Then, she copied the statement in her own handwriting. We took it to the bank where she signed it and had it notarized. From there, we went to lunch and then straight to the police station. We spoke with the officers who again warned us they had no way to stop Andrew, because Mom insisted she was not afraid of him. She had no bruises where he shoved her. The notarized statement did not impress them. The officers suggested she move across state with me. They could not guarantee her safety if she stayed in her house. Andrew was dangerous. She seemed to agree it was time for her to move. As usual, however, she said whatever satisfied the listener. But Mom had other plans.

That same day, Mom informed me her driver's test was scheduled. She forgot to write down the time, so I called the testing center. I also asked how long the test would take and how much it would cost. They told me three hours and about four hundred dollars. I let Mom know her test was scheduled for the next day. I gave her a choice: She either took the test or turned in her driver's license to the DMV. She said it was a hard decision, but she agreed to turn in her license. I was amazed at her response. I did not waste even a moment. We immediately drove to the DMV office. While we were there, we also obtained a photo ID for her and two letters - one for the car dealership and the other for her insurance company.

Next, we picked up some groceries for Andrew and then drove to the drugstore where Mom could buy cigarettes for him. I apologized to the drugstore workers for Andrew's very bad behavior in their store. I told them Mom was coming home with me; Mom even agreed. Again, I was amazed and thankful.

When we arrived at Mom's house, Andrew was waiting in the driveway. He was troubled about a letter he received in the mail. He said he had to go to the jail – right then. I informed Andrew that Mom could not drive him anywhere. She no longer had a driver's license. When I asked him what the letter was about, he told me it was none of my business. He went home angry.

We proceeded into Mom's house to pack everything she needed for her trip to my house. In a few minutes, Andrew rang the doorbell. I refused to open the door. I was determined to protect Mom and me from his continuing anger. Again, he demanded to go to the jail, and rudely reminded me it was none of my business. I warned him to go home, or I would call the police. Andrew did not leave, so I called the police station. When he saw the patrol car arrive, Andrew hurried to his house. Mom and I walked out the front door to speak with the officers. I let them know we were very glad they were there with us, and that we would appreciate their continued presence; it would allow us time to load the last of our belongings into my car. I also informed them she would be living near me. Again, Mom agreed. The officers were very happy to know she would be living in a safe environment. They had been concerned about her safety for a long time. They agreed to stay until after we drove off down the street. What a relief! Then Mom voiced her concern, "Andrew needs to go to the jail." One officer checked Andrew's status and confirmed that Andrew was wrong. He did not need to go to the jail. (It amazed me when Mom remembered Andrew's need, but was unable to remember anything else. She was focused on him.)

Before we left for my house, Mom and I wanted to make sure Andrew had enough food. We purchased his groceries, but knew it was not safe for us to approach Andrew's house. The officers agreed to walk across the street and deliver the groceries to his door. Mom and I drove three hours back across the state. We sang hymns together and enjoyed the ride. It was a very nice trip.

That was Monday. By Tuesday morning, Mom wanted to go home. She insisted she would not move away from her home. All she could think about was her home and Andrew.

A case worker from the Florida Department of Children and Families and a police officer visited my house for a wellness check. Since I drove Mom to the police station in her town, DCF was sent to investigate any possible abuse. I met with investigators for a pre-conference, and then they spoke to Mom – alone. Mom assured them everything was fine. The results, as usual, included informing me very little could be done unless she was afraid of Andrew and was willing to file a police report. I gave them copies of my documentation, but in the end, they directed me to get an Elder Attorney and have her declared incompetent. She needed to move over here where it was safe. They also recommended contacting an Alzheimer's group for support – which I have done.

The problem in dealing with Mom and Andrew was very complex. When I questioned the case worker about the cost of the legal aspects of what he recommended, he suggested getting a loan on my house to pay for it might be a good idea. Really? With the minimal help I received from every agency I contacted, I was not interested in getting a loan on my house! At that rate, I was more interested in having the Durable Power of Attorney and Rep. Payee positions cancelled. But not yet. I hadn't given up, yet.

In the afternoon, Mom and I had a long talk with her repeatedly interjecting that she wanted to be in her house. I advised her I had already arranged an appointment with a local independent/assisted living facility the next day at 10 a.m., and we would be keeping it. All I asked her to do was to go with me and keep an open mind. Then I let her know I did not want to talk about any more of this again that day. So, we talked about other things, and she was fine.

Andrew called. He wanted to talk to Mom. I advised him that I put him on speakerphone, just like he always did to me. He didn't sound pleased. He wanted to know when she was coming home. She told him that we would be returning in a few days. He wanted to know what was going to happen to the car. She let him know that the car would have to go back to the car dealership. Andrew was very angry because she previously promised him he could have the car. He was surprised to learn that the buyout on the car was about $9,100.00. He continued to complain about the car, as well as the price. Andrew finally hung up.

Chapter 11: August
Safe Harbor: Rejected!

On the first of August, we visited the senior living facility where we met with the Director of Sales and Marketing. The visit was wonderful. We learned all about available activities, trips, visits to doctors, and shopping. They organized a buddy system to help newcomers make friends and learn where all of the amenities were located. The facility served wonderful breakfast, lunch, and dinner meals, prepared by a chef. There were plenty of choices at every meal. They also provided classes, and if there was anything they did not offer they would attempt to add it. They even had resources to make the move easy and shared information about possible funding for widows of Veterans. We took a tour of the clubhouse and the villas. One apartment was a model, and the other was one recently vacated. Two were located on the water, one on a canal and one on a lake. All were absolutely beautiful! The monthly payment included electricity, water, housekeeping, and repairs. I asked Mom if there was anything she did not like. She said that she liked everything. After about an hour and a half visit, we went home for lunch. We talked all day about how great this arrangement would be for her. I could come every week and visit, take her shopping or to some activity, and bring her home for family visits. She talked about moving in a positive way, asking a few questions about how things would work.

Come evening, she wanted to go home. I reminded her, at home she had no transportation to get food or go to the doctors. She said she would take a taxi. I reminded her that the police could not protect her from Andrew. She didn't care. She wanted to go home. I explained: It was like when Dad got transferred to another Air Force base. When it was time to go, you just went and made the new place your home. She had only lived in her current house for three years. Still, she just wanted to go home. Then I thought for moment and asked, "Did you mean your old home in Ft. Myers where you grew up?" She looked at me a little strange and specifically asserted that she wanted to be in her house, "the house across the street from where Andrew lives."

The following day was Thursday. We had an appointment with Mom's lawyer. Yes, it was on Mom's side of the state, requiring the usual six hours of driving. As soon as Mom woke up, she desperately wanted to go home and stay home. I asked her what she would use for transportation, once she was home. Again, she said that she would take a taxi. I cautioned her that if she went shopping and took a taxi, she could not have the taxi wait for her; it would be too expensive. She would need to call another taxi to get home. She seemed frustrated at the idea. I suggested she try to find a taxi phone number in the phone book. She had no idea how to do it. After about 20 minutes of flipping through the pages, she just sat there. In the past, even when I left her exact phone numbers, she was unable to call and take care of any business. A taxi was obviously not the solution.

After we met with the lawyer, we planned to stop by Mom's house. First, we went by the drugstore where she bought cigarettes for Andrew. We also stopped at Walmart to purchase a basket for his bicycle. If Andrew was going to shop for his own food, he needed a basket to carry the groceries home. Mom insisted on having some time to visit with Andrew. While they visited, I planned to pay for her lawn care, buy groceries, and purchase a couple of sub sandwiches for Andrew. Mom walked across the street to take the cigarettes to him. When she knocked on his door, he opened it, took the cigarettes, and told her to, "Get on about your own business." He closed the door, refusing to even talk to Mom. Not too far away, I was paying the neighbor for cutting the grass. I had a good view of Andrew's front door. As Mom left his house, she waved to me, indicating she left the stuff at Andrew's and was walking back across the street to her home. I headed for Mom's house. When I heard about Andrew's continued rudeness to her, I had not had time to purchase any groceries. My plan had changed. Instead of purchasing food, I slid an envelope under his garage door. The envelope contained one hundred dollars to pay for food. I placed the two bike baskets on his front porch and then walked back to the car. We left for my home. I immediately tried to call Andrew on my cell phone. I wanted to tell him about the location of the money and his responsibility to use his Food Stamps and the money to purchase food. He hung up on me right away and would not answer the second call. At that point, I figured when he called me looking for food, he would be willing to listen.

The next day was Friday. We were at my house. As soon as Mom woke up, she was immediately crying. "I want to go home." My husband, who was already awake and having coffee, spoke gently to her and explained all the reasons why she was better off at our house. He asked her for suggestions. If she had any solutions to the transportation, food, or doctors' issues, we wanted to know. We were diligently searching for solutions. Mom had no ideas. She just wanted to go home.

In a calm voice, I informed her she could not go home yet. I declared, "We are going to wait on God for the answer." None of us had answers, and we needed the wisdom only God could provide. We prayed. At that very moment, I received a revelation. I doubted Mom had ever waited on God for anything in her life. She was always so quick to fix everything for Andrew. Waiting on God was part of trusting Him. If she had never waited on God, then this would be a good experience for her.

By Saturday, Mom was distraught. She wanted to go home! I asked her how she would purchase groceries. She said she would walk. I suggested we try walking to my grocery store; it was fairly close to my house. This experiment would prove how far she could walk. Mom previously lived in my area for ten years. Under normal circumstances, she knew the way to the grocery store. So she took the lead, and I followed. We managed to walk about a half mile before she made a wrong turn. I announced it was time to return to my house. She was happy and thoroughly exhausted. I reminded her that although she made it a small portion of the way to the store, she would still need to walk home with her groceries. We walked back to the house and drove to my grocery store. Yes, we really needed to get groceries. She didn't talk about walking anymore that day. Obviously, walking was not the answer. I reminded her that we were still waiting on God. When it was God, she would know it. The answer would be amazing and right.

I was scheduled to sing a song at church on Sunday. So Mom and I practiced a song we used to sing together, "Canaan Land is Just in Sight." We practiced again on Sunday before we went to church. We were sounding great! As soon as we arrived at church, she started crying about wanting to go home. Many people tried to comfort her and pray for her. She finally settled down when the service began and was fine for the rest of the morning. We sang, and everyone loved our song. Many people complimented her and insisted we sing again another time. Mom loved to sing. She especially loved hymns.

Later that day, some friends visited my house. Again, Mom cried. She wanted to go home! My friends attempted to encourage her by saying that being at my house was a good thing. They prayed for her. After the prayer, Mom chose to leave the room.

The next day was Monday. I had previously scheduled a personal, early morning doctor's appointment and decided to take Mom with me. This would allow my husband some much needed rest before returning to work on Tuesday. Mom and I sat in the waiting room of the doctor's office. When the nurse called me into the examining room, I asked Mom if she wanted to come with me or stay in the waiting room and watch TV. She said that she would wait there. It wasn't long until she started crying and telling the people I wouldn't let her go home. The nurse quickly informed me, so I asked her to bring Mom to me. As soon as Mom sat down, she was crying about going home. I reminded her that both Sam and I would like to see her living in her home, but it was not time for her to go home. She still needed medical visits. It was not safe for her at home. She had no way to get food or travel to doctor visits. Finally, she calmed down and returned to the waiting room. She was fine.

The doctor's visit was for me, but when my doctor observed all that transpired with Mom, he confirmed what I already knew. With all of the negative issues limiting Mom's ability to safely live alone, she needed to be placed in assisted living. I let him know that I had already located a very nice senior facility. He talked about his own experience with his aging dad. An assisted living facility worked well for his family. I knew it wouldn't be long until I would have to make the decision. My mom's inability to think clearly made it very difficult to reason with her. And when you could tell she actually understood, it wasn't long until she forgot and we went back to square one – crying. She was crying to go back to an unsafe environment. Could I keep her near me? Only time would tell.

Mom had not been to see a doctor in a long time. Even when she could drive, it was not a priority for her; this was a problem. I called my dentist's office to make an appointment for Mom. She thought she needed a tooth filled. Her front tooth had a black spot on the gum line. She ended up needing both front teeth filled. My wonderful dentist was able to fit her into his very tight schedule. I then scheduled an appointment for her with a podiatrist.

Andrew called on Tuesday. He asked if he could speak to Mom. I said he could, but first I wanted to tell him that I tucked one hundred dollars in an envelope and slid it under his garage door last Thursday. He complained, "Nobody is ever considerate of me," and hung up.

A few hours later, Andrew called again. He asked to speak to Mom. I told him that he could and put the phone on speakerphone. Mom started off in a quivering desperate voice. I reminded her to speak to him like an adult. Andrew shouted out, "This call is being recorded by the Federal Government and the police!" I calmly informed Andrew that I had a Durable Power of Attorney for Mom. He hung up.

Later in the evening, Mom commented, "I hope Andrew hasn't turned his back on me." I questioned why he would do that. She said, "It is because I came over to your house."

Mom and I talked a long time about Andrew. He needed to be held responsible for his behavior. Every time she protected him from consequences, she hurt him. She seemed to understand for the moment, but by the next day, her focus returned to going home. Again I reminded her, we were waiting on God to see His provision for her. She seemed to willingly accept this answer. I prayed with her, and she calmed down.

Every day, Mom had her "I want to go home tears." She was desperate to see Andrew. It had only been one week. Finally, she said she was afraid Andrew might do something to her house. It was true, he might. Her concern, however, did not provide ample reason to take Mom home. We reminded her that to go home without being able to get food or go to the doctors, was not a good idea. Not safe. She continued to insist, but offered no solutions.

A new revelation: She informed me she did not like riding back and forth across state. I voiced my own dissatisfaction, saying that I didn't like it either and had been doing it for most of a year. Even though we didn't like the travel, it was not a good enough reason to return her to live in her house. The next day the same thing, tears and

"I want to go home." My same response, "We are waiting on God." Each day we allowed only a minimal time to talk about home. If Mom needed time to calm herself down, she was gently guided to her bedroom. This helped everyone to have a good, peaceful day.

Did God provide the answer? Yes. My husband saw a commercial on TV for a group that provided assistance for the elderly. I called, and sure enough, the number was no longer working. Then I remembered I had also seen a TV commercial for GrannyNANNIES. I spoke with a counselor on the phone. We discussed a few options and worked out a plan to provide help for Mom. The Granny Nanny, a certified assistant, could drive Mom to the bank, grocery store, doctor's office, and wherever else she needed to go. She could also cook and do light housekeeping. Even though it was part-time help, it was what we could afford. When she needed to visit the doctor, we would add another day. I decided to try this option. Was Mom thrilled? Absolutely not! Oh she wanted to go home; however, she did not want help. But that was the only way she could go home.

The counselor also suggested Meals-on-Wheels. When I previously tried to get meal service for Mom, there were no openings on their routes. I called Meals-on-Wheels one more time, and they were able to accommodate two on Mom's route. Mom and Andrew would receive daily meals.

Now, both of these solutions were worth the wait. As time went on, I looked for additional resources, but for now, I was satisfied she could reasonably live. I was ready to drive Mom home. We waited on God, and He provided.

The next day, we left my house about 8 a.m. and drove directly to Mom's house. Mom and I unloaded her things from the car and spent a good hour at the grocery store getting a variety of food. We spent almost two hundred dollars, leaving very little cash. As we left the store, I asked Mom if she knew why we spent so much on groceries. She did not answer. I reminded her I didn't want to leave too much cash for Andrew to steal. She was curiously quiet. I asked her if she believed Andrew ever stole money from her in the past. She looked at me and in a very serious tone of voice insisted, "Andrew told me he would never steal my money." It was settled in her mind. The truth: He stole from her all the time. Now, I regretted having returned her to her home. The collision of enabling and Alzheimer's disease created so many complex issues, some marginally resolved, others looming in the future. Even with this latest revelation of Mom's obsessive love and trust in Andrew, there was no point in trying to tell her otherwise. Not today.

We took the groceries home. After we divided them into hers and his, Mom took a few of Andrew's items over to his house. It took what seemed to be forever before he answered the door. When he did answer, he did not hug her and barely spoke to her. He took the groceries and sent her home. For now, she didn't seem to be disturbed about Andrew's rejection.

Mom had other things on her mind. As I prepared to return to my house, Mom complained she did not want someone cleaning her house or telling her what to eat. Regardless, if she wanted to live on her own, she would have help.

It was getting late, and I was exhausted. I had three hours of driving time ahead of me, and it would soon be dark. In my haste to leave, I forgot to get the car key from Mom. I called her the next morning and let her know I forgot to take the new key. I instructed her to take the key off her key ring and place it in her dresser drawer. I waited for her to do it. I reminded her she was not to drive. She told me the key was put away, and she promised not to drive. When I called her in the late afternoon, she announced she had driven to town to buy sub sandwiches. I was very upset and repeatedly insisted, "Do not drive." It was against the law for her to drive. She did not have a driver's license. Again, she promised she would not drive. Again, I reminded her to place the key in the drawer.

Then she started crying, "I don't have anything. I'm all alone, and I can't drive." She was breathing exceptionally hard. I attempted to calm her down. I assured her I loved her, and it would be OK. I reminded her that Maureen, the Granny Nanny, was coming the next day, and I would be back in a few days. She seemed to calm down.

I called later that same afternoon. She was very upset with Andrew. When she took cookies and a banana to him, he refused her peace offering and sent her home. I encouraged her to give Andrew some space. I reminded her that Andrew had not gotten into trouble while she was at my house last week. I asked her if she wanted him to grow up. She admitted she did, but immediately returned to lamenting Andrew's rejection.

Finally, it was the Granny Nanny's first day. I called Mom and reminded her that Maureen would be at her house that morning to help her. Again, she seemed a little troubled. She didn't want help. I waited and called back a little later. Maureen arrived and immediately Mom decided she really liked her. When I phoned, they almost didn't hear the phone ring. They were singing and playing the piano together. What a great start! They even attended the same church. They had much in common. I phoned and talked to Maureen in the morning and then later in the day to make sure everything was going well. Maureen cooked, washed laundry, encouraged Mom to take a bath, and reminded her to take her meds. It was a very good day. The next visit included a trip to the bank and grocery shopping. I created a very detailed list to ensure both Mom and Andrew received all the basics – healthy food and a few treats. Maureen was a treasure. She was above and beyond what we prayed for. She took care of Mom as if she was family. I thank God for sending us Maureen.

New challenges awaited us. With the addition of Granny Nanny expenses and Mom's determination to drive without a license, it was time to take the car back to the dealership where it was originally purchased. My plan was to use the money from the car payments and car insurance to pay for the Granny Nanny. It promised to be a very full Friday, with more to do than humanly possible. I prayed and asked God for help. Even in the midst of these storms, I knew God was still working in our situation.

Finally, it was Friday. As soon as I arrived, Mom and I went to the DMV and requested a copy of the car's registration. Later I learned Andrew appropriated the original copy and hid it in his house. He thought having the registration gave him some control over ownership of the car. He desperately wanted the car and thought he could keep me from selling it.

Next we went to the bank that held the car loan. Mom owed $9,100 on the car. Being a realist, I was aware the dealership might not give us enough money to pay off her loan. Just in case, I asked the bank if they provided some type of financial assistance to finish paying off the loan, since Mom's Alzheimer's disease made the sale of the car necessary. The bank called it a settlement. I was instructed to contact the bank after I finished finding out how much the dealership would pay for the car. The bank would make their determination at that time. My focus was not on the negative possibilities. In faith, I just kept pressing on, looking for God's provision. He had already revealed a settlement existed.

Returning the car to the dealership presented its own challenges. I checked to see if AAA would tow her car to the dealership, but was informed AAA only towed vehicles that were not working. From that information, and being the only licensed driver in the family, I needed to make three 30 mile trips: I had to drive to the Toyota dealership in my car, get a driver to drive me to Mom's house, and then drive her car back to the dealership. Oh yes, and while en route with Mom's car, I needed to stop and have it detailed. Mom and Andrew had not been taking care of her vehicle. The car was a filthy mess. Andrew treated Mom's car as badly as he treated his house.

I took Mom to lunch and then drove back to her house. When I attempted to start her car, all I heard was a click. Mom's car would not start! Immediately, I knew God was working on our behalf. While we waited for AAA to come, Mom and I cleaned the trash out of her car and threw out the stained mats. AAA arrived within the hour. The service technician inspected her car and informed us the problem was probably with the fuel pump. Mom and I followed behind the tow truck in my car. What a blessing! I did not have to make multiple trips to get her car to the dealership. I also didn't have to spend the extra time and money to have the car detailed.

When we arrived at the dealer's service department, the mechanic inserted the key into the ignition. The car started right up! It turned out that the new key Mom and Andrew secretly had made, was the only key that worked. Mom and Andrew informed the dealership that the other keys were lost. For security purposes, the programming was changed on the new key. When I tried to start the car at Mom's house, the car wouldn't start because I used the old key. Only the new key worked. Yes, God does work in amazing ways.

Next, we met with the used car salesman. To demonstrate Mom's "need" to return the car, I asked Mom to tell the salesman how much she originally paid for her car. She said, "I paid $100 for a new Corolla." (The payments were always $299.99 a month, but Mom was adamant the car only cost a total of $100.) This in itself proved Mom was experiencing some dementia, three years ago when she bought the car.

The salesman arranged for a good payoff. Mom owed $9,100, and the dealership offered $8,000. I called the bank and reminded them about Mom's Alzheimer's disease and her inability to drive. They forgave the rest of the debt. I was so thankful. God orchestrated the whole day.

For He is able to do exceedingly abundantly above all that we ask or think, according to the power that works in us, to Him be the glory (Ephesians 3:20-21, NKJ).

After we arranged for the sale of Mom's car, we drove back to her house. I then walked across the street to Andrew's house to deliver a letter from Social Security. The letter appointed me as Andrew's new SSD Representative Payee. Andrew refused to answer the door. I knocked on his bedroom window and heard a groaning sound. I knew he was there. Standing outside on the lawn, I read the letter to him. I also informed him that I left a copy of the letter and a phone book at his front door. Mom told me later that she carried both into his house.

The next day was Saturday. When I called Mom, she was upset about the loss of her car. I reminded her that although she could not drive, she needed to be thankful for what she could do. Her pity parties did not help her. They were not in faith. She needed to trust God. At least she was living in her home, she had a Granny Nanny, she had food, and she lived close to Andrew.

I must confess, I did not tell Andrew the car was going to be sold that day. I did not want to create a hostile environment on a day when I had so much to accomplish. As soon as Andrew found out, he called the dealership and angrily declared he owned the car. Toyota promptly called me and questioned Andrew's ownership of the vehicle. I assured them Andrew did not own the car, and we still wanted it sold. I emailed Toyota a copy of the Durable Power of Attorney. Concerned, he said that Andrew sounded irrational. I explained about Andrew's mental condition and told him to call the police if there were any problems.

Ever since I took over managing Mom's finances, I consistently reduced the amount of money available for Andrew to steal. Finally, all the bills were getting paid. With no money to steal and the loss of

Mom's car, Andrew had very little reason to allow Mom to come into his house. Her obsession for hovering over his every move and doing everything for him suffered a huge loss when he could no longer extract money from her. Every day Andrew allowed Mom to give him food, but then insisted she leave. She spent a lot of her time sleeping. She even said she would consider moving near me. I let her know that when she was ready, I had a place for her where they would take good care of her. She said it sounded good. She would let me know, but she was not quite ready.

A few days later, Mom was positive she wasn't leaving her house. She also informed me she wanted to get a bicycle and ride it to town. I reminded her Andrew already owned a bicycle, but she had better be careful. She might fall. And at almost 90 years of age, if the police saw her riding a bicycle away from home, they would be concerned about her safety. She gave up on the bicycle idea.

Chapter 12: September/October
The Storm Rages On!

It was Sunday. Mom was very upset because she could no longer attend church. We devised a plan. On my next visit, our first priority was to locate a church for Mom in her community. She was pleased with the plan. Right away, the church arranged a ride for Mom with her new Sunday School teacher. The teacher already provided rides for a few other senior ladies. After Mom's first Sunday at church, she announced that she liked the church a lot. She really like her Sunday School teacher, and best of all, the church sang hymns.

I continued to call Mom multiple times every day, reminding her to take her meds and about upcoming events. One day, before Maureen arrived, Mom informed me she did not like anyone giving her a bath. I suggested that if she bathed and washed her own hair before Maureen arrived, she would not need assistance. I asked Mom how long it had been since her last bath. Mom was silent. She said, "About a week." I let her know that meant she needed to wash her body and hair. She also needed to put on fresh clothes, or else she would smell like she had not taken a bath. My explanation seemed reasonable. By taking her own bath, Mom discovered they had more time for shopping and other activities. If not, Maureen's visit began with bath time. I knew Mom was still capable of many things. She just needed to be reminded. After Mom's first assisted bath, she became very willing to take her own bath in preparation for Maureen's arrival.

I knew Mom still needed to visit a podiatrist. I had previously made an appointment for her with a podiatrist located in my community, but she insisted on returning home before she could keep the appointment. I asked Mom for the name of the podiatrist in her town. She did not remember his name. I told her I needed the doctor's name in order to make an appointment for her. All she could tell me was his office was in a pink building on the main road. After a lot of detective work on the Internet and phone, I finally located the doctor and made an appointment for her.

Things seemed to be working better for Mom, but then there was Andrew. Life for him was also changing. It had been more than a year since Andrew was in possession of his Food Stamp card. With his limited income, Food Stamps were a necessity. I encouraged him to request a new card and was subjected to vile obscenities when I reminded him. When the card arrived, Andrew refused to entrust it to Mom so she could buy his groceries. Since Andrew no longer had access to Mom's car to take him to town, he had two options: He could give the card to Mom, or he could provide his own transportation. I already made sure he had a bicycle, and of course, he could walk to the store. Until this point in time, Andrew's groceries were totally purchased through Mom's funds. Andrew chose not to entrust his card to Mom, but he still needed groceries.

My plan was to reduce the amount of Andrew's groceries that were bought with Mom's money. Mom's new grocery list for Andrew only included foods that supported basic living. She bought the food he needed, and he was to use his Food Stamp card to buy the food he wanted – a good plan. All extras were to be bought with his card. It would have worked, but Mom liked to share her extras with him. She continued her well established enabling ways, leaving her with less. Her favorite was ice cream, chocolate with almonds. It didn't take long until she learned that if she gave her ice cream to him, she would not have enough to last the week. And since Andrew was not allowing her to visit him, it became easier and easier for her to keep her goodies for herself. So with time, the plan worked fairly well. Andrew, of course, was angry with me, but that was nothing new. It was past time for him to experience using his own funds for his own purchases. He didn't starve. He still got the basics. Plus, he received Meals-on-Wheels.

The second Sunday in September, Mom informed me she and Andrew attended church that morning. I was shocked and pleased. Andrew needed to be in church. I learned later that he had a personal agenda. When Andrew saw Maureen, he shared with her he was going to get a woman from the church to clean his house. That information concerned me. I called the pastor of the church. He had already observed that Andrew had some problems. Wisely, the pastor included Andrew in his Sunday School class so he would be there to control any issue that might arise. In addition, Andrew had a history of liking to speak out in church. On that Sunday, he shared some New Age beliefs, which were not well received. During a phone conversation with the pastor, I expressed concern that Andrew might request someone to clean his house. I told him, "Andrew needed to clean his own house."

I was also concerned about Andrew riding in the car with Mom's Sunday School teacher. The pastor agreed these were real concerns, and thanked me for calling. Mom's Sunday School teacher phoned me a few days later. She advised me her husband did not want her transporting men in her car. And that is exactly what I shared with Mom.

Her teacher also let me know that on the second Sunday she was to pick up Mom, Andrew was not ready for church. Instead, he sent a note telling the teacher he needed her to purchase cigarettes for him, before she drove the rest of the ladies to church. When Andrew first visited Mom's new church, he did not go seeking to get closer to God. He was looking for someone else to enable him. I am glad the pastor was quickly aware of Andrew's attempts to highjack church members for his purposes. Since the church was about half a mile from his house, if Andrew really wanted to attend church there, he could easily reach it by foot or by bicycle.

Years ago, I tried to get Mom to take Andrew to the Salvation Army Church. I worked with them on many occasions and knew they would be able to help Andrew, if Andrew indeed wanted help. Andrew's prompt response was, "They are just a bunch of losers." Andrew was not seeking help then, nor was he seeking help now. When Andrew was ready to repent, to be sorry for his sins and actively trust God to help him change, God would be ready to listen. Until then, Andrew continued in his pride.

Andrew was becoming less and less welcome in the community and in his own neighborhood. The bank, the grocery store, Mom's previous church, the sandwich shop, and the drugstore did not want Andrew in their establishments. He was too abusive and disruptive. With no transportation, he frequently tormented neighbors with repeated calls into the middle of the night, demanding they take him to get cigarettes or liquor. Some neighbors moved out. Others were not able to leave. After a few complaints, the police no longer took them seriously, even though they knew Andrew was dangerous and could harm them in one of his many fits of rage. When Andrew got mad at his next door neighbor for rejecting his advances, he hit her. She immediately called the police and was willing to file a police report. When the police arrived and discovered she did not have a witness, they said they didn't believe her – end of story.

Enabling not only wreaks havoc in the family, but the neighbors and the community also suffer. Although Mom was diagnosed with moderate Alzheimer's two months prior, she could still manage many of her daily functions, with reminders. What she hid from view in the past became known in the community. Everyone loved Mom, but could not tolerate Andrew. She wanted her son to be loved, but that was impossible now. He spewed vile obscenities everywhere he went. He blatantly demanded money and even stole from Mom. With no one willing to file a report, and the police even encouraging the advantages of less paperwork, the possibility of another violent act was not inconceivable. Then they would deal with him. At least, that is what the police told me.

Just when I thought the car situation was behind us, a gentleman from the dealership left a message on my answering machine, requesting I call him. He received a call from Andrew which concerned him very much. When I returned the call, he shared with me that Andrew was verbally abusive to Mom while they were on the phone. Andrew demanded the car be returned. When the phone conversation ended, the gentleman called the police and requested that they perform a wellness visit at my Mom's house. I expressed my appreciation for his call to the police; it was the right thing to do. For the next few days, I received repeated calls from Andrew demanding the car's return, followed by abruptly hanging up. The final time we spoke about the car, he let me talk long enough to tell him the car was sold. With one last verbal assault, he railed out at me, "Burn in hell!" and then, of course, he hung up.

After I spoke with the salesman from the dealership, I immediately called Mom to see if she was OK. She insisted that everything was fine. She told me she was at Andrew's house when the police came to the door. Andrew answered the door and spoke with the officers. They did not speak to Mom. Andrew assured them that everything was fine. That meant the police were satisfied with the abuser's answer, not even checking on Mom's account of what happened. Then again, since things calmed down, she probably would have confirmed everything was fine. But things weren't fine.

Later in the afternoon, I called Mom. She said she understood Andrew couldn't have the car. I reminded her that the conversation had been very ugly that morning. She agreed. She tried to change the direction of our conversation and insisted that Andrew never hurt her. I responded, "He hurt me. He destroyed my family, murdered

85

my father, and treated my mother horribly." In a quiet voice, she said, "I know it." I let her know I was praying for God to make it clear to her when it was time for her to move near me. She decided she was tired and needed a nap. She didn't like to be reminded of the reality of her situation.

Being Andrew's Representative Payee only added to my challenges. Andrew didn't like the loss of spending money. He called me in a fit of rage, because there was no money in his bank account. I explained that Social Security required a new bank account be established when the Rep. Payee changed. This account would be used to pay his bills. I informed him he was already getting his spending money on Tuesdays from Mom. This, of course, was a drastically reduced amount from what he was accustomed to receiving. He yelled at me and declared that he would never get someone to be with. (Translated: a woman) I responded insisting, "That has nothing to do with me." He began screaming vile names at me and hung up. In a few minutes, Andrew called back. By then, I was on the phone with someone else. He left a message. His remark was minimally intelligible, but none the less, vile.

I called Andrew's doctor's office. They confirmed that Andrew phoned them a lot. They asked if everything was OK. I replied, "Not really." I told them Andrew was very angry about me being his Rep. Payee. Andrew no longer enjoyed money for drugs and prostitutes. I asked if any government agencies would provide Andrew with some mental health services. She said she would check into it and call me back. No one called.

The next day, Mom was scheduled to go to the Podiatrist. Maureen took Mom to the doctor's office and stayed with her the whole time. This was so much better than me trying to run back and forth every single week. Mom let me know she was very glad to be getting some help for her toenails. I reminded her about the appointment I made for her in my town. When she cried so much about going home, I cancelled the appointment. She declared that she did not know why she acted that way.

When Mom arrived at the doctor's office, her blood pressure was 236/101. She was dizzy. Maureen drove her to the hospital emergency room. With medication, her blood pressure finally came down to 124/72. This was a huge wake-up call for Mom. She needed to take her medicine. She could not pretend to take it or only take it when she felt like it. Waiting until later was not an option, because later she would forget. I called to remind her every day. We created a whole list of reminders which started each day. But with Mom insisting on living in her home, it was up to her to actually take the medicine. She could not afford a Granny Nanny every day of the week.

Andrew, however, was very consistent. For months, he continued to accept food from Mom, but immediately insisted she go home. One day, he allowed her to come into his house. She washed a multitude of dishes, and then he called her a vile name and sent her home. It was sad, terribly sad.

Andrew continued to make demands. Mom continued to protect her boy. She continued to attempt to hover over him. He continued to reject her. These habits were entrenched from the early years of their lives. With assistance, Mom could probably have lived on her own for some time, if it weren't for the Andrew she created, but could no longer control.

Chapter 13: November
Sailing to Safe Harbor

He stilled the storm to a whisper; the waves of the sea were hushed (Psalm 107:29, NIV).

I prayed God would somehow give Mom enough clarity of mind to be willing to leave her home and Andrew. I purposed to wait on God, knowing His ways are higher than mine. At the end of October and again in early November, Mom ended up in the hospital with bouts of dizziness. They were caused by her inability to correctly take any of her medicines, especially her blood pressure medicine. A neighbor drove her home after the first event, but within a couple of days, she was back in the hospital. This time, I drove across state to take her home. As I walked into her hospital room, I gently whispered, "It's time. It's time for you to come with me." Without argument or confrontation, she said, "It's time." Mom dramatically changed. She was cooperative and talking very positively about the move. Only God could create this radical change in her. And the greatest miracle – by the amazing grace of God – she never argued with me again.

Mom and I loaded my car with clothing and household items to start the moving process. Mom stayed at my house a few days until we could arrange for her move to the assisted living facility. With mid-level Alzheimer's disease, Mom needed the stimulation and resources I could not adequately provide at home. I visited her multiple times each week with many outings in the community and visits with the rest of the family in my home.

From the beginning, Mom loved the place. Her studio apartment, three delicious meals a day in the beautiful dining room, activities, and many people with which to chat and spend time, were all very positive changes in her life. She even started playing the piano again, something I had not seen her do in years. Her former days were filled with mindless, lonely hours watching TV news. Now, there was joy and peace. And although Alzheimer's generally prevented Mom from being forthcoming with any information, she surprised me one day. Without any prompting she declared, "This is a fun place to live." It was a very good move for Mom.

Some people might think I should have kept Mom in my home. Believe me, with her amazing change in attitude, that did cross my mind a few times. As we were moving Mom into her apartment, the nurse at the assisted living facility confirmed I was doing the right thing by making this move now. She said, "Too often, people try to manage at home until they are so burned out the relationship between parent and child is severely damaged. By moving Mom in while your relationship is good, your time together will be very positive – spent in fun, relaxing activities and ending in good memories for all." I was very thankful for her wise counsel.

What about Andrew? Throughout the years, I asked Mom to require responsible behavior from him. It would have been easier if this had been done early in his life, but that was then, and this is now. A few months before Mom moved to assisted living, I asked her one last time what she thought would happen to Andrew when she died. She had no idea. I tried to explain, requesting one more time she quit enabling his irresponsible and sinful lifestyles. I reminded her she was leaving an awful situation for me. She had no answer.

This day had to come, either by Mom's move to assisted living or at her death. With no one to enable him, Andrew grew decidedly more hostile. And yet with each time, I repeated and held to the rule about acceptable behaviour. He discovered that I was not Mom, nor did I plan to pick up enabling where Mom left off. Neither whining nor demands worked with me. When he cooperatively spoke to me about a specific need, I gave him an honest answer. I continued to pursue help for him.

Then on Christmas Eve night, he called my house and in graphic detail threatened to kill me with a chainsaw. At that point, I needed to make a decision: Either I file a police report or ignore his threat and become an enabler like Mom. For my protection and his benefit, I went to the police station and filed the report. I hoped he would finally get some help.

I attended his initial court hearing. The local victim's advocate was present to support me. When I informed her about Andrew's history, she suggested I request a Mental Health Court hearing for him. As soon as the judge invited me to speak, I immediately made my request known. I then gave detailed information about Andrew's ongoing abusive behavior and desperate need for help. With a regular hearing, he would have been released in a matter of weeks. Now, the Mental Health Court hearing made him eligible for extensive evaluation and treatment. During the hearing, I also provided documents that allowed the court and mental health workers to know an in-depth history of what transpired since he was very young, to include the murder of our father. (These documents are not readily available unless a family member has wisely kept copies.) The seriousness of Andrew's mental health condition was obvious. His threat to murder me, combined with a lifetime of abusive and violent behavior, made it clear to the authorities he needed help. He was moved to a state mental hospital. As long as he is a danger to himself and others, he needs to remain confined. My husband and I pray for him every day.

Chapter 14:
Worse than Death

A young husband and wife were concerned and sought counseling. Their family was caught up in a lifetime of enabling. The wife loved her husband and in-laws very much, but her in-laws were constantly enabling their other adult son. He was an unemployed alcoholic, who enjoyed the fact that his parents paid all of his bills and even gave him an allowance. When he was stopped for DUI, his parents paid his court costs and proceeded to chauffeur him wherever he wanted to go. The husband and wife were very concerned about what would happen when the enabling parents died. This couple did not want the enabled brother to become their problem.

The counselor logically advised the husband and wife to come to an agreement about how they will proceed when his parents die. The optimum solution would result in the brother taking responsibility for his own life. It would not be easy, and from my observation, would require tough love, especially when the consequences for poor choices became a reality.

Enabling is a very real concern today. I believe there are many families in similar situations. When the parents die, life may be very difficult. Know this: If the parents live and suffer dementia or Alzheimer's disease, it will be much worse. It will become "The Perfect Storm." Dependable adults will be left with the enabled sibling who is constantly making demands and living irresponsibly.

They will also experience every challenge and phase of Alzheimer's with parents who have developed coping mechanisms such as stubbornness, concealing information, lying to ensure that they are still in control, and I could go on and on.

Is my story over? No. I could have taken you through the stages of Alzheimer's and let you experience all of the life-changing disabilities that come with this terrible disease. Many are the ones my family and I have yet to face. I do not think sharing that information would have further served my purpose. As difficult as it is to lose a loved one to death, facing the challenge of coping with Alzheimer's disease while dealing with an out of control adult who has lived through a lifetime of enabling, is something no one should have to experience. It is worse than dealing with death. Death is final. Alzheimer's, encumbered with enabling, will control your family until someone has the courage to put a stop to the destruction. Is that person you?

Chapter 15:
Your Legacy

I pray that these two books, When Compassion Turns to Enabling and When Enabling and Alzheimer's Collide, will provide you with insights and strategies to change the future for your family. There is no time to waste. Your future will be here before you can comprehend it.

My message is simple: Enabling must be stopped while the enabler still has clarity of mind. Once dementia or Alzheimer's disease is present, there will be no way to protect the enabler from the one who has been enabled.

Use your time to share this information with your spouse, your family, and the enabler. Stand together, holding each one accountable for his or her personal decisions. Pray together and trust God to help your family change while there is still time to prevent this story from becoming your family's legacy.

Chapter 16:
Greater than the Storm!

Was there any joy in the journey? The difficulty of the storms I faced cannot compare with the joy I have experienced in God's presence. I am overwhelmed by His unfailing love. He sustained me, comforted me, rescued me, and allowed me to know Him in ways I never imagined. I am changed. I am forever grateful!

Sarah

When Compassion Turns to Enabling

When Enabling and Alzheimer's Collide

To learn more about Mary Willock Ministries or to invite Dr. Mary Willock to be a guest speaker on enabling or many other life-changing topics, you can reach her through www.marywillock.net.